WAYNESBURG
WAYNESBURG, PA.

D0651813

301   A561u
Andreski, Stanislav
The Uses of Comparative Sociology
87473

APR 1 0 '72

SEP 21 '74

OCT 5 '86

THE USES OF
COMPARATIVE SOCIOLOGY

THE USES OF COMPARATIVE SOCIOLOGY

Stanislav Andreski

UNIVERSITY OF CALIFORNIA PRESS

BERKELEY AND LOS ANGELES 1965

University of California Press
Berkeley and Los Angeles
California

© *1964 by Stanislav Andreski*

Printed in Great Britain

CONTENTS

CONTENTS

BOOK THREE
Case Studies

FOREWORD

THE PRESENT BOOK grew out of my long-standing concern about the neglect of comparative method in contemporary sociology which I first voiced in the foreword to my *Military Organization and Society* published by Routledge & Kegan Paul in 1954 under my original surname of Andrzejewski. I am glad to be able to say that my strictures have lost some of their applicability owing to the appearance in the meantime of a few important works based on comparative study. Although some points of my criticisms expressed in that foreword seem to me now to have been over-emphasized, I have the satisfaction that I have succeeded in helping to revive interest in comparative studies.

A book which would attempt to cover the field of comparative sociology would amount to a comprehensive treatise on all the aspects of social life in their manifold variety. The mere size of the present book proves that its purpose is more restricted. What I tried to do here is to show the fruitfulness of comparative analysis, illustrate its difficulties and pitfalls, and clear certain misunderstandings surrounding its methodology.

The text is divided into three parts: Book I is focused on methodology, Book II deals with substantive general problems, and Book III contains case studies. The division is by no means water-tight because a discussion of methodology without reference to concrete applications must remain on the level of unrealistic pontification; and one of the chief contentions of the present work is that the difference between a case study and a comparative analysis should be a matter of emphasis and focus rather than of exclusive divergence.

Book II is divided into parts dealing with a few out of many aspects of social life which could be illuminated with the aid of comparative analysis. They were chosen not because I regard them as more important than other aspects, but simply because I felt that in these fields I could illustrate best the fruitfulness of comparative method. The same consideration governed the choice of cases selected for treatment in Book III, where my aim was to show how the understanding of a concrete case can be augmented by considering it from a comparative point of view.

High selectivity also characterizes Book I. If I tried to give a comprehensive picture of the philosophical foundations of the social sciences, I should have to cover the ground which has already been well treated in a number of excellent works. And as needless repetition is one of the greatest blights of sociological literature, I did not attempt to expound the general principles of logic and methodology, concentrating on problems on which I felt that I had something relatively new to say, and on points on which confusion still prevails.

In preparing the final draft of the present work I have been greatly helped by my wife and my good friend Ernest Gellner.

STANISLAV ANDRESKI

1964

'Le philosophe, comme le navigateur, doit se méfier de courants; plus ils sont forts, plus il doit s'en écarter.'

Augustin Cournot

Le philosophie, comme le navigateur, doit se
méfier de courants; plus ils sont forts, plus
il doit s'en écarter.

Augustin Cournot

BOOK ONE

Philosophical and Methodological Foundations

CHAPTER ONE

DESCRIPTION AND THEORY

ACCORDING to the popular distinction between fact and theory fact is something certain, whereas theory is something most likely to be false. The correct distinction, of course, is between statements about particular events, and generalizations (that is to say, statements about open classes of events); and there are no grounds for supposing that the former must always be more certain than the latter, because sense data and other evidence about particular events are interpreted in the light of assumptions about what is likely and what is not, what can cause what and so on. On the other hand, as everybody knows or at least should know, generalizations cannot be correct unless they are supported by observations of particular events. To repeat another commonplace of philosophy of science, the growth of knowledge absolutely requires an intimate and proper relationship between observation and theoretical speculation. The unsatisfactory state of contemporary sociology derives from the lack of balance and mutual stimulation between theory and description, partly due to the sterile character of the most influential recent attempts at sociological theorizing.

Bareness of Unguided Description

It does not require much philosophical sophistication to realize that the mere accumulation of factual data cannot contribute much to our understanding, or even help us decisively in practical action. In order to act effectively, we must be able to foresee the consequences of our actions, which means that we must know the causes of the phenomena which we handle. Auguste Comte had in mind precisely this when he propounded the basic tenet of positivism *savoir pour prévoir, prévoir pour pouvoir*. Now it is quite

15

obvious that accumulation of disjointed bits of information cannot by itself bring forth the knowledge of causal relations; nor can it be intellectually satisfactory because, though it may enable one to make a living, it permits no intellectual development, for the simple reason that the capacity of human memory is limited. The available store of useful and interesting information about social life has long ago exceeded the retentive capacity of even the best endowed human mind. There are not the slightest grounds for supposing that any living scholar knows more details about social life than Montesquieu or Machiavelli. If the knowledge of some of us might be considered to be superior to that of these illustrious thinkers of the past, it is because we know different things – not because any of us has stored in his mind a larger number of bits of information. One assortment of bits of information can be regarded as better than another not less numerous only if it differs in the nature of the items it contains. That one assortment of data may be more valuable than another for some specific task calls for no explanation, but of two equally numerous and relevant collections of pieces of information one can be regarded as superior only if it contains more general propositions from which deductions about particular cases can be made, thus absolving us from the necessity of memorizing. The chief use of generalizations is precisely this: that we may know more without having to remember more; for we do not have to remember what we can deduce. A glance at the history of the sciences of nature shows how purely retentive knowledge is being continuously replaced by theorems of increasingly wide reach.

Theoretical undernourishment of descriptive studies gravely impairs their fruitfulness, and condemns them to dullness and repetitiveness; because, unless it concerns a case never studied before, a sociographic study can be interesting only if it brings to light information which was not until then appreciated, or shows hitherto unnoticed connections between already known facts. It is sheer mysticism to imagine that such insights can be obtained from pure immersion in the situation. Such an immersion is no doubt necessary, but only a mind well furnished with a stock of hypotheses (in their majority inevitably conceived by others) can see from a novel point of view a situation well known to others. The history of the natural sciences shows very well how without new ideas the marginal utility of new observations rapidly declines.

There is nothing new in what I am saying: it is simply an attempt to re-assert old truths, well known to anybody who has studied the philosophy and history of science, in a context in which they are blatantly ignored. Apart, however, from infantile illnesses through which other sciences have passed, sociology suffers some special diseases as well.

Terminology and Jargon

Once upon a time Condillac put forth a dictum that 'science is but a language well made'. Without great exaggeration one could say that a large part of sociology is but a language badly made. What seems to have happened is that sociologists, mesmerized by the wonderful achievements of the exact sciences, and seeing that these sciences employ abstruse terms, have mistaken the external paraphernalia for the essence: they came to feel that abstruseness makes a science, ignoring why and how the terminologies of the exact sciences evolved.

The principal reason why every science developed a special terminology is that colloquial words do not divide reality in such a way as to single out entities which exhibit regularities of behaviour, describable by a system of interconnected theorems. As Whewell beautifully puts it: 'the fundamental principle and supreme rule of all scientific terminology is that terms must be construed and appropriated so as to be fitted to enunciate simply and clearly true general propositions'. If we follow the terminological debates among early physicists and chemists, we can see very well that consciously or unconsciously this aim has been on the mind of all those whose verbal innovations came to be incorporated into the body of science. Now, what happened in contemporary sociology is that the term-coining activity became dissociated from the purpose which alone can justify it, for there is no merit in incomprehensibility for its own sake. Neologisms and even more pernicious circumlocutory and ambiguous phrases are put into circulation, without being at all needed for formulating testable hypotheses.

Ever since Mach (or even Occam) economy has been recognized as one of the ideals which every scientific formulation must strive to approach. We can leave aside the great metaphysical problem of whether there is economy in the structure of the universe, because the mere incapacity of human mind to operate upon a large number of discrete ideas at once, requires some simplicity in formulations devised as aids to understanding. This can be seen very well in the example of mathematical terms. Take, for instance 'logarithm': its use is justified solely by economy of words, because it could be replaced without any loss or alteration of meaning by the following expression: 'a number which is related to a second number in such a way that it indicates how many times we must multiply by itself a specified third number in order to obtain the said second number'. Even the word 'multiply' is not absolutely necessary, because we could replace 'multiply by itself' by 'add to itself as many times as the number of units it contains'. Likewise, terms like 'derivative', 'limit', 'integral', and so on, can be replaced by complicated expressions which do not contain them. These examples show that a new term can also be justified on the ground that it can serve more efficiently the same purpose as a more complicated expression. In the light of this criterion most sociological neologisms fail miserably because, far from subserving economy, the great majority of them can be replaced by ordinary words with considerable gain in brevity and clarity. In a widely known book by George Homans, *The Human Group*, we read (on page 422): 'a social system is in moving equilibrium and authority exists when the state of the elements that enter the system and of the relations between them, including the behaviour of the leader, is such that disobedience to the orders of the leader will be followed by changes in the other elements tending to bring the system back to the state the leader would have wished it to reach if the disobedience had not taken place'. Without any loss of precision and a substantial gain in clarity, the meaning of this cumbrous phrase could be conveyed by saying that authority exists where there are effective sanctions against disobedience. Examples of this kind abound not only in Homans' book but throughout sociological literature, as can be verified by any intelligent person who takes the trouble to translate ponderous statements of various sociologists into plain language.

There is one advantage of neologisms which is peculiar to the study of society: namely, the possibility of eliminating the emotive charge, with which nearly all words relating to social relations are loaded. Thus, instead of saying that a person is lazy, we might say for the sake of greater impartiality, that 'his responses to stimuli which motivate individuals to expend their energies are below the average'. One can doubt, however, whether anything can be gained thereby, because everybody who understands this phrase still knows that it means that the person in question is lazy. Anyway, so long as we move on the level of rudimentary abstraction, an attempt to eliminate valuative words from the sociological vocabulary is a fruitless task, because as soon as a more neutral substitute for a colloquial word is put into circulation it acquires the same emotive charge. Moreover, people who insist on eliminating emotive nuances should replace ordinary words with verbal inventions which are not longer: instead of 'lazy' they should use something like 'gok'. True, it would be difficult to show that the gains of such a wholesale substitution would be worth the enormous burden of learning a vocabulary far more extensive than that of any physical science. Nevertheless, such a procedure would be preferable to the present practice of replacing simple words by cumbrous phrases which thwart intelligible discourse. The author of a certain book on industrial sociology cannot be so unintelligent as not to know that one suffers from fatigue when one is exhausted; nevertheless, he enunciates as a great discovery that 'fatigue reaction index is negatively correlated with the distance which separates the actual state of an individual from the point of physiological exhaustion'. Such examples show very well the disastrous results of flouting the principle of economy. The preoccupation with eliminating plain words is in any case superfluous, because as science progresses its concepts automatically become so abstract as to be immune from corrosion by colloquial usage. This applies even to social sciences: although Keynes' 'multiplier' sounds plain enough, it stands for a genuinely sophisticated concept, and for this reason has in no way been twisted. So it would be better to forget about such purisms, and concentrate on unravelling causal relations.

In order to elevate the controversy above the level of personal preferences which cannot be explicitly justified, I propose the following formal criteria of admissibility for neologisms: (1) every sociological term must be clearly translatable into ordinary words; (2) it must stand for an idea which cannot be adequately expressed with fewer than five ordinary words. Weber's term 'charisma', for instance, satisfies these criteria, as it replaces the phrase 'the ability to command through sheer force of personal magnetism, without having at one's disposal an apparatus of coercion'. These criteria constitute only the preliminary conditions of admissibility of a new term, the final being (to repeat Whewell's words) that it is 'constructed and appropriated so as to be fitted to enunciate simply and clearly true general propositions'.[1]

If a really useful and sophisticated sociological terminology develops, it may be necessary to introduce terms which cannot be defined in ordinary words although there is no reason to imagine that they would not be translatable into such words at more than one remove. It has been argued that new concepts are most useful when they cannot be defined in terms of the previously existing concepts. It seems to me, however, that this may be true in epistemology which deals with basic irreducible categories of thought, but not in an empirical science. The development of the terminology of mathematics and the natural sciences suggests that the progress of knowledge reduces rather than augments the number of primitive concepts which cannot be defined but only apprehended by perception or intuition.

Nebulous verbosity hampers thought in many ways, but above all because it deludes people into accepting renaming as discovery. Some people imagine, for instance, that the formulation of the dichotomy between 'universalistic' and 'particularistic' social systems constitutes a contribution to knowledge, whereas in reality it only amounts to a renaming of the old dichotomy between open and segmented societies – that is to say, between societies in which there is social mobility and the ones in which membership of groups is hereditary. For distinguishing the kinds of criteria on the basis of which individuals are assigned to various positions in a society, the predicates 'particularistic' and 'universalistic' are mere substitutes for 'personal' and 'objective' or 'impersonal'. The term 'particularistic' might be worth adopting, as it is more precise in such contexts than the word 'personal'; but 'universalistic' suggests too much, and it is difficult to see what can be gained by speaking of 'universalistic' instead of 'objective' criteria and of 'universalistic' instead of 'open' societies or groups. The replacement of the old distinction between achieved and inherited status

[1] The readers acquainted with my *Military Organization and Society* will remember that in that book I have sinned against the second formal criterion of admissibility advocated here. The neologisms introduced there were clearly defined, and they were used to express what I still consider to be true general propositions, but most of them were not necessary.

by the dichotomy between 'achieved' and 'ascribed' status amounts to a regression because, whereas the predicates 'achieved' and 'inherited' exclude each other, 'ascribed' and 'achieved' do not. A rank in an army is both achieved and ascribed: achieved because a soldier has to work for it (no matter whether honestly or not), and ascribed because a promotion is an act of ascription of status. In contrast, a status acquired through accumulation of wealth in independent business activity is only achieved, as no act of ascription takes place. Furthermore, without twisting the meaning of 'ascribe' we cannot equate 'inherited' and 'ascribed' because inheritance need not involve any definite act of ascription. Who has ascribed Mr Nelson Rockefeller to high society? Rather than replace 'inherited' by 'ascribed', it seems more logical to distinguish three kinds of status: independently achieved, ascribed and inherited; bearing in mind that every concrete case represents a mixture of elements of these ideal types. Thus the status of president was ascribed to John F. Kennedy by the electoral body, but this ascription was achieved through his own efforts which, however, would most probably have been fruitless if he had not inherited great wealth and the concomitant status.

By employing the illogical nouns 'in-group' and 'out-group', instead of 'group' and 'outsiders' or 'other groups', and resorting to other similar substitutions, many people delude themselves that they move on a higher level of discourse. Referring to the fact that courtship is more conspicuous in spring than in other seasons, Chappel and Coon say in their *Principles of Anthropology* that 'men originate to women with higher frequency'. The word 'originate' may sound more scientific than the old-fashioned 'courting', but in fact it is less so, because it is less precise: origination in the sense of initiating interaction covers many kinds of behaviour apart from courting, and the phrase in question might be legitimately interpreted as referring to an increase in handbag snatching.

There are countless other examples of purely verbal innovations which have passed for discoveries. For instance, it was known for a very long time that people often adopt habits and viewpoints of circles to which they would like to belong but do not. It remained, however, for R. K. Merton to make a great discovery by baptizing this simple finding with the high-sounding name of 'reference group theory'. Self-explanatory terms like 'circle of aspiration' or 'aspired-to group' would neither overawe the laymen nor give the initiated the feeling that they belong to an exclusive craft. For the same reason the devotees of the reference group theory speak of 'anticipatory socialization' instead of 'imitation', notwithstanding their finding that individuals who imitate the standards of a circle to which they aspire make themselves unpopular in the group to which they belong.

How pernicious is this kind of verbiage can be seen from another quotation: from Homans. On page 135 of the book mentioned above, he says, 'that persons who interact with one another frequently are more like one another in their activities than they are like other persons with whom they interact less frequently'. Plainly, the pompousness of his phrase prevents our author from realizing that he is uttering a childish tautology. Lately another fountain of impressive words became available for the purpose of making spurious discoveries: namely cybernetics.

Cybernetics

The word 'cybernetics', though first invented by Ampère in order to designate the science of government, was given currency by Norbet Wiener in a book called *Cybernetics, Control and Communication in Animal and Machine*, published in 1948. Cybernetics is used nowadays in two distinct though related senses. The first (particularly current outside English-speaking countries) need not concern us here, as it denotes the branch of electronic engineering devoted to construction of computers and servo-mechanisms. The insights gained in this activity stimulated Wiener and others to ponder about the common features which all self-regulating systems must exhibit, thus creating a body of knowledge known as cybernetics in the second sense of this word, that is to say, in the sense of a general theory of self-regulating systems of whatever kind.

The idea that there are principles common to different realms of being is not new. Descartes' biology, for instance, was so strongly mechanistic, that he resorted to the extraordinary metaphor of two clocks antecedently synchronized, in order to reconcile his interpretation of the body as nothing but a machine with his belief in the existence of human soul. The debate between mechanism and vitalism continued throughout the history of modern biology, and still continues, though in a slightly abated form. Electronic technology had a great impact on this debate by showing that teleologically oriented behaviour, previously considered to be the characteristic which distinguished animate from inanimate matter, could be built into a machine.

The analogy between an organism and society has been noticed long ago. It was implicitly recognized, for instance, in coining names for leaders, derived from roots signifying 'head' in various languages. In the debate between the patricians and the plebeians in ancient Rome, the former resorted to a metaphor assigning to them the function of a head, in order to persuade the latter to obey. We arrive at full comprehension of the organismic analogy with Francis Bacon, who thought that it could help greatly to devise proper methods of governing. During the second part of the 19th century the recourse to this analogy inspired many sociological works. The writers posteriorly classified as organicists were by no means so one-sided as Sorokin and some other historians of sociology would have us believe. *Bau und Leben des sozialen Koerpers* (1875), whose author Albert Schaeffle was accused of equating organism and society, contains a chapter which bears the title 'Society is not an Organism'. Herbert Spencer – to take the most famous exponent of this approach – explicitly stated that although he conceived his sociological theories by contemplating this analogy, he upheld them solely on the basis of inductive confirmation. It cannot be denied that the organicist point of view led to some valuable insights: it taught sociologists to view society as a system of finely balanced interdependent parts, which function or undergo transformations only under certain specific conditions; it also introduced the idea of function. The originality of the so-called functionalist school of anthropology lay (apart from their insistence on greater thoroughness of field work than was hitherto customary) in interpreting ethnographic materials in accordance with these notions. The most serious drawback of the organicist approach was the encouragement it gave to the ubiquitous inclination to pass as genuine discoveries the mere changes of names, which in this case took the form of labelling social phenomena with biological terms – the vice exactly analogous to that of most sociological fans of cybernetics.

The extension of comparison to all realms of being long antedated cybernetics: Herbert Spencer, for example, conceived his

First Principles as applicable to all entities. In 1913 a Russian economist and philosopher Bogdanow wrote a book called *Tektologya – A General Science of Organization* (republished in Moscow in an expanded form in 1923), where he attempted to analyse common principles inherent in all structures from that of a crystal to that of a state. It even deals with mathematics as the most advanced mental structure, and treats such topics as forms of fusion and fission in different realms, and their various permutations.

The foregoing remarks ought to help us to assess justly the contribution which cybernetics might make to sociology. Contrary to what many people seem to imagine, this contribution cannot consist of the concept of feedback, because although self-regulation and teleological behaviour are something revolutionary in engineering, they have long been recognized as essential features of life: the biologists knew long ago about afferent and efferent nerves, and the organicist sociologists of the last century pointed out that an analogous flow of messages is a necessary condition of existence of any human organization. Those sociologists who continuously speak about feedbacks needlessly imitate the vocabulary of engineering, motivated probably by their inferiority complex with regard to the engineers, and also, perhaps, by the deep totemistic urge which prompts man to worship the source of his sustenance.

Is there anything, then, that a sociologist can gain by studying cybernetics? Yes, but only if he contents himself with indirect profit. The concepts of system, function, equilibrium, teleological behaviour entered our intellectual armoury a long time ago, but the knowledge of some of the conditions of equilibrium or teleological behaviour is new. For example, it is by no means obvious to the unaided common sense that a system containing a large number of variables can attain equilibrium quickly only if the relations between the variables can be expressed by what the mathematicians call step functions; that is to say, only if the variables do not react to small variations of other variables. Likewise, a sociologist might gain something from knowing how permutations of negative and positive connections between factors (of stimulation or inhibition, so to speak), or the order or relative magnitudes and time lags of reactions, can make equilibrium stable or unstable or impossible, cause oscillations, or produce vicious or virtuous circles known as positive feedbacks, and so on.

Owing to the impossibility of measuring many crucial factors, the equations of electronic engineering cannot be applied to sociology. Even in economics, with its far greater scope for measurement, attempts to apply cybernetic models (whether symbolic or material) proved interesting but of little help in predicting actual behaviour of the economy. A cybernetic philosophy of causal relations can be illuminating, but only in so far as it can suggest discoveries of hitherto unknown relations between observable social phenomena. Unfortunately a book which would distil from technical manuals a philosophy of relations between factors has not yet been written as far as I know. Wiener's *Cybernetics* is too technical and not philosophical enough. *An Introduction to Cybernetics*, by Ross Ashby, does not really deal with cybernetics but with preliminary and ancillary matters. More useful, as far as suggestions for sociological analysis go are *Design for a Brain* by the same author, and *Thinking by Machine* by Pierre de Latil. *La Cybernétique* by T. Guilbaud (of which there is an English translation) is a useful little book which does not jump to unwarranted philosophical conclusions.

Applications of Frameworks

In addition to the neo-totemism mentioned above, another archetypal urge operates in sociology: the desire for the philosopher's stone – for something that would relieve us of the burden of laborious studies. One form of this creed is the belief that all difficulties can be solved with the aid of some concept or techniques imported from another discipline, maintained in the face of complete lack of evidence in its favour. In fact, the history of natural sciences shows that no advances were made by people who tried to *apply* conceptual frameworks: the great discoverers were interested in how and why things happen, and in order to find out they had recourse to any helpful ideas or techniques which they knew. The conceptual frameworks of the sciences grew by accumulation and ordering of correct solutions of definite problems. All the talk, which one hears nowadays in sociological circles inspired by Talcott Parsons and George Gurvitch about frameworks of reference and applications of conceptual systems, amounts to putting the cart before the horse – it is a sterile logomachy.

25

Often the insistence on applying 'frameworks' amounts to no more than an addiction to meaningless repetition of this word. There are many other examples of verbal fads of this kind. No doubt owing to the militarization of science, the word 'strategy' came into the fashion and replaced 'method' without any gain in discernment. On the contrary, as with most fads, this substitution has led to an impoverishment of the language because, instead of two words with distinct though overlapping meanings, only one is used indiscriminately – so indiscriminately indeed that people talk pleonastically about 'strategy of conflict', as if there could be a strategy without a conflict.

One of the most futile fads centres around the word 'role', whose metaphorically sociological usage dates from the 18th century at the latest. Although this metaphor has by now become utterly commonplace, the suddenly developed addiction to repeating it interminably has been baptized as 'role theory'. This 'theory' consists of pompous, nebulous and incredibly lengthy re-statements of what has been common knowledge for a very long time: namely, that in every group the members play different roles which sometimes are complementary and sometimes contradictory; that sometimes individuals change or exchange their roles; that often one person acts in several roles which may be mutually reinforcing, but also may be incompatible; that a group can act effectively only if the roles of its members are in harmony. These platitudes can be equally well expressed without ever using the word 'role', which proves that this fad in no way leads to an improved understanding.

Classification

A good simple classification must satisfy the minimal formal requirements of exhaustiveness and exclusiveness – which means that every item which belongs to a category must fall into one of its sub-categories, and that no item should fall into two sub-categories at once, although with classifications which concern reality there are bound to be borderline cases. This means that at each stage the principle of classification must be the same. A compound classification ought to consist of simple classifications which comply with these requirements. Naturally, within these formal limits (which, incidentally, are valid for ideal types too) many variants are possible, whose value depends on the degree to which they approach the ideal of economy, and above all on the extent to which they facilitate discovery of regularities. The advantage of knowing that a bat, a horse, a man, and a whale are mammals is that we do not need to memorize all the organs of these animals, but only their specific differences and the generic features of the mammals.

Facilitation of discovery and economy of remembering are in fact two aspects of the same thing, because it is the existence of true general propositions that enables us to deduce properties of an entity from an assertion that it belongs to a category which figures in these propositions. On the other side, clear classifications often created conditions for subsequent discovery of regularities not envisaged by those who formulated the classifications. To take one example: Linnaeus, by working out the first classification of animate beings which satisfied the criteria of formal logic, enabled Darwin to conceive the theory of evolution. Here we have a beautiful example of the supremacy of logical order in the growth of knowledge.

The work of classifying is of great importance, but a good classification must not only satisfy the formal criteria of logic but also order the phenomena in such a way as to exhibit order inaccessible to common sense. Unfortunately, when we examine the works of the creators of frameworks of reference – and above all the writings of George Gurvitch, the most prolific classificator in contemporary sociology – we find ourselves in a topsy-turvy world of verbalisms unrelated to anything that can be observed, and which constitute a kind of mental treadmill which prevents one from seeing the outside world.

How weak is the power of analysis, and how low is the level of discernment of the subleties of human interaction, embodied in contemporary efforts in sociological systematics, can best be seen by confronting these writings with the best products of jurisprudence such as, for example, *Causation in the Law* by H. L. A. Hart and A. M. Honoré.

Theorizing from above

One of the features of the approach of Talcott Parsons and like-minded writers which condemns their efforts to sterility is what might be called theorizing from above: they attempt to construct a framework which then can be exemplified by factual data. This sequence is not just a matter of exposition – in which case it would be perfectly legitimate – but of stages of work, as can be seen from the lack of any evidence of inductive reasoning. In this respect these theorists resemble theologians and Marxists, though not Marx himself, and contrast sharply with all the writers whom posterity recognized as great: from Aristotle and Polybius, Machiavelli and Montesquieu to Malthus and Herder, Tocqueville, Marx, Durkheim and Weber.

The verbalist school of sociology disregards, moreover, another important lesson of the history of science: namely, that in all the sciences theorizing proceeded from lesser to greater generality. Even in mathematics many specific theorems were known before a more general theorem was invented from which the former could be deduced; and only in this century have mathematicians attempted (unsuccessfully, I believe) to deduce the whole of mathematics from a few basic propositions. In physics the Galilean laws of falling bodies were incorporated into the more general Newtonian laws of motion, which in turn were found to be a special exemplification of even more general laws of theory of relativity – to mention only the barest outline of the most famous of analogous sequences. Such evidence shows conclusively that a theoretical system can be good only in so far as it incorporates more limited discoveries of the predecessors. On this score too, much of recent theorizing must be judged as defective as it tends to fall either into ancestor worship or the equally sterile patricide – whereas what is needed is critical selection, modification and dovetailing of the work of our forerunners.

I must add that I have selected Talcott Parsons as the chief butt of the criticisms contained in this paragraph not because he exemplifies most uncivilized antics of contemporary sociology, but for the opposite reason. He is unquestionably a serious scholar of great learning, who, far from being guilty of intellectual patricide, has on the contrary, the great merit of making American sociologists interested in the heritage of Max Weber; so, if one can show that certain basic errors crippled even his efforts, one has proved one's point.

The Magic of Numbers and Formulae

Some ancient philosophers already maintained that measurement is the beginning of true knowledge, and nobody can deny that our ability to predict the behaviour of a phenomenon must remain very restricted unless we can measure it. It does not follow, however, that no knowledge whatsoever is possible without measurement, nor that such knowledge cannot be worth having – which is precisely the conclusion which many sociologists have adopted, in the mistaken belief that only thereby they can maintain the scientific character of their discipline. But the true scientific spirit consists of trying to obtain the nearest approximation to truth which is possible under the circumstances, and it is puerile to demand either perfect exactitude or nothing. Those who refuse to deal with important and interesting problems simply because the relevant factors cannot be measured, condemn sociology to sterility, because we cannot get very far with the study of measurable variables if these depend on, and are closely interwoven with, immensurable factors of whose nature and operation we know nothing. A weakness of this kind diminishes the usefulness of economic theory: notwithstanding the great sophistication of statistical techniques and mathematical models, it remains incapable of predicting such *par excellence* economic phenomenon as inflation, because it excludes from its universe of discourse immensurable but causally crucial factors, abandoning them to the step-motherly care of sociology (with which most economists want nothing to do), or simply relegating them to the category of those things which are being equal.

Many people falsely imagine that 'figures' constitute the proof of exactitude. In fact, the presumed measurements may not at all measure what they are supposed to measure. The tabulated results of answers to questionnaires, for instance, indicate with precision solely the frequency of certain kinds of written responses under very specific conditions: they do not measure any attitudes other than attitudes towards the given questionnaires, and we can only surmise what might be the relationship between such responses and behaviour in real life. It does not follow that investigations employing questionnaires are useless, but only that we must realize that the exact numbers which they supply stand for very approximative assessments of what really matters.

There is nothing wrong in trying to make our knowledge of society as rigorous as we can; and formalization may, under certain circumstances, further this aim. Its use is justified, however, only if it in fact makes comprehension easier. Mathematical symbolism provides such an aid; complicated as mathematical formulae are, they are much easier to grasp than their verbal translations. But they help us to understand the world around us only in so far as they describe exactly the real (not just imaginary) behaviour of things to which they are supposed to refer. Otherwise they merely serve the purpose of decoration.

All mathematicians and philosophers agree that mathematics is a deductive system; which means that, by carrying out transformations upon the symbols, we can make explicit in the conclusion what was implicit in the premises. Mathematical operations cannot increase the precision of initial measurements. Nevertheless, many sociologists and psychologists seem to imagine that by merely putting mathematical formulae on paper, they enhance the exactitude of their statements. In some books on so-called group dynamics, we find formulae for friendship and similar attributes which nobody succeeded in measuring. Some of these formulae contain even derivatives and integrals, although one might think that the very name of infinitesimal calculus suffices to convey the idea that it can be applied only where very precise measurement is possible. Such sociologists seem to ignore another simple truth: namely that in practical calculation the error of the conclusion in proportion to the error of initial measurements increases with the number of operations, and their remoteness from simple addition.

In addition to disconnected decoration, there are two methods of employing mathematics spuriously. One of them is illustrated by Stuart Dodd's *Dimensions of Society*. There, the premises and the conclusions are stated verbally and amount to exactly the same thing couched in different ways; elaborate calculations are inserted in between, but are quite superfluous as the whole argument is tautological.[1] The other method consists of making sure that the formulae will not be falsified by experience, by telling us how to measure some of the variables but not the rest. Thus, in his

---

[1] I am using 'tautological' in the sense current in ordinary speech – which means that a conclusion consists of simple rephrasing of the premise – not in the technical sense in which it is employed by Wittgenstein.

book *Nationalism and Social Communication*, Karl Deutsch gives us an equation which pretends to show what determines the strength of nationalism. Among the determinants figure such fairly measurable variables as attendance at schools and circulation of publications, but whether they really produce the effects attributed to them cannot be ascertained, because the author does not tell us how to measure nationalism. Notwithstanding his apparent concern for exactitude he does not even explain to us what he means by nationalism, although he manages to tell us what is consciousness (which was hitherto regarded as one of the primary undefinable ideas) by defining it as 'processing and feedback of secondary symbols in an information processing system'. As *Nationalism and Social Communication* is a fairly big book, the preparation of which must have required a certain effort of will, we can understand better the remarkable ideas contained there in the light of the author's statement that 'will is the ability to inhibit, partially or wholly, any further learning'.

In virtue of its name, sociometry must be mentioned in a discussion of the applicability of mathematics to sociology. Practised widely, and directed by its founder Jacob Moreno, from his institute in New York, it presents a formidable combination of research technique with therapy. The latter employs various though related methods. The first is called psychodrama: it consists of getting people together and persuading them to act as if in a play on the themes of their personal troubles. Thus, for example, if some man is worried about his wife's infidelity, but afraid to do anything about it, he has the opportunity of venting his rancour in make-believe. In view of the attraction which the acting profession has for many people, it would not be surprising if such games sometimes helped. Sociodrama is the same thing except that here some wider social implications enter into play: people have the opportunity of pretending to upbraid their bosses, shout down policemen and so on. The 'Theatre of spontaneity' is the third method of treatment: it consists of getting people on something like a stage, and persuading them to do whatever comes into their minds. What happens to spontaneity when somebody has an impulse to murder or rape is not explained. The therapeutic powers of these procedures are, no doubt, enhanced by the fact that (as Moreno tells us in the preface to his book *Who Shall Survive*) 'the origin of sociometry is like the origin of Godhead'.

As a technique of investigation sociometry consists of getting groups of people to tell the sociometrist who likes or dislikes whom, and how much, listing the results, and then drawing pictures which show who is in and who is out, and how much. This account must suffice, as it would be presumptuous to offer further comments on the work of a man who says in the same preface that he had two precursors, Jesus and Socrates – particularly as he improved substantially upon his illustrious forerunners in respect of earning capacity.

The lesson of all this is that we should not take mathematical formulae in sociological publications at their face value, but enquire whether they in fact subserve some purpose other than the desire to dazzle the readers; whether they permit deductions which could not otherwise be made, or at least, whether they make some complex web of relationships easier to grasp, and whether their premises are sufficiently precise to lend themselves to formal operations.

No good worker bandies about his tools needlessly, and the same precept holds good for sociologists. Mathematics, particularly if approached from the point of view of its philosophy, provides a wonderful training in clear thinking, and for this reason, any intellectual who has the requisite ability, and can spare the time, can benefit from acquainting himself with the mathematical manner of reasoning. Apart from being a good 'mental hygiene' (as Comte called it), some knowledge of mathematics bestows the advantage of being able to discern spurious from genuine uses thereof. But it is worth noting that writers on social matters who were mathematicians did not obtrude mathematics needlessly: the writings of Auguste Comte, Augustin Cournot, and Bertrand Russell bear no traces of this foible.

What has just been said is also true of the new branch of mathematics known as the theory of games, which enjoys great vogue, and has been acclaimed as the saviour of the social sciences. Personally, I do not see how it can – in its present state – be usefully applied to sociology or even realistic economic theory. Its postulates – such as *a priori* knowledge of possible outcomes, the unchangeability of values placed on them, perfect rationality, the strict alternation of moves of the partners (which rules out the advantage gained by speed), separateness of courses of action and so on – are so remote from the real human rough and tumble that they make it useless as an instrument of sociological analysis, let alone prediction. Possibly, further developments of the theory of games may lend themselves to useful applications, but it is a mere pretence to claim that this day has arrived. Naturally, nothing can be achieved without trying, and there is no reason for not contemplating the applicability of the theory of games to sociology, or not publishing accounts of such cogitation, but the authors ought to state clearly that so far it is just a play of ideas.

Some acquaintance with the theory of games might, perhaps, be profitable to a sociologist, particularly if it is derived from a book like *Games and Decisions* by Luce and Raiffa, which stresses the ideas rather than techniques. Apart from training in reasoning, the chief advantage of such acquaintance is that the awareness of the contrast between the idealized model and real life might bring to attention some hitherto unnoticed important features of the latter.

Techniques of Field Research

To judge by the enthusiastic eulogies, one could think that some fantastically powerful instruments of observation have been invented, which can do for sociology what the microscope did for biology, and the telescope for astronomy. Unfortunately, all these techniques do not amount to very much: a few tips on how to goad people into opening their souls at interviews (not much more sophisticated than those traditionally given to police interrogators), some hints on how to prepare questionnaires, on how to make records, how to tabulate and file the results; a few pieces of advice on how to procure personal documents and discount their biases, and on how to enter into participant observation. All these things are useful in their proper place, and if treated as accessories, but become extremely pernicious if idolized. In the latter case, they function as labour-multiplying and thought-saving devices. Unlike the microscope and the telescope, these 'tools of social science' have not brought new worlds within our purview: all they have achieved has been to make it easier to avoid certain errors of observation.

Excessive reliance on prefabricated techniques constrains thought. Questionnaires ask only questions adumbrated beforehand by their framers. Forms and tables often induce their users to reject problems which do not fit into them, and in this way function as blinkers. The proneness to these foibles is enhanced by the trend towards research by large teams, where the ubiquitous tendency of a bureaucratic apparatus to stamp out independent thought manifests itself with full force.

There is a saying that 'those who can – do, and those who cannot – teach'. It could be applied to scientific work by paraphrasing it as follows: 'those who can – discover, and those who cannot, take up methodology'. Both sayings are, of course, caricatures of reality, but like all passable caricatures, contain a grain of truth; for it cannot be denied that there exists a phenomenon which might be described as 'a flight into methodology' from the problems which are either too difficult or too dangerous. This is not to deny that, in view of the advantages of the division of labour in science as in industrial work and sports, there must be some people who devote themselves to studying how others do it. On occasions such people can give to those 'on the firing line' some useful advice. On the whole, however, there is little evidence in the history of science that great discoveries were due to new ideas on methodology. On the contrary, most radical changes of view on this matter seem to have followed important scientific discoveries; which seems natural enough, as methodology is basically reflexion upon the causes of the investigators' successes and failures.

Methodology is prophylactic in its essence. In the same way as hygiene can help us to avoid some contagions but is powerless to ensure health, methodology can warn us of pitfalls but will not help us to conceive new ideas. The so-called methods of induction are in reality methods of verification: they tell us how to test hypotheses but not how to arrive at them. Indeed, the latter process is just as much a mystery as it was in the days of Socrates: all that is known is that, in order to conceive fruitful original ideas, one must have talent, must immerse oneself in the available knowledge and think very hard.

The over-emphasis on methodology and techniques, as well as adulation of formulae and scientific-sounding terms, exemplify the common tendency (which also manifests itself in such diverse phenomena as miserliness and barrack room 'spit and polish') to displace value from the end to the means: something originally valued solely as means to an end comes to be valued for its own sake, and the original end is forgotten. A sociologist obsessed with frameworks, jargon and techniques resembles a carpenter who becomes so worried about keeping his tools clean that he has no time to cut the wood.[1] These tendencies are reinforced by the feeling of helplessness in the face of an unmanageable complexity of social phenomena, and the fear of dabbling with dangerous issues, which lurk throughout the field of sociology. The result of all this is that it is forgotten that unfettered thought is the most essential of research methods.

A Good Description

When is a description good? The answer, clearly, depends on its purpose. In the same way as there are no tools good for everything, so there are no descriptions which are good from every point of view: a description of a man which would provide an appropriate basis for selecting a chief engineer, will contain no information which a tailor needs, and most details of the latter will be of no use to a coffin maker. This difficulty cannot be circumvented by giving a full description, because such a thing cannot exist; reality is inexhaustible, and nothing can be described completely – not even the end of one's nose.

With descriptions which have a practical aim in view the criteria of adequacy are fairly evident; with purely cognitive descriptions the matter is more elusive. One criterion which applies to all descriptions is economy. In view of the fact that reality is inexhaustible but our capacity limited, widely spread skill in judging what ought to be left out and what included constitutes an indispensable condition of intellectual progress. Judged from this point of view, most sociological publications are sadly defective: they insist on telling the reader everything that the author knows, irrespectively of whether there are any grounds for doubting that the reader knows it too. Sometimes the authors tell us what literally everybody knows: thus from a study of Irish villagers we learn that 'the care of children is mainly the task of women'. An interesting description omits what can be justifiably taken for

---

[1] In his recent book *Words and Things*, Ernest Gellner has castigated an analogous tendency in British philosophy, consisting of an exclusive preoccupation with the meaning of concepts without attempting to use them for tackling important problems.

granted, and dwells upon the unexpected: without, however, insinuating thereby that the curious is the norm.

Economy of expression is partly a matter of stylistic skill, but even more the result of being able to discern what is important and what is not. But what does importance mean without reference to a definite practical aim – importance in general? I can think of only one thing which it can mean: namely, causal efficacity. It follows that a cognitive description (ie a description without any practical aim in view) is good in so far as it gives in an economical form the information about factors which have produced a given situation or are maintaining it in its present state. In view of what has been said earlier, it is obvious that a good description must be analytic and be based on recourse to all relevant theoretical generalizations. What happens with the authors who produce good descriptive analyses without having much knowledge of theory is that they have a good intuitive grasp of the theories implicit in their work – which is possible owing to the rudimentary state of sociology. However, as an intuitive grasp can be only imperfectly transmitted by demonstration, it cannot provide foundations for a rapid cumulation of knowledge.

The number, size and complexity of social entities, and above all their continuous transformations create a need for the work of description, even when no new theoretical issues demanding fresh evidence have been raised. Even within the assumptions of unaided common sense the need for descriptions will always remain, but such work alone can never amount to scientific progress.

Conclusion

The most general lesson which emerges from the foregoing discussion is so plain that it would not be worth mentioning were it not continuously disregarded: it is that a sociologist must continuously ask why. When theorizing, he should try to find out why things always happen the way they do; when describing and analysing a concrete case, he should try to discover why it is as it is. It is the failure on this score that makes so many sociological works so boring. Statistics, questionnaires, techniques and conceptual frameworks are all very well, but they should be treated as tools taken out of the box when needed – not as idols paraded around and worshipped. Methodology is the mental hygiene of the scientist, but excessive preoccupation with it is just as incapacitating as obsessional washing.

I know very well that intricate epistemological problems stem from the semantic analysis of the little word 'why'. But sociologists who are not philosophically inclined should not worry unduly: semanticists have uncovered various shades of meaning of 'why', but have by no means disproved the legitimacy of this good old word. Only by asking why, and trying to give concrete answers, will the sociologist avoid the pitfalls of sterility and verbalism.

CHAPTER TWO

UNCERTAINTY PRINCIPLE, SELF-FULFILLING PROPHECY AND OTHER DIFFICULTIES OF SOCIOLOGICAL ENQUIRY

IT HAS OFTEN been remarked that the magnitude and complexity of social phenomena make them into an exceedingly intractable object of study. As Charles A. Beard said, speaking of sociological history, 'after all, physics, complex as it may be, is relatively simple as compared to a subject which includes physicists and physics, and everything else mankind has ever said and done on earth'. In order to avoid repetition of what has been said many times before I shall consider only a few methodological lessons which can be drawn from an examination of some consequences of the disparity of size and longevity between a sociologist and the objects which he studies.

A sociologist moves between Scylla and Charybdis: if he shuns difficulties connected with the study of large-scale social phenomena and turns his attention to small groups, he comes up against the residual, but apparently irreducible indeterminacy of individual behaviour, as well as against another equally irremediable limitation, caused by alterations in the state of an observed object by the process of observation. Physics encountered this barrier (I am referring to Heisenberg's uncertainty principle) only after three centuries of phenomenal growth, when particles commensurate with waves of light began to be studied – that is to say, phenomena very far removed from ordinary human perception. In sociology, on the contrary, this limitation operates on the level of small groups, that is to say, on the level of the only phenomena which can be directly perceived, for nobody can see a state or any other large human aggregate; we can only infer their existence from fragmentary observations and received information. So long as in studying a small group we are interested in exemplifications of norms which prevail in a wider society, we need not worry about the effects of the process of observation on our findings. People do not deviate from the customs of their society just because they are being watched; rather the contrary. In contrast, peculiarities which distinguish particular small groups from other similar groups can be greatly affected by observation. The presence of an observer will not alter people's religious beliefs, but if I move into a house in order to study the dynamics of the domestic quarrels of its inhabitants, I might see things which would never have occurred without my presence: quarrels might cease and I might become a scapegoat; or alliances might be reversed, or I might be drawn into the battlefield and so on. These difficulties partly explain why the study of small groups remains so far rather unfruitful: in spite of the enormous outlay of resources, the results are far inferior to what has been obtained by critically collating reflections based on practical experience of affairs. The tragedy is that so many workers in this field delude themselves that they are making discoveries when they couch bits of common sense in nebulous pseudo-scientific jargon. It must also be remembered that small groups existed since the beginning of human species, so that common sense had time to develop some means of understanding their behaviour, whereas large groups are something very new in relation to the biological and linguistic evolution of mankind. Moreover, common sense is helpless when elements which have to be taken into account are very numerous: a housewife needs no statistics for making her plans, but without elaborate statistical calculations the planning of national economy will end in a calamity. In business management, likewise, abstruse systems of data processing, operational research and other intricate techniques are useful only in firms which are so large that unaided common sense cannot grasp the situation. The possibility of experiment, which is widely considered to be the chief advantage of studying small groups, is largely illusory because the really important social bonds, which constitute the vertebrae of every enduring human aggregate, cannot be reproduced artificially. In view of these circumstances, it seems that only a much greater infusion of genuinely creative imagination than that which has so far been forthcoming could rescue this field from its present impasse.

A physicist or a chemist, when he finds an explanation unconvincing, can usually check it by repeating the relevant experiments: he can see with his own eyes a confirmation of his deductions. But what can we do if an explanation of the fall of the Roman Empire does not convince us? Even leaving apart ascertainment of causes, what can we do if we distrust our information on some simple matter of fact which is beyond the reach of our personal perception? Examine the relevant documents? But that may take years. Ask another specialist or see what is said in various books? How do we know that the very sources on which the whole edifice is built tell the truth? Some may say that historical materials are in any case useless, and that we must concentrate on contemporary events. Very well then, how can I check the truth of what a statistical yearbook tells me about the number of inhabitants of a city – even of the city in which I live? How do I know that Nasser really exists, or that Somoza's rule in Nicaragua is tyrannical, or that the rate of industrial growth is higher in China than in India, or that in the United States sons of immigrants commit more crimes than either the first or the third generation, or that there is a Manus island and that its inhabitants really practise the customs described in a book whose authorship is ascribed to a person called Margaret Mead? In all such matters, we accept information on trust which is often misplaced. If we are careful, we attempt to form some estimate of the veracity of some of our sources, try to ascertain and discount their biases, look for inconsistencies, read between the lines and so on. Always, even when ascertaining most elementary facts, we make judgements based on circumstantial evidence, which means that we proceed on various assumptions about what is, likely or unlikely, possible or impossible, what follows from what, what is incompatible with what and so on. For this reason one of the most essential parts of the training of a student of social processes is acquisition of the skill in evaluating information. Courses on sociology and psychology usually include some instruction in techniques of interviewing. The even more important art of critical examination of written documents is taught only in courses in historiography. Either kind of instruction is of limited use unless supplemented by a fairly wide personal experience of varieties of human behaviour. This, incidentally, is

one of the reasons why a very young person can become an outstanding mathematician or physicist but not an outstanding
historian or sociologist; the other reason being the greater relative
importance in the study of society of mere bulk of necessary
information as compared with pure power of reasoning. Reliance
on circumstantial evidence – and, therefore, on the test of consistency – leaves very wide scope to prejudices and wishful thinking
of all kinds. It strengthens dangerously the element of circular
verification, whereby an opinion is regarded as confirmed because
factual evidence which testifies against it is rejected as unreliable,
because it does not accord with some implications of the said
opinion. Personal experience of a variety of social situations is
unimportant as far as the amount of information is concerned, for
the bulk of it must unavoidably be second hand; its importance
lies in the way it helps one to judge the veracity of supplied
information.

Saddened by the awareness of so many weaknesses of our discipline, we might find some consolation in the knowledge that,
after all, physicists also have to rely on the test of consistency.
The fairly old doctrine of empiricism, recently reformulated more
rigorously by logical positivists, according to which science is
constructed upon the foundations consisting of what these
philosophers call 'protocol sentences' (that is to say, of descriptions
of immediate perceptions) has been demolished by Karl Popper
who, taking up the arguments of Kant and Cassirer, pointed out
that even the names of most ordinary things have 'dispositional
content', which means that they imply a number of assertions
about the regularities in the behaviour of objects which they
designate. By using the word 'thermometer' for instance, we
assume various regularities in the behaviour of quicksilver, the
existence and transmission of something called heat, and so on.
Long before Gestalt psychology and the studies of Piaget, a
Scottish philosopher and psychologist, G. F. Stout, showed how
the growth of a child's knowledge of the external world and of
itself consists of working out coherences. In the same way, though
on a higher level of abstraction, the growth of science consists
mainly in adjusting our beliefs so as to eliminate contradictions.

The view that coherence is the main criterion of truth may be
criticized on the ground that reality is full of contradictions. To
say this, however, is to use the word contradiction rather vaguely.

87473

Reality is full of conflicts, oppositions and contradictions between uttered statements, but it is a fundamental axiom of all science, as well as of practical reasoning, that there can be no contradiction between true descriptions of real events. Physicists, archaeologists, detectives, judges, shoemakers and merchants, all assume it without question. Indeed our very concept of reality – our distinctions between illusions, delusions and true perceptions – is based on this axiom. We call illusions data provided by one of our senses which do not agree with data provided by other senses, or with antecedent or subsequent perceptions. We deem to be hallucinations all those perceptions of an individual which are not confirmed by perceptions of others, in spite of belonging to a category of publicly confirmable perceptions. In this case reality is defined with reference to inter-personal coherence of perceptions. To say this does not imply the acceptance of Hegel's view that 'truth is coherence', and the rejection of so-called correspondence and pragmatic theories of truth, associated respectively with the names of Bertrand Russell and William James. As a matter of fact these theories (or rather definitions) in no way clash. On the contrary, it is quite plain that all scientific and practical reasoning proceeds on the assumption that correspondence implies coherence, which in turn implies utility for the purpose of prediction, and the other way round: utility of a proposition implies correspondence between its meaning and the events to which it refers, and coherence with other propositions which exhibit these characteristics.

The strength of the exact sciences is in the fact that over enormous areas there are relationships of mutual implication between propositions, which are supported by independent observational evidence. In the social sciences not only do we have no network of strict mutual implication, but we are still trying to eliminate glaring contradictions. So we labour under several disadvantages at the same time: firstly, in a far greater measure than natural scientists we have to rely on second hand information which we cannot check directly; secondly, we are much less able to procure factual information which might bear upon our hypotheses; thirdly, in virtue of the uncertainty of most statements, we have to rely to a much greater extent on the test of coherence, which we cannot apply so rigorously as does a natural scientist because our statements are more involved and less precise. Our predicament stems mainly from the disparity in size and longevity between ourselves and the objects of our study. Cosmology and geology provide the nearest analogies in physical sciences.

Being so puny in relation to society a sociologist cannot experiment. This is so obvious that it calls for no comment. When some people talk about experimental sociology, they are attempting to cash in on the prestige of physical sciences by twisting the meaning of 'experiment'. What merits more emphasis are some consequences of inevitable delays in obtaining information which throws light on our hypotheses, due to the necessity of relying in this respect on others. There are many examples of such delays. Pareto presented his system, centred around what we now call vertical social mobility, at the beginning of the present century (its final formulation was published in 1916), but it was only within the last few years that serious efforts were made to obtain extensive statistical data on this point. Even so, the systematic information gathered so far bears upon only one aspect of the problem raised by Pareto, because it refers almost solely to the numbers involved, and throws no light on the equally basic question of the methods by which social ascent is achieved. Similarly, only now have we factual basis for deciding some of the issues which Max Weber raised fifty years ago, or Marx one hundred years ago. Besides inevitably slowing down the progress of sociology, such delays have another consequence of extreme importance to methodology: namely, that any important contribution to sociological theory must be tentative. A thesis which can be fully proven by the existing data cannot be original, because, if it had not been current among the workers in the field, they would not have gathered the relevant information. A physicist can conceive a hypothesis, and often (though by no means always) can prove it himself by a series of experiments carried out for this purpose. A sociologist can formulate his hypothesis, try to show with the aid of data which happen to exist that it seems to be valid, and hope that it will not be entirely discarded by later investigators. If his successors find after many years that there is 'something in it' he achieves the status of a great thinker, for more often than not 'there is nothing in it'. Thus steps of successive approximation and modification which may take place in a laboratory during one series of experiments, are here spread over generations. The very important practical lesson which emerges from this argument is that if, unintelligently aping physicists and chemists, we demand that no thesis must be put forth unless it is fully substantiated by factual data, we condemn sociology to sterility. Intuition and surmisal play is, of course, an indispensable role in the process of discovery in any field; the peculiarity of sociology and related sciences lies in the greater need for publishing unproven products of speculation. Naturally, in order to be fruitful, a contribution to sociological theory must take into account available data, but it must outrun them.

The lag of proofs behind theses and the consequent pullulation of unverified theories, have some very unfortunate effects: they give a wide scope to unscholarly sensationalism. When controls are slack many people succumb to the temptation of choosing the line of least resistance, and instead of enduring hard work with uncertain prospects, organize a publicity campaign for their goods. Coteries with strong vested interests in their patent medicines form themselves, which to methodological difficulties add an even more formidable barrier of malevolent prejudice.

Human beings not only react to being observed, but are also influenced by what is said about what will happen to them, or about what they themselves will do. There are many examples of people who were apparently in good health but then sickened and even died, after being told by a person whose word they believed that they would do so. A rumour that certain shares will fall may become the cause of the anticipated event. A belief in the inevitability of a war or revolution may in fact bring it about, in spite of the falseness of the grounds on which it was originally based. Thus, there are circumstances under which a fulfilment of sociological prediction creates no presumption whatsoever in favour of the premises which supported this prediction. This gives to sociologists an opportunity of committing a fallacy which is absolutely unknown in natural sciences, and which Robert K. Merton has called the 'fallacy of self-fulfilling prophecy'. There is no way of eliminating this handicap which severely restricts the area of verifiability in sociology. We can only draw a prophylactic conclusion that a causal analysis is most satisfactory when it deals with events which occurred contrary to the expectations of persons whose actions brought them about.

In his remarkable *Histoire des Sciences et des Savants* (published in 1875) Adolphe de Candolle expressed doubt whether the study of society would ever attain the status of a science. His chief argument was that in dealing with human beings, lying is too profitable to allow a custom of honest investigation of human affairs to strike roots. This argument has considerable force: inanimate objects respond neither to threats, nor to lies nor to entreaties, whereas human beings do. Even a most objective, strictly factual finding – such as, say, figures concerning incomes of some individuals or groups – may affect adversely somebody's interests, and therefore bring hostility upon a person who made or divulged it. Since the time when Candolle wrote his book we witnessed grandiose and phenomenally successful attempts at falsifying information on every aspect of social reality. A whole treatise could be written on this topic, and it is clear that the obstacles to development of sociological knowledge which stem from vested interests and passions are far more lethal than purely methodological difficulties, formidable as these are.

To deserve his place in society, the sociologist must try to enlighten people about the causes and consequences of their collective actions; and in doing so he cannot avoid bringing to light what many would like to conceal, destroying cherished illusions and wounding susceptibilities. Indeed, no important contribution to our understanding of social phenomena can be made without offending adherents of various dogmas as well as those who are incapable of viewing their loyalties, enmities and material interests objectively. The price of writing honest sociology is exposure to resentment or even wrath; and one can escape from this dilemma only by confining oneself to minute details or dwelling upon irrelevancies or taking refuge in nebulous verbosity, unless one is unscrupulous enough to write solely with an eye to applause regardless of the truth.

In the study of society the reasoning still proceeds on the basis of assumptions of doubtful validity. But whereas any new idea is readily rejected for want of conclusive proofs, the current assumptions escape questioning by never being explicitly stated. The evidence adduced in support of the theories put forth in the present book would certainly not be accepted as conclusive in the exact sciences: as everything else in sociology they must remain tentative approximations. Nevertheless, before the reader dismisses them on these grounds, let him consider whether the generally accepted views rest upon any firmer proofs; and let him remember that negation requires equally conclusive evidence as an affirmation. Moreover, notwithstanding the absence of generalizations as certain as those of the exact sciences, practical decisions concerning human affairs have to be made; and they ought to be guided by theories which are most likely to be true in the light of the available knowledge, rather than by sheer guesswork or mental inertia. Waiting for certitude amounts to resigning ourselves to acting in almost total ignorance.

CHAPTER THREE

DETERMINISM, TELEOLOGY AND EXPLANATION

LOGICAL POSITIVISTS chose as one of the corner-stones of their approach to philosophy the view that meanings of words are the matter of choice and convention, and that there is no such thing as true or real meaning. Nevertheless some of them forgot this principle when it came to the words 'meaning' and 'truth' themselves; so that in some books, which show how silly it is to raise the question of real or true meanings, we find chapters called 'theory of meaning' or 'theory of truth', where we find assertions about what meaning and truth *are*; whereas, according to the said view, we should speak only of definitions of 'truth' and 'meaning' and their relative usefulness. Something similar can be said about the treatment of the word 'explanation'. If we consider various ways in which 'explanation' is used, we find that the only common denominator is psychological rather than logical; so that we can say that an explanation is a statement which satisfies the curiosity of a person who asked for it. For the sake of avoiding ambiguity, the problem of explanation ought to be treated as a problem of deciding which kinds of explanation should be accepted as scientific, rather than a problem of finding out what a scientific explanation *is*.

We can define adequately causal (or strictly determinist) explanation of a particular event as a statement which tells us why this event was an inevitable consequence of antecedent events. More precisely this idea can be expressed as follows; in order to constitute an admissible explanation of an event E a statement must contain: (1) a specification of a rule according to which there is a type of event T, every exemplification of which is invariably followed by the occurrence of an event of the type to which E belongs; (2) an assertion that an event C which belongs to the type T did occur at an appropriate time and place. When a detective answers the question 'why did this man die' by saying 'he was shot through the heart', he makes an assertion about the occurrence of the shooting, which carries an implication that shooting through the heart is always followed by death. Often a connection between two events is so remote that it cannot be subsumed under any known general rule, and is explained, therefore, by splitting the chain of events into several links, each of which can be subsumed under some recognized general rule. An explanation of a regular connection between two types of events ought to consist of specification of a more general rule from which the said regularity can be deduced; as has been pointed out by various methodologists, the mere formulation of a general rule describing the regularity in question should be regarded as a discovery rather than an explanation.

A satisfactory explanatory premise must imply not only the assertion to be explained but other conclusions as well. If it does not, we have a tautology which can neither be falsified by further evidence nor connected with other findings. Molière understood it intuitively when he ridiculed a physician who explains why opium makes people sleep by saying that it possesses a dormitive power. Though old, this methodological rule is often broken in contemporary sociology, as can be seen from the examples of purely verbal discoveries mentioned in Chapter One.

The canons of admissibility mentioned above carry no implications as to the nature of events to which an explanation refers: such events can be mental as well as physical, macroscopic as well as microscopic, and so on. Sociological and historical explanations, in so far as they are adequately causal, are simply explanations of events studied in sociology and historiography, and differ from explanations employed in other disciplines not in logical structure, but only in the nature of events to which they refer. Dealing with human conduct we must have recourse to interpretations in terms of mental processes which we know by introspection, and which are not open to public observation. No valid epistemological objections can be raised against this procedure; for unless we assume some basic likeness of human minds, the very process of communication, including conveyance of knowledge about the physical universe, is senseless and illusory. The mere intent to communicate presupposes the belief in existence of other minds, capable of experiencing thoughts and feelings similar to ours. For this reason, an assertion of belief in either sollipsism or physicalism is denied by the mere fact of being uttered.

It is still fairly fashionable among historians (and used to be much more so) to talk about 'historical explanation' as something *sui generis* – something logically different from other explanations. In the light of what was said earlier it is clear that our view on this matter must depend on the canons of admissibility of explanations which we recognize. Nevertheless, it is clear that if we take a wide sample of pieces of reasoning which have been offered as historical explanations, we can easily see that they satisfy no set of methodological requirements that have ever been formulated – that they are narratives of sequences of events, whose only common denominator is that they somehow satisfy many people's curiosity.

Some scholars have claimed that the distinctive attribute of historical explanations is that they purport to explain unique events, whereas the physical sciences deal exclusively with regularities. The first remark which suggests itself in this respect is that geology, cosmology and the theory of evolution of species offer explanations of processes which, as far as we know, are absolutely unique. A more important point, however, is that the only kind of admissible explanation of a unique event consists of showing either that it comes under a known general rule, or that it can be resolved into elements which all come under some known rules. This means that a unique event can be explained only in so far as it consists of recurrent elements. Elements of irreducible uniqueness (which can be found in many natural phenomena as well, though to a lesser extent) can be apprehended but neither explained nor described – for even description involves analysis of a phenomenon into elements which are sufficiently recurrent to fit meanings of words. It follows that a historical explanation which is admissible must invoke, or at least imply, some general rules denoting regularities in social processes, and therefore must belong to the category of sociological explanations; in other words a historical explanation is a sociological explanation of events described in historiography, in so far as it is an explanation as distinct from a narrative.

In the course of the foregoing discussion the word 'cause' appeared several times, and so I must say a few words about the place of this concept in scientific explanation. The view that sociology, like other sciences, has no need for the concept of cause has been put forth by Pareto, who arrived at this conclusion by reflecting upon the absence from physics equations of any references to causes. Like some later methodologists, he forgot, however, that books on physics, apart from mathematical equations, contain verbal accounts of experiments, which distinguish clearly between variables which can and those which cannot be manipulated; and this distinction is reflected in mathematics in the distinction between dependent and independent variables. Moreover, whenever time is treated as irreversible the idea of causation is implicit. The argument that we had better drop 'cause' from our scientific vocabulary because it is anthropomorphic (as it stems from our experience of action), has no force as far as social sciences are concerned – no matter what validity it might have in other fields. A greater weight is carried by the argument that a cause has to be a sufficient condition of its effect, but it is beyond the powers of our limited minds to specify all the conditions which make up a sufficient condition; an event (whatever it might be) can be invariably followed by another event only under certain conditions, which in turn depend on further conditions, which in their turn depend on still other conditions, and so on until we exhaust all the attributes of the universe. For instance, it might be said that the existence of mankind constituted a part of the cause of the death of a beheaded man, or that the existence of tools was also a part of that cause, or even the fact that the earth did not collide with another celestial body. This argument is not convincing because, although an event called 'the beheading of a man' could not happen unless mankind, the earth and tools existed, such an event if it occurs is invariably followed by an event called the 'death of a man'; we can speak, therefore, unambiguously of the former as being the cause of the latter, if we accept the simple definition that a cause of an event is an event of which the first is a necessary consequence. The plurality of causes (that is to say, the possibility that each of several antecedent events constituted a sufficient condition of occurrence of the event E) enhances the difficulty of ascertaining them, but in no way undermines the epistemological status of the concept of cause.

Many people believe that human behaviour can be studied

scientifically (ie with a view to discovering regularities) only on the assumption that there is no such thing as free will; that negation of its existence constitutes an essential part of scientific outlook. Any doubt in this matter amounts to a sacrilege in the eyes of 'scientific' psychologists. Nevertheless, at the risk of being regarded as a retrograde obscurantist, I propose to reconsider it once more. I shall attempt to show that a solution, which provides a quite satisfactory basis for the methodology of social sciences is not difficult to find: indeed, it seems to be just a common-sense solution.

The debate about free will well illustrates how dangerous abstract words can be, and how easily they can become divorced from the reality which they were intended to describe. For centuries philosophers talked in terms of an antinomy: man is either absolutely free or an automaton whose actions are completely determined by preceding physical events. In contrast, simple common-sense introspection shows that neither is the case: only madmen have feelings of omnipotence, and only the very ill have feelings of complete impotence. The rest of us are aware that we can control certain bodily and mental processes but not all. I know that I can decide now either to continue sitting or to get up, but I cannot control my feelings in the same way: I cannot make myself angry or hungry, or gay or frightened by a simple act of will; on the contrary, the law of reverse effort applies in these matters.

The awareness of some freedom of will is one of the primary data of consciousness, and as such irrefutable. No inferences from any scientific generalizations can undermine it for the following reasons. Propositions of natural sciences are series of signs which enable us to predict observations, which are interpretations of perceptions. Perceptions, which provide in the final instance verification of scientific theories, are visual, auditory and tactile – but only those perceptions which can be attested by many observers are regarded as objective. Objective data is merely another word for publicly confirmable perceptions. Perceptions which cannot be confirmed by more than one person are called subjective data: toothaches, for instance. Science must rely on publicly confirmable perceptions because it is a collective endeavour, but it does not follow that all perceptions which are not confirmable in this way can be disregarded. No dentist can convince me that I do not have a toothache when I feel one; all he can do is to enlighten me about causes thereof. Likewise, no inferences from observations of moving bodies, noises and so on can convince me that I cannot decide whether to put my hand on the table now or not. Indeed, my awareness of being able to decide this is not more open to doubt than my awareness that I see a table now, or that two and two make four; and it is far more evident than the assertion that the earth is round, or that I have a liver. Perception of being free to decide about some of my actions forms an essential part of perception of my own existence. To Descartes' dictum 'I think, therefore I am' we can add 'I decide, therefore I exist'. It follows that I cannot assert a belief in non-existence of freedom of will without denying my own existence. Now, it seems reasonable to suppose that an utterance, which implies that the person who uttered it does not exist, cannot be true; or at least, that we cannot accept a view which asserts our non-existence, for the obvious reason that if we do not exist then we cannot accept anything.

As Isaiah Berlin inimitably puts it in his book on Historical Inevitability (Oxford 1954, pp. 30-1, 33-4):

'The proposition that everything that we do and suffer is part of a fixed pattern; that Laplace's observer (supplied with adequate knowledge of facts and laws) could at any moment of historical time describe correctly every past and future event including those of "inner" life, that is, human thoughts, feelings, acts, and so on, has often been entertained, and different implications have been drawn from it; belief in its truth has dismayed some and inspired others. But whether such determinism is a valid theory or not, it seems clear that acceptance of it does not in fact colour the ordinary thoughts of the majority of human beings, nor those of historians, nor even those of natural scientists outside the laboratory. For if it did, the language of the believers would reflect this fact and be very different from that of the rest of us.

'I do not here wish to say that determinism is necessarily false, only that we neither speak nor think as if it could be true, and that it is difficult, and perhaps impossible, to conceive what our picture of the world would be if we seriously believed it; so that to speak, as some theorists of history (and scientists with a philosophical bent) tend to do, as if one might accept the determinist hypothesis, and yet to continue to think and speak much as we do at present, is to breed intellectual confusion. If the belief in freedom – which rests on the assumption that human beings do occasionally choose, and that their choices are not wholly accounted in, say, physics or biology – if this is a necessary illusion, it is so deep and so pervasive that it is not felt as such. No doubt we can try to convince ourselves that we are systematically deluded. But unless we attempt to think out the implications of this possibility, and alter our modes of thought and speech to allow for it accordingly, this hypothesis remains hollow; that is, we find it impossible even to entertain it seriously, if our behaviour is to be taken as evidence of what we can and what we cannot bring ourselves to believe or suppose not merely in theory, but in practice. My submission is that to make a serious attempt to adapt our thoughts and words to the hypothesis of determinism is scarcely feasible, as things are now, and have been within recorded history. The changes involved are too radical; our moral categories are, in the end, not much more flexible than our physical ones; we cannot begin to think out in real terms, to which behaviour and speech would correspond, what the universe of the genuine determinist would be like, any more than we can think out, with the minimum of indispensable concrete detail (ie begin to imagine) what it would be like to be in a timeless world, or one with a seventeen-dimensional space.'

Very important methodological consequences follow from this *reductio ad absurdum*. If human will is at least partially free, then we must abandon in the social sciences the ideal of absolute predictability. Since the formulation of the principle of indeterminacy even the physicists gave up this ideal of absolute determinism. Anyway, in spite of all the progress of physiology and chemistry, the psychic has not yet been reduced to the physical, and it follows from the foregoing arguments that we must view social life not as a continuum of uninterrupted causal chains, but rather as consisting of broken causal chains. We may strive to extend our ability to predict, but it is important to realize that we shall not find determinacy everywhere, because then we might think about where it can most probably be found.

The conclusion that decisions are not entirely determined by antecedent events does not nullify the possibility of prediction because a decision is a choice: a choice out of a finite number of alternatives. For this reason, when trying to discover elements of predictability, we ought to concentrate on limitations of choices. It is quite clear that no amount of freedom of will can affect the fact that I cannot eat my cake and keep it, or that if I devote more of my time to some activity, I shall have less for other pursuits. Furthermore, by making certain decisions we limit the freedom of action of others: if Mary does not wish to marry, John's field of choice is correspondingly reduced. In some cases there is only one possible course of action for a set of persons although there are alternatives for the individuals. For example, in a group which meets to discuss something the members may have freedom of choice about the order of speaking, but as far as their collective behaviour is concerned, they have only two alternatives: speaking in turn or failing to communicate properly. At most one could say that the third alternative is to split into smaller groups, but then the first two alternatives would reappear on a smaller scale. Certain features of collective actions can be predicted easily and safely: for instance, if we take some fairly large collection of persons, we may not be able to foresee whether they will embark upon some collective action or not, but we can predict with confidence that if they do then they will have to form within themselves a hierarchy of executives. It appears, in view of the foregoing argument and examples, that in our search for predictability we must look for constraints (structural constraints, if you like) on choices. This view seems to support the conclusion which Gaetano Mosca reached on entirely unphilosophical pragmatic grounds, that in making political forecasts we should begin with the elimination of impossible outcomes.

Reasoning along these lines we reach further conclusions. It has been observed long ago by Buckle and Quetelet that whereas it is impossible to predict whether any given individual will or will not commit suicide, or post a letter without a stamp, or perform some other unusual action, statistical incidence of such actions in any large population fluctuates within very narrow limits. If the argument about free will is correct, then this is not a consequence of inadequate knowledge, but something that is rooted in the nature of social phenomena. This was the view upheld by Quetelet, as can be seen from the following quotation from his *Du Système Social* (Paris 1848, p. 69–70):

'Que l'on ne croie pas que les mariages forment la seule série de faits sociaux qui procèdent avec tant de régularité et de constance. J'ai fait voir ailleurs qu'il en est de même des crimes, qui se reproduisent annuellement en même nombre et attirent les mêmes peines dans les mêmes proportions. Même constance s'observe dans les mutilations que se font des individus pour échapper au service militaire, dans les sommes exposées autrefois dans les maisons de jeu de Paris et jusque dans les négligences signalées par l'administration des postes par rapport aux lettres non fermées, manquant d'adresses ou portant des adresses illisibles. Tout se passe, en un mot, comme si ces diverses séries de faits étaient soumises à des causes purement physiques.

'Devant un pareil ensemble d'observations, faut-il nier le libre arbitre de l'homme? certes je ne le crois pas. Je conçois seulement que l'effet de ce libre arbitre se trouve resserré dans des limites très étroites et joue, dans les phénomènes sociaux, le rôle d'une cause accidentelle. Il arrive alors qu'en faisant abstraction des individus et en ne considérant les choses que d'une manière générale, les effets de toutes les causes accidentelles doivent se neutraliser et se détruire mutuellement, de manière à ne laisser prédominer que les véritables causes en vertu desquelles la société existe et se conserve.

'La possibilité d'établir une statistique morale et d'en déduire des conséquences utiles, dépend entièrement de ce fait fondamental que le libre arbitre de l'homme s'éfface et demeure sans effet sensible, quand les observations s'étendent sur un grand nombre d'individus.'

It follows that the study of large aggregates is more likely to yield predictive knowledge than the study of small groups, and that the current stress on the latter is probably misplaced.

If we stress the element of choice in social behaviour we cannot avoid invoking the concept of purpose, which is anathema to those who tend to imitate the external paraphernalia of natural sciences, but not their spirit. In these sciences the exclusion of teleological explanation constituted an essential step in the elimination of the anthropomorphism which impeded their early growth. Naïvely following this example, some psychologists took it as their aim to eliminate anthropomorphism from the study of *anthropos* as well. To say that water seeks or desires the lowest point does not appear to be a very useful way of describing what happens, but if we answer the question 'why is he bending down?' by saying 'he wants to find a lost coin', our statement is perfectly admissible even if it be wrong on point of fact. If the foregoing argument about free will is correct, then teleological explanations of this kind are not only admissible but often the only possible.

It is often asserted that teleological explanations must be ruled out because they assume causation of earlier events by the later. Now, a moment's reflection shows that this argument is false. A correct teleological explanation of why I am running towards the station is that my desire for the event 'my-going-in-the-train' is the cause of the event 'my-running-towards-the-station', not that the event 'my-going-in-the-train' is the cause of the event 'my-running-towards-the-station'. The latter version is clearly absurd because I may fail to catch the train, in which case the event 'my-getting-to-the-station-after-the-train-had-left' would have to be the cause of the event 'my-running-towards-the-station'. An explanation which refers to purpose assumes no causation which runs against the direction of time for the obvious reason that a process called purpose precedes or accompanies action which it causes. A teleological explanation of this kind is perfectly legitimate so long as there are grounds which justify imputation of purpose. Now, purpose is a mental process which we know by introspection; and we must assume that it occurs in other human beings, unless we uphold solipsism and doubt existence of other minds like ours. I also believe that we can justifiably impute purposes to higher animals, as we in fact do in everyday speech. As to the rest of the universe, we have no means of knowing whether something resembling human purposes operates there, and therefore, in empirical science we should refrain from imputing purposes to entities other than human individuals. We cannot legitimately say that the purpose of lungs is to oxidize blood, because we have no grounds for supposing that lungs can entertain purposes; all we can say is that lungs oxidize blood. How and why they came to do it is a question which cannot be answered by referring to a purpose. Without more justification, historians used to attribute (some of them still do it to this day) purposes to historic processes or to entities such as civilizations. Many historians make statements about 'the mission' of Alexander or Caesar, explaining actions of these gentlemen in terms of the needs of posterior civilizations, without, of course, saying anything about the nature of such retroactive guidance. This kind of reasoning, of which one can find innumerable examples in older historiography, is so obviously inadmissible that it calls for no further comment.

Explanations of human actions in terms of purposes can be called teleological but, though never entirely verifiable, they constitute a special kind of causal explanations. If we say that John entered the cinema because he decided to do so, we envisage an antecedent mental event called decision; and we assume that the circumstances were such that John could choose whether to enter or not to enter: that the cinema existed and was open at the time, that John was near it and was not separated from it by impassable obstacles, that he was not paralyzed and so on. A possibility of performing an act and a decision to perform it constitute jointly a sufficient antecedent of its occurrence; and therefore an explanation which indicates them adequately is strictly deterministic, even though the occurrence of one part of the sufficient antecedent (the decision) cannot be directly perceived by individuals other than the actor.

Writers on methodology usually distinguish four types of explanation: (1) the deductive, (2) the genetic, (3) the probabilistic, (4) the teleological or functional. The deductive is the same thing as the strictly deterministic or adequately causal, and therefore no more needs to be said about it. The genetic explanation is simply a concatenation of unitary explanations, in so far as it is a genuine explanation and not merely a narrative of past events. The structure of the probabilistic explanation is the same as that of the deterministic: it is also deductive, with this difference that what is deduced is probability instead of necessity. It must be remembered that no given probability can constitute either a necessary or a sufficient condition of occurrence of an event: it cannot be a necessary condition because the event in question could have occurred even if it were less probable, and it cannot be a sufficient condition because the event could fail to occur even if it were more probable. As necessity cannot be deduced from probability, probabilistic explanations of single events are inconclusive. Probabilistic explanations can explain fully only frequencies in terms of other frequencies.

The so-called functional explanations assume teleological

guidance other than human purpose. They are highly questionable unless they are interpreted as simply descriptions of consequences; but as the problem of functional explanations in sociology links up with the whole programme of 'functionalism', we must defer its examination to the next chapter.

One point connected with the present discussion must be noted: it is that if we do not regard universal determinism as an indispensable basis for the study of human behaviour, we need not object to the idea of personal responsibility. Many psychologists criticize administration of justice based on the idea of free will and responsibility without realizing that, if valid, determinism applies to everybody: if a criminal cannot avoid committing a crime, then neither can the judge avoid sentencing him, nor can the executioner avoid quartering him. Unless we assume that individuals can make decisions, and are responsible for at least some of their deeds, there is no reason why we should regard any action as good or bad, or try to refrain from doing harm to our fellow beings; and moral exhortation is meaningless.

The complexity of social phenomena compels those who study them to be usually satisfied with an explanation of a type to which natural scientists rarely resort, and which might be called possibilistic explanation, because it consists of a statement which tells us why a certain event could occur. Whereas a causal explanation of an event refers to sufficient conditions of occurrence of an event, a possibilistic explanation specifies only the necessary conditions of its occurrence. Here is a very simple example of a possibilistic explanation: to the question 'how could he have won on the lottery?' we answer 'because he had bought a ticket'. Explanations offered by historians are at best partial possibilistic explanations, as they specify at most only some of the necessary conditions of occurrence of events which they discuss; normally they are not even that but simply narratives of events, whose mutual relationships are only dimly surmised.

If the arguments advanced on the preceding pages are not mistaken, then it is not only the complexity of the subject matter which condemns the study of society to recourse to possibilistic explanations. If there is an element of intrinsic indeterminacy in human actions, then adequate causal explanations are ruled out in all cases where the action is determined by the personal choice of one or a few individuals. This, however, does not mean that we can find causal explanations nowhere. In the first place, as Quetelet pointed out, with large numbers the effects of the exercise of free will by the individuals cancel each other out, unless one of them can impose his will upon the others. Secondly, there are structural constraints, a few examples of which were given earlier.

It is as certain as any equation of physics that a conjunction of a rapid growth of population with stagnation of production will cause impoverishment. It is equally certain that no large mass can embark upon a collective action without successive subdivisions into units, delegation of authority and an elaborate network for conveying information. In contrast it is by no means certain that if there is an army there must be war, although there can be no war without an army. In other words, the existence of an army is a necessary but not sufficient condition of occurrence of war.

The necessity of recourse to possibilistic explanations ought not to dissuade us from searching for adequately causal explanations, because we can never be sure beforehand where they can and where they cannot be discovered. We may justifiably believe that our knowledge will never be complete, but this is no argument for abandoning the efforts to extend it.

CHAPTER FOUR

COMPARATIVE METHOD, FUNCTIONALISM AND EVOLUTION

WHEN COMTE invented the name 'sociology' he had in mind a science of the most general aspects of social life. In the process of professionalization sociology became a rag-bag – an extraordinary mixture of things ranging from the most pedestrian housing surveys to the most abstruse disquisitions on the nature of society. As it happened, sociology became a residual discipline, and its limits negatively defined: it can be described as the study of those aspects of social life which have no special disciplines devoted to them. This is the reason why the study of the family belongs to sociology, whilst the study of the economy does not. It is not surprising, therefore that no satisfactory definition of sociology in its present shape can be given.

A coherent nomenclature and rational delimitations between the branches of learning concerned with social phenomena would unquestionably be more helpful than the present hodge-podge produced by haphazard precedents and struggles between academic pressure groups, but we should not overestimate the importance of neat delimitations. Problems do not respect frontiers between conventional academic disciplines. Even the boundary which divided such hitherto well-separated disciplines as physics and chemistry has vanished. In the study of society the divisions between its various branches are particularly arbitrary because, unlike the division between botany and zoology, they are not based on the separateness of the objects, but merely on the differences between various aspects of the same thing; and therefore they are more abstract and arbitrary than the differentiation of medical specialities in accordance with the organs which they study. In order to put the matter in the proper perspective, it might be worth mentioning that in medicine serious shortcomings have been attributed to the narrowing of the horizon, due to excessive specialization, and to the absence of specialists in generalities. 'In industrial organization, and in the natural sciences, still further subdivision of special functions may do more good than harm. But in the social sciences and in the art of government it can be overdone. The tendency of experts to build little empires, to entrench themselves in their own ruts, and to raise barricades against the neighbouring ruts, is indeed comic, but its consequences may be tragic. The enthusiasm with which academic experts draw arbitrary lines between history and economics and sociology, or between subdivisions of each of these branches of learning, and the rage with which they turn on those who trespass in the borderlands, reflect a morbid condition of Western intellectual life.' (Hugh Seton-Watson, *Neither Peace Nor War*, London 1960, p. 250).

Attempting to introduce some order into the matter of the boundaries of sociology, we cannot circumvent the necessity of accepting locally disparate bases for various delimitations. For example: jurisprudence and the sociology of law study the same rules and regulations, but, whereas jurisprudence looks at them from the point of view of normative exegesis, sociology of law treats them simply as social events whose causes and consequences have to be described and explained. Until very recently it could be said that political science was hortative, whereas political sociology was objective; nowadays, however, the only distinction one can think of is that whereas a political scientist confines himself to the study of political phenomena in themselves, a political sociologist is principally interested in the inter-relations between political and other aspects of collective behaviour. In practice this delimitation is not observed.

As the most sophisticated of the social sciences, economics is naturally most inclined towards a splendid isolation, even though the economists cannot agree on how to define its nature and to delimit its scope. In reality this inability to define the subject stems from the quest for the impossible: namely, a definition which would insure that there would be no overlap between the province of economics and those of the other branches of the study of man in society. For example: one of the more popular definitions of economics describes it as the science of optimal allocation of scarce resources; and indeed, economic problems are problems of allocation, but this characteristic does not distinguish them either from the principles of strategy, or from the rules of scientific methodology or from the canons of the fine arts. The oldest conception of economics – which views it as the study of activities connected with production and circulation of material goods – seems to be the best, so long as we do not seek watertight divisions and are prepared to accept that the predicate 'economic' refers only to an aspect of human activities, and does not exclude other predicates such as 'political', 'religious', 'legal' and so on. Indeed there are no purely economic facts or acts; and we can legitimately speak of economic activities only on the tacit assumption that we mean thereby activities whose economic aspect is most conspicuous.

The study of economics could be fruitfully pursued in isolation from other branches of social enquiry only during the brief period of *laissez-faire* capitalism. Naturally, even that system was not independent of non-economic factors: its emergence and continued existence depended on very specific circumstances of a predominantly political and religious nature. Nevertheless, for several decades, especially in Britain, these factors were relatively static, or at least did not directly produce abrupt economic effects; and for this reason could be left out of economic analysis. This relative autonomy of the market disappeared several decades ago, and nowadays an economic study which entirely neglects non-economic factors cannot have much relevance to reality. Incidence of inflation, for instance, cannot be predicted without an analysis of the forces on the political arena. Indeed, no further important advances in economic theory seem to be possible without very substantial advances in the study of other aspects of social life, which would throw new light on the workings of the factors taken as given in economic theory, and place that theory in a wider and more correct perspective.

Of all the labels for branches of learning 'anthropology' seems the most confusing. In continental Europe it used to designate the study of races, although in Germany it was also employed to cover metaphysical disquisitions on human nature. Recently, however, the desire to tap funds earmarked for anthropology by American foundations induced the Continentals to adopt the Anglo-American usage. If one looks into the contents of books in English which go under the heading of anthropology, one finds there human biology, linguistics, archaeology, human geography, early history of mankind, history of technology and of the art of writing, accompanied by a treatment of every kind of social institutions with the exception of those specific to industrial civilization. If we remove the restriction that anthropology deals only with primitive societies, the term will cease to designate any logically distinguishable speciality. Actually, were it not for cultural inertia, it would be desirable from the point of view of aesthetics as well as convenience to use 'anthropology' in the widest sense justified by its etymology, and put it in the place of the ungainly expression 'behavioural sciences'. For the study of primitive peoples there is the etymologically more appropriate term 'ethnology', although in Britain it acquired a faint flavour of disrepute connected with the now out-dated dispute between 'functionalists' and 'diffusionists'. As to social anthropology, the only possible difference between it and sociology is that the former studies primitive and the latter more complex societies, otherwise they are different names for the same thing; for all the other delimitations which have been proposed sound like mere justifications of academic vested interests. Logically, social anthropology is a branch of sociology, specializing in the study of relatively simple and isolated aggregates such as tribes or peasant communities. With the disappearance of isolated primitive societies social anthropology will be unable to function as a sociographic discipline, and will be able to preserve its traditional subject matter only by becoming a branch of historiography. Those social anthropologists who will insist on field study will become indistinguishable from other sociologists.

Dealing with relatively simple and isolated entities, anthropologists were sometimes able to study all the facets of a culture, and this comprehensive type of study is known as cultural anthropology. Obviously, the mere bulk of the items of a literate, let alone industrial, civilization rules out the possibility of examining them in the same manner. Nevertheless, there seems to be a need for a branch of learning which would study the relations between various aspects of complex cultures, preserving the 'integralist' viewpoint of cultural anthropology, though necessarily differing from it in the method which would have to be adapted to mass phenomena, and moving on a higher level of abstraction. Musicology, philology, history of arts and sciences, and other analogous disciplines deal with parts of culture, but the problem of inter-connections is left out of the purview. The most appropriate name for the advocated branch would be culturology, notwithstanding the recent attempts to appropriate this term for a particular doctrine. The writings of Alfred Kroeber (such as *Anthropology, Style and Civilizations* or *Configurations of Culture Growth*) would most fitly be classified as culturology.

The perniciousness of barriers between disciplines appears particularly evident when we contemplate the relationship between sociology and historiography, for no progress in sociological theory is at all possible without constant employment of historical data. Anyway, the present is fleeting, and even accounts based on personal observation soon become historical documents. From the point of view which might be approximately described as biological or cosmic, sociological theories appear as mankind's attempt to draw lessons from its past experience.

There is no contradiction between the search for synchronic concatenations between various institutions of a society and the enquiry into their past evolution. This point is well brought out by Evans-Pritchard (*Anthropology and History*, Manchester 1961, pp. 10/11) who has the rare distinction of having made important contributions to 'functionalist anthropology' as well as to histo-riography:

'The tendency in the past, and even today, to overestimate what are called functional ethnographic studies of primitive societies at the expense of developmental studies, and even to ignore historical facts altogether, has prevented us from testing the validity of some of the basic assumptions on which our studies have for long rested; that for example, there is an entity which can be labelled "society" and that such an entity has something called a "structure", which can be further described as a set of functionally interdependent institutions or sets of social relations. These are analogies from biological science and, if they have had their uses, they have also proved to be highly dangerous. On them has been based the argument that just as we can understand the anatomy and physiology of a horse without requiring to know anything about its descent from its five-toed ancestor, so we can understand the structure of a society and the functioning of its institutions without knowing anything about its history. But a society, however defined, in no way resembles a horse, and, mercifully, horses remain horses – or at least they have done so in historic times – and do not turn into elephants or pigs, whereas a society may change from one type to another, sometimes with great suddenness and violence. Do we then speak of a society at different points of time or do we speak of two different societies? Except in a few very remote parts of the world, there are no primitive societies which have not already undergone vast changes. New social systems have come into being, and it is precisely in relation to such historical changes that such terms as "society", and "function" have to be defined. Indeed, I would say that a term like "structure" can only be meaningful when used as an historical expression to denote a set of relations known to have endured over a considerable period of time. Some have tried to wriggle out of the difficulties involved in the study of primitive societies in process of rapid transformation by extending the organic analysis and saying that they are then in a pathological condition, but though there may be a means of discovering what is normal to societies of a certain type in the sense of what is general in, or common to, them, one cannot speak of "normal" in the sense of the physiological analogy, because what is normal in a certain type of society may be abnormal in the type of society into which it is developing, and vice versa. I do not think that Durkheim succeeded in giving a satisfactory definition of social pathology.

'Moreover, I think it must be accepted that far from the history of a society or of an institution being irrelevant to a functional study of it, we only fully understand it when we can view it not only in the present but also retrospectively, for, as we all know from our personal experience of events, there is a sense in which it is true that we can know more about the past than about the present. We know what its potentialities were and what were its enduring qualities. De Tocqueville knew much better than anyone who took part in the French Revolution what, sociologically speaking, was happening at the time, and he even had a greater knowledge of the plain facts. Indeed, it has often been pointed out that vast social changes have taken place without even the clearest contemporary minds being conscious of what was happening, and – here now is the point I wish to establish – the nature of the institutions involved in the process of change could not adequately have been understood till placed in the crucible of history.'

There is no difference in the type of information or the method of reasoning between social and institutional (or better structural) history and descriptive sociology. The only difference is that by convention (not even always observed) descriptions of chronologically remote cases belong to historiography, whereas descriptions of situations existing at the time of writing belong to sociology. In contrast, the difference between theoretical sociology on one side, and descriptive sociology and history on the other, is of an epistemological nature; in theoretical sociology, descriptions and analyses of individual cases are used in order to establish generalizations, whereas in historiography and sociography (to use the better name for descriptive sociology and social anthropology) theoretical generalizations help and guide the analysis of concrete cases, which remains the principal aim. Almost needless to say, there are many variants which combine in varying measure both approaches. The body of ideas which concern the most general problems of social life is sometimes called general theory, sometimes comparative sociology, because wide ranging comparisons constitute the only method of testing hypotheses which refer to such problems.

Comparisons (verbal or numerical) enter into all induction, but by common acceptance comparative method designates only comparisons which draw upon data from different societies. To be precise we should have to define what we mean by a society; but let us leave this problem for the moment and follow the vague current usage, as its vagueness does not matter for the purpose of the present argument.

Some people have questioned the wisdom of having recourse to a wide range of data, instead of concentrating on a more detailed study of two or three cases. The answer to this is simple: in order to ascertain the limits within which a connection between two factors holds, we must vary the other circumstances as widely as possible. Fortunately, however, there need be no 'either or' in this matter: various combinations are possible, and here as elsewhere science can proceed by successive approximations. On the basis of an analysis of a fairly narrow range of data, a hypothesis can be formulated which may be later modified in the light of wider (or at least different) evidence; and this process can go on being repeated. Ideally, comparative analyses should be carried out within all accessible ranges of data – narrow as well as wide.

A comparison of two situations which differ in every aspect save one constitutes an application of the method of induction which John Stuart Mill called The Method of Agreement, whereas a comparison of two situations which are alike except in one respect falls under Mill's Method of Difference. We know, of course, that no discoveries can be made by mechanical application of Mill's (or anybody else's) methods: the crucial step is always the discovery of the factors (or rather the invention of isolates) which exhibit regularities in their permutations; and in this task the investigator obtains little help from ready made formulae. These difficulties, however, beset the use of both methods in equal measure, and their relative usefulness depends on the nature of the problem. As there is a great deal of confusion on this point, it must be emphasized that comparing does not amount to equating, and that there are no logical reasons why a comparison should be focused on resemblances rather than differences. To repeat again: it all depends on what kind of question we are trying to answer.

Misuse of comparative method by older writers like Westermark, who did not really compare but merely listed resemblances with almost complete disregard of the contexts in which they occurred, or the equally unthinking but highly mechanized use thereof by our contemporary G. F. Murdock, must be contrasted with such masterpieces of inductive reasoning as Durkheim's *Suicide* or the comparative essays of Otto Hintze.[1]

The real founders of sociology did not compare without a further aim: they resorted to comparisons in order to work out and prove their theories, which can be done only if the relevant information is stored in a single mind. Gathering specialists on different areas or periods, or putting under the same covers contributions which would otherwise appear under different covers, may prepare the ground for comparative sociology, but does not amount to cultivating it.

Three important practical lessons emerge from the foregoing

[1] Commonly, adequate verification is secured by selecting easy and trivial substantive problems. Among the works which deal with truly important substantive issues Durkheim's *Suicide* approaches most closely methodological perfection. It is therefore surprising that the pronouncements on methodology in his *Rules of Sociological Method* are so mediocre.

argument. The first is that, as problems do not respect administrative divisions of academic institutions, the fear of trespassing on other people's fields hampers progress. The second is that, in view of the arbitrariness of these divisions and the mutual dependence of different aspects of social life, there is need for specialists in general sociology – which ought not to mean elementary sociology but the study of the most general problems of social life and of the relations between its various aspects. Raymond Aron proposes the name 'synthetic sociology' for this type of enquiry. The third lesson is that, for the same reasons, all students of society (and sociologists in particular) should have some acquaintance with the related disciplines: getting together into interdisciplinary colloquia specialists who know nothing about each other's fields cannot produce any substantial results.

The advocacy of comparative or synthetic sociology presented on the foregoing pages is not intended as a criticism of field work or any other type of study. Many different approaches and methods are necessary for the progress of science, and nothing is more pernicious than faddism and conformity, or attempts to foist upon everybody one's preferences or interests. It is worth noting in this context that only in economics can one find theorists who deny the value and necessity of empirical study. In sociology the current of hostility flows only in the opposite direction. There are many 'field workers' who decry all works based on 'second-hand' information, and insist that only works based on personal observation have any value. This point of view is partly disingenuous as it affords an excuse for not reading much. What its proponents do not realize is that it negates the value of their own work; for if nothing useful can be said on the basis of knowledge obtained by reading, then it is utterly futile to write reports on field work.

Comparative method came to be associated with evolutionism, and for this reason it was attacked by the functionalists as well as by the diffusionists and the exponents of fact-finding without preconceptions, who attacked each other as well. These disputes were inspired by a sectarian spirit rather than rational arguments, as in fact there is no logical incompatibility between these approaches. In the thought of Herbert Spencer – the spiritual father of both the evolutionists and the functionalists – the ideas of function and evolution were mutually supporting.

The works of the functionalist anthropologists are distinguished from the writings of earlier ethnographers not only by more thorough field work, but above all by the adoption of what might be called an integralist viewpoint, the essence of which is the search for relations of mutual dependence between various social institutions and aspects of the studied society. It must be stressed, however, that only in dealing with primitive societies was this approach entirely new, as literate societies had been treated from this point of view by some much earlier writers. Fustel de Coulange's *Ancient City* was written in the spirit of functionalism long before this term was invented. De Tocqueville's *Democracy in America* is far from being a straightforward description of the institutions of the United States; and is perhaps even more 'functionalist' than Malinowski's studies of the Trobrianders. Throughout it De Tocqueville tries to unravel relations of mutual dependence between various aspects of social life in America, with the aid of constant recourse to comparisons with Europe. The reflections upon what he saw during his travels, innumerable remarks contained in his letters, and even the ostensibly purely historical work on the Revolution are all inspired by the same combination of functionalist and comparative approach.

De Tocqueville practised 'structural-functional' analysis without ever saying anything about the methodology. In contrast, Herbert Spencer formulated all the relevant concepts but never analysed any concrete society from this point of view. The pages of the volumes of his *Descriptive Sociology* are invariably divided into sections under the headings Structure and Function, but they bear no trace of any attempt to disentangle precisely the web of inter-relations. The formulations of the concepts, however, are far superior to those of the present day exponents of 'functional-structural analysis', who extol Max Weber, Pareto, Toennies but contemptuously dismiss Spencer who put forth ideas which they regard as their own discoveries. Our verdict on Malinowski would have to be equally severe if we judged him by posthumously published scraps of theorizing. But there is no proof that he would have allowed his scrap-books to be published under the pretentious titles of *Dynamics of Culture Change* and *Scientific Theory of Culture.* These notes would cease to be trite only if they had been filled with interesting analyses of concrete cases. Altogether Malinowski was a great interpreter of primitive societies but a mediocre methodologist and theorist. The only 'functionalist' whose formulations add something to what Spencer said was Radcliffe-Brown, but he told me many times that he regarded himself as a Spencerian.

In the preceding chapter I have suggested that functional explanations in sociology seldom amount to more than descriptions of effects. So let us take an example. In a number of primitive societies men have an obligation to avoid their mothers-in-law. Having demolished Freud's contention that the function of this custom was to prevent incest, by pointing out that the mother-in-law was not the most likely relative with whom incest might be committed, Radcliffe-Brown put forth the thesis that the function of this custom is to prevent strife between the lineage of the husband and that of the wife. We can agree with Radcliffe-Brown that the custom in question has the effects which he imputes to it, but what is not clear is the legitimacy of the expression 'its function is to . . .'. If instead of saying that 'the custom of mother-in-law avoidance reduces conflicts', we say 'the function of the custom of mother-in-law avoidance is to reduce conflicts', what have we added? Why should we speak of the function if we simply mean the effects?

It seems that a recourse to the concept of function is fully justified only if we are entitled to imply that the effects of the operation of an element are a sufficient condition – or at least a necessary condition – of its existence. When Radcliffe-Brown says that the function of the custom of mother-in-law avoidance is to reduce conflicts, he does not mean merely that this custom has this effect, but he also insinuates that it came into existence and continues to exist because it has the said effect. The thesis is plausible. He points out that always there is a conflict between the claim of a mother upon her daughter and the claims of the husband; and that in a small society, where those who have insulted each other cannot get away from each other, an open quarrel represents a serious danger to the entire social fabric, particularly as there are no organs of authority which can maintain peace by force. But all this constitutes no proof that this custom had to arise or persist, for it is not inevitable that the society in question must persist.

Imputations of function are most securely based in relation to practices instituted deliberately in order to achieve definite aims.

When we say that the function of a train inspector is to prevent people from riding without paying, we imply more than just that that is what he does. There might be conscientious passengers who take it upon themselves to combat this type of fraud but we would not say that this activity was their function. What entitles us to speak of the function of the inspector is that the effects of his activity constitute a necessary condition of his continuing in this role; that if his activity would make no difference to the numbers of free riders he would disappear as an element in the system. But supposing the custom of mother-in-law avoidance somehow ceased to reduce quarrels, what is the evidence that it would then disappear? The great weakness of functionalist interpretations is that they practically never adduce evidence that the imputations of function are justified. They do not specify the nature of the teleological mechanisms which they assume; and the entire argument proceeds on the level of vague surmisals which may or may not be correct. Indeed within the usual framework of static analysis the validity of such imputations can seldom be examined, because it is only by observing permutations that we can unravel causal relationships.

Radcliffe-Brown, like Durkheim, often used the term function in the wider sense discussed above, which implies some kind of circular causality; but when it came to definitions he restricted its meaning to effects, and defined 'function' as the contribution which an element makes to the continuing existence of the whole. This definition, however, creates the danger of purely tautological arguments; for if we take a part out of a whole to which it belonged, then the whole can no longer be what it was. We can say meaningfully that an element contributes to the continued existence of the whole only if its disappearance destroys not only the relations between itself and the other elements, but also the relations of the other elements to each other. When the head is removed, the relations which existed between the heart and the lungs, or the kidneys and the bowels, disappear. Clearly without postal services an industrial society could not continue to exist, but is it equally certain that the division into classes is equally indispensable? Light can be shed on the latter question only by a study of variations. In other words only a comparative analysis can justify an imputation of function which goes beyond the obvious.

Another great weakness of interpretations in terms of functions is that they presume knowledge which is not available as far as social phenomena are concerned. A statement that something contributes to the continuing existence of the whole can be made with justification only if we know a great deal about the relations between parts other than the part to which function is imputed. As this is seldom the case in sociology, it seems more advisable to search firstly for simpler relations of mutual or unilateral dependence.

Equally great difficulties stem from resorting to the word 'whole' or the equivalent term 'system'. In biology it has a fairly definite meaning, but what is a social whole? An isolated tribe may fit this concept well enough, but apart from such cases where are the boundaries of social wholes? What is the point of speaking about the continued existence of the whole, when this whole is continuously changing, so that we do not know where its identity in time begins and ends?

Analysis in terms of function falls on the horns of a dilemma: the wholes to which it refers are definite only where they are static and isolated, whereas the relations of dependence between the parts can be discovered normally only by observing changes. The conclusion therefore emerges that the concept of function, though not entirely useless, can seldom be profitably applied except in the study of organizations deliberately set up for pursuance of definite goals, in which case the nature of the teleological mechanism is fairly transparent.

Even more dubious is the concept of dysfunction. Anything that changes an existing structure can be regarded as dysfunctional from the point of view of its perpetuation. In a less trivial sense, the concept of dysfunction can be used without further specification only on the assumption that divergence from the type is pathological, which (as pointed out earlier) is a workable approximation in biology but not in sociology. Without such an assumption the concept of dysfunction can have definite meaning only with reference to a specified goal. We can say that bribery in the police force is dysfunctional from the point of view of its efficacity in catching law-breakers; but whether it is dysfunctional from the point of view of the stability of the society as a whole cannot be decided without unravelling multifarious causal connections, and in many cases can be decided only by hindsight. In pre-Castro Cuba, for instance, the entire social structure was embedded in corruption on which important branches of the economy depended for their subsistence. It is certain that without corruption the Cuban society and economy would have been very different from what they were. We can say, therefore, that corruption was functional in the Cuban society of that time. On the other hand, the army crumbled before the onslaught of the *fidelistas* chiefly because of the all-pervading corruption in its midst. Therefore, corruption must have been dysfunctional, as it eventually contributed to the destruction of the social order. Without it, however, this order would have disappeared even earlier or would not have come into existence at all – so corruption must have been functional after all. A predicate which can be affirmed and negated with equal justification cannot be useful as a tool of analysis.

The most judicious interpretation of functionalism is that it is a programme of search for relations of mutual dependence between various aspects of social life. As a doctrine asserting that all institutions have functions, in the sense of contributing to the maintenance of the society in its given form, it is either tautological or unwarranted. It seems that the mathematical concept of function (that is to say, of dependence between variables) constitutes a better analytical tool.

In addition to greater clarity Herbert Spencer's structural-functional analysis had another important point of superiority over the more recent variants: namely, it gave reasons why we should believe that various features of social structure normally contribute to the maintenance of the whole. The explanation was that the struggle for existence between societies, with the attendant elimination of the unfit, ensured that only those societies survived which consisted of functional parts. Spencer's evolutionism is the only convincing justification of functionalism that has been advanced.

Spencer's theory of social evolution is one of the most securely based generalizations of sociology; and the disdain in which it is held by all those who never took the trouble to read it well shows how widespread is the addiction to fads in the study of society. Spencer conceived evolution as the general movement of human societies towards increasing differentiation and integration, and the concomitant increase in size. There can be no doubt about the existence of such a trend in the history of mankind; and as far as prehistory is concerned we have now archaeological proofs, whereas

Spencer had to rely on deductions from the rudimentary ethnography of his day. Nor did Spencer ever maintain that all societies must pass through the same stages – the notion which was later baptized as the doctrine of unilinear evolution. On the contrary, the mechanism of evolution operates, according to him, through destruction and absorption of the simpler by the more complex entities.

If by evolution we mean a unidirectional trend as opposed to mere diversification, then it can be observed only in the realm of the superorganic. The evolution of the species has proceeded in all directions. True, the higher (ie more differentiated and integrated) organisms have appeared later than the more primitive, and have descended from them, but they did not displace them, whereas the more complex societies have been and are continuously destroying and absorbing the simpler societies, and becoming ever more complex themselves.

Even the quest for origins of institutions (for which the evolutionists have been so often castigated) need not be always futile. True, the early evolutionists commonly chose as the objects of this type of enquiry the family and the religion, which are precisely the institutions of whose origins we can never know anything certain, for the simple reason that there are no records of any societies which do not have them in some form. But an enquiry into the origins of stratification or the state need not be purely speculative because instances of their emergence or absence have been observed and recorded.

Except in his treatment of the family, where he could not think freely, Herbert Spencer made substantial contributions to our understanding of society, which have by no means been nullified by later thinkers. Indeed, it is surprising how the theories of the great sociologists of the past – who more often than not either ignored or rejected each other's views – dovetail if we sift them judiciously.

CHAPTER FIVE

IDEAL TYPES, THE POSTULATE OF NON-VALUATION AND *DIE VERSTEHENDE SOZIOLOGIE*

THE WAY IN WHICH most textbooks on the history of sociology classify Max Weber's contribution provides a good example of how people tend to affix labels by seizing on trifles: the pigeon hole assigned to him bears the label 'understanding sociology – *verstehende soziologie*'. If we take the word understanding at its usual connotation, we arrive at the conclusion that Max Weber had a monopoly on understanding society. This seems to be a slight exaggeration, although most sociological publications (including those which invoke Weber's name in vain) could very well be classified as 'non-understanding sociology'. Weber's distinction (not very clearly formulated) between 'understanding' and 'explaining' refers to something that has been known to philosophers for a very long time: namely, that we interpret actions of other human beings by attributing to them the feelings and thoughts which we should have if we carried out such actions.

As Fichte showed, the validity of this procedure can never be proved; but neither can it be disproved, and nobody can utter its denial without contradicting himself, for the mere intent to communicate presupposes it. This analogy from subjective experience is not nowadays used in interpreting the behaviour of objects other than the higher animals. Its continuous application does distinguish the study of man and society from other branches of learning, but in no way distinguishes the thought of Max Weber. In fact, dustmen, historians, detectives, pimps, philosophers all have to rely on their subjective experiences in order to be able to explain and predict the actions of others. Even the most astringent behaviourists, who avoid humans and concentrate on rats, speak of organisms 'seeking' and 'escaping'.

Weber, naturally, never claimed that he invented the procedure of *verstehen*, or that it was in any way peculiar to his way of thinking. It was the commentators who committed this folly. Moreover, when dealing with definite sociological problems as distinguished from the discussion of the method of sociology – Weber (as far as I can recall) never refers to the distinction in question. In *Wirtschaft und Gesellschaft* there are only a few phrases on this matter.

Naturally, he devotes more space to it in his methodological writings, but I do not think that there is anything in that discussion which has not been said better and earlier by some philosopher. I must confess that in spite of my great admiration for Weber, I find his formulations of philosophical problems to be rather mediocre: he laboured under the baneful influence of the main current of German philosophy, with its habits of ponderous and elusive verbosity. (This was not so when it came to inductive theorizing, based on concrete data.) Notwithstanding this weakness, some of his thoughts on the methodology are of fundamental importance.

Three ideas constitute the essence of Weber's contribution to the methodology of the social sciences: firstly, the paradigm of reducibility of sociological concepts to actions of individuals; secondly, the paradigm of ethical neutrality; thirdly, the concept of the ideal type. The paradigm of reducibility amounts to a prophylactic rule. The practice of explaining the meaning of words denoting social conditions and positions in terms of the actions of individuals is as old as analytical thought. If we look up a dictionary for the meaning of 'unemployment', we find it defined as 'a condition when large numbers of workers have no jobs'. 'Ruler' is given as 'one who rules', and so on. Yet, abstract terms, which refer to phenomena which cannot be directly observed in their totality, tend to be bandied about without the least concern for their meaning. Millions of people (including many professional sociologists) talk about 'socialism', 'democracy', 'imperialism', 'nationalization', 'social integration' and what not, without ever stopping to consider what these words mean in terms of the concrete actions of real persons. Formulating his paradigm Weber simply erected into a methodological canon what was always the practice of all sound thinkers; but it was an important step forward because it makes a great difference whether a procedure is intuitive or reasoned out, and there is great merit in having said something that ought to have been obvious but was not, and still is not to most people. A further merit of Weber was that he stuck to methodology, and steered clear of the futile ontological problem, to which many of his contemporaries devoted their energies, which sidetracked even Durkheim, and which to this day haunts the precincts of some methodological seminars: namely the question of whether it is the society or the individuals that really exist. I cannot recall any statements of Weber on this point, but I feel sure by inference that he took it for granted that the parts exist just as 'really' as the wholes. Weber, however, was not unique in this respect, for Auguste Comte and Herbert Spencer had perfectly clear ideas on this matter, and the reification of social processes by the Durkheimians was a retrograde step.

The requirement of *wertfreiheit* – which has been translated as value-freedom or ethical neutrality, but which I propose to call the paradigm of non-valuation – has often been misunderstood. Some people interpreted it as enjoining upon the sociologist Olympian indifference to the ills of mankind. Even apart from anything that Weber wrote, his passionate advocacy of various causes shows that this was not what he had in mind. His paradigm of non-hortation can best be regarded as a methodological and semantic rule for classifying propositions, in accordance with which we include in sociology only non-valuative propositions. Naturally, in view of the emotional loading of all the words which describe human relations, the strict adherence to this ideal would silence us for ever. But this is no argument against trying to approach it, because the same is true of ideals such as logical consistency or clarity, which are universally upheld, though only intermittently attained. The validity of a methodological precept is not a matter of truth, but of heuristic utility, and by definition a precept cannot be *wertfrei*. We must, then, examine the claim of this paradigm on the assumption that knowledge of social phenomena is valuable.

The first argument in its favour is that, when dealing with matters which arouse our emotions, we must discipline our reasoning, so as to avoid wishful or hate-inspired thinking.[1] The adherence to the canon of non-valuation – ie careful separation of judgements of value from judgements of fact – is extremely useful for this purpose. Secondly, the paradigm in question can be recommended on the grounds of semantic expediency. People differ considerably in their valuations, and it is often difficult to infer from the words of praise or denigration what features the objects exhibit, other than the capacity to please or displease the utterer. This difficulty might be obviated if all publications carried as a preamble a full exposition of the author's values, but, plainly, the acceptance of the paradigm of non-valuation provides a far more economical solution. The third reason for recommending this paradigm is that by excluding numerous controversial issues, it enables people who disagree on many values, but share the wish to advance the knowledge of social phenomena, to collaborate in the furtherance of this end. In short, non-valuation in analyzing social phenomena commends itself for the sake of objectivity. Objectivity, incidentally, can be defined as the freedom of reasoning from the influence of the desires, other than the desire to know the truth. Only in this sense can objectivity be approached, if not attained, for obviously no reasoning can be independent of the concepts with which it operates, or of the knowledge on the basis of which it proceeds. Arguments for or against the admission of any given proposition into the body of accepted sociological knowledge cannot, of course, be free from judgements of value: they presuppose positive valuation of truth, consistency and of other ideals of scientific thought. They belong, however, not to sociology itself but to its meta-language, to use the expression current among contemporary philosophers.

The concept of ideal type is rather difficult. In the first place, it might be said that to talk about an ideal type is like talking about

---

[1] In a recent discussion in the pages of *The Observer* occasioned by H. J. Eysenck's pronouncements on 'tough-mindedness' versus 'tender-mindedness' all the contributors misunderstood this distinction and confused it with that between 'hard-heartedness' and 'tender-heartedness'. But when William James introduced these expressions he meant by 'tough-mindedness' the courage to face the stark truth, and to draw appropriate conclusions no matter how distasteful they might be; and by 'tender-mindedness' he meant the lack of such courage and the consequent inclination to believe what one likes to believe – in other words, wishful thinking. In this sense gentle Socrates and Spinoza were tough-minded, whereas Nero and Hitler were tender-minded. Indeed, megalomania by definition implies tender-mindedness.

wet water, for any type, being an abstraction, is ideal and not real in the sense that a given material object is real: there exists this horse and that, but not a horse in general. The difference between an ideal type and a type pure and simple lies not in the abstractness of connotation but in the definiteness of denotation: whereas the types established by biological systematics have referents which fall under them and nowhere else, this is not the case with ideal types. No horse in general ever lived, but there are many horses which satisfy perfectly the specifications of 'horsiness', whilst nothing like a perfectly rational organization has ever been observed. The idea behind the concept of ideal type is that social phenomena, in virtue of their manifold and fluid nature, can be analysed solely in terms of the extreme forms of their characteristics, which can never be observed in their purity. This idea is perfectly sound but was presented in a manner somewhat lacking in clarity. It might be even argued that Pareto's treatment of the problem of conceptualization in sociology was less open to criticism. Pareto pointed out that all concepts of physical sciences are idealizations: that no movement without resistance of the medium has ever been observed (but only surmised in case of celestial bodies), that nothing perfectly straight has ever been found, that vectorial analysis assumes movements which never take place, and that social sciences must proceed likewise. As far as social sciences are concerned, the most useful idealizations can be found in the most mature of them, which is not surprising: the concepts of economic theory, such as perfect competition or static equilibrium, provide the best examples of ideal types. On the other hand, there is nothing very 'ideal' about Weber's own typologies. When he talks about bureaucracy or feudalism or capitalism, he moves on the level of abstraction which is not very far removed from observable reality. Moreover, there is nothing methodologically new in Weber's handling of typologies: he is doing exactly the same as did all the other good thinkers, beginning with Aristotle. The originality lay not in methodological novelty, but in substantive implications of the features, which on several occasions he singled out for consideration. For example his distinction between producing and consuming towns – *Produzentenstadt* and *Konsumentenstadt* – is of fundamental importance to the problem of the conditions which permitted the rise of capitalism, but there is nothing logically distinctive about these concepts. The master's touch reveals itself in the way he used them as the tools of analysis. On some occasions his typologies are less illuminating, or even useless: this is the case, I think, with his classification of the forms of rationality, as well as with that of the types of actions. On these points common-sense notions seem to be better.[1] What I have said so far may have sounded almost as a denigration. This is far from being my intention. I regard Max Weber's contribution as the most monumental that has been made to sociology, but I feel that the relatively less valuable parts of it have attracted the greater share of attention. To say that other parts of his works are more impressive, is not to claim that the methodological writings are without importance. On the contrary, I am convinced that merely for formulating the methodological ideas discussed above Weber merits a place in the history of sociology. His supremacy, however, is due to his unsurpassed ability for making or suggesting inductive generalizations. This kind of work requires, in addition to a gift for theorizing, a profound knowledge of a wide range of factual data; and in this respect Weber was unrivalled. Nobody who glances through any of his major works can fail to be impressed by the astounding array of detailed information. True, the same can be said about writers like Frazer, Ratzel, Westermark, Spengler and Toynbee, but there is a great difference between them and Weber. In the first place, they had nothing useful to say in the way of theoretical generalization. Frazer and Westermark were interested in establishing a sequence of evolutionary stages, and Ratzel in showing the influence of geographical environment. Actually their works constitute useful encyclopaedias of customs, beliefs, and institutions. Toynbee has a theory but it is vague, tautological and unverifiable. The theory of challenge and response, for instance,

---

[1] Weber's muddled classification of social actions into types such as *Wertrational* and *Zweckrational* played no part whatsoever in his substantive explanatory theories; nevertheless, it was adopted by Talcott Parsons as the foundation stone of his own system, in preference to Weber's more substantial discoveries. In *Structure of Social Action* Parsons devotes about 600 pages to showing that the chief merit of Weber, Pareto and Durkheim was that they pointed the way towards 'the voluntaristic theory of action' finally formulated by him. Translated from the tenebrous language in which it is couched, this theory amounts to saying that in order to understand why people act as they do, we must take into account their wishes and decisions, the means at their disposal, and their beliefs about how the desired effects can be produced.

is purely tautological. We are told that a civilization develops when it responds successfully to a challenge; but how do we know that it has responded successfully, except by seeing that it has developed? Toynbee provides no criteria for independent assessment of the two variables. *The Study of History* has considerable value, but chiefly as a source-book of recondite pieces of informations. Whilst Frazer and Westermark catalogued customs, and Spengler filled his books with spurious analogies between superficial features of mostly fictitious entities, Weber compared social structures and their functioning, noting differences as carefully as resemblances, and trying to relate isolated features to their structural contexts. When information on the structure of the society in which he was interested was lacking, he made truly herculean efforts to extract it from the sources. Each volume of his *Religionssoziologie* would merit praise even if it were the single product of life-long work. In spite of many serious errors, the parts devoted to China and India still stand unrivalled as 'holistic' (or if you like, functionalist) analyses of these societies, revealing their inner springs, and showing the mutual dependence of culture and society. His original insights into the functioning of these societies are too numerous to be discussed here in detail, so one example must suffice: Weber was the first to raise the problem of the distinctive features of the Chinese towns, and of how these were related to the structure of the state and of the economy. After fifty years there is still nothing better of this kind. Étienne Balazs – the sinologist who has done more than anybody else to fill this gap – recognizes Weber as the source of his inspiration. To appreciate the magnitude of Weber's achievement, it must be remembered that when he prepared his *Religionssoziologie* next to nothing was known about social and economic history of China. He extracted his information on the structure of the Chinese society and its development from translated dynastic chronicles, reports of travellers and the pages of the *Peking Gazette*. The amount of effort and perspicacity necessary for this task must have been prodigious. The same is true of his treatment of India. In the case of ancient Israel his task was somewhat lighter because the subject had been better studied; and so the factual mistakes appear to be fewer. The history of the economic and political institutions of the ancient Mediterranean world had been studied intensively even before Weber was born, and his contemporary Eduard Meyer

WAYNESBURG COLLEGE LIBRARY
WAYNESBURG, PA.

attempted a synthesis in a remarkable essay on *Economic Development in Antiquity*. During the sixty years since the appearance of *Agrarverhaeltniesse in Altertum*, many excellent works appeared in this field, the most comprehensive being those of Roztovzeff and Heichelheim. Nevertheless Weber's sociological history, concealed under the modest title, remains unique. For it is neither an economic history, nor a social history (as it is commonly understood), nor a political nor a military, but a truly structural history, which shows how the economic changes influenced religion, how the innovations in tactics brought about the transformations of social stratification, how the distribution of political power impeded the growth of capitalism and so on. All the time he tries to trace dynamic relations between various aspects of social life. His treatment of historical data is just as functionalist as were Malinowski's analyses of the Trobriand society; and in its light, the dispute between the functionalist and the historical schools of anthropology, which raged in the twenties and thirties, appears puerile.

Max Weber was a great historian, but at least in his later years he studied history mainly in order to make comparisons. His case studies are strewn with references to other situations, and with generalizations or hints at possible generalizations. When writing about the prophets of ancient Israel, he presents a theory about the relations between peasants and town traders and usurers, about the destruction of tribal solidarity by the monetary economy and the bureaucratic state, and about how social protest of the peasants tends to be connected with movements for religious reform. At the end of his analysis of the causes of the fall of the Roman Empire he draws a comparison with the modern Occident, and throws in a prediction that 'as in the antiquity, the bureaucracy will become the master of capitalism in the modern world . . . for capitalism is now the chief agent of bureaucratization'. This was written before the end of the last century.

Weber was not the first to resort to comparisons in order to arrive at generalizations. Indeed, all the thinkers that have left their mark on the history of sociology did precisely that. Aristotle, Ibn-Khaldun, Bodin, Machiavelli, Montesquieu, Buckle, Spencer, Roscher, Mosca and many others – they all used comparative method. The moral of this incidentally, is that the aspirants to Weber's mantle should postpone their attempts to produce another

Economy and Society until they acquire a comparable range of factual information. Weber's achievement shows, moreover, that the knowledge of other societies, and the consequent ability to compare, aids enormously the analysis of any given society, and particularly the discovery of causal relationships. His superiority over his most distinguished predecessors was largely due to the progress of historiography. Montesquieu could not have used similar data because they just were not available. Today it is possible to correct Weber on a number of points because during the forty years which have elapsed since his death relevant information has accumulated. His greatness can be measured by the profusion of extremely interesting hypotheses which can be found in his works. For instance: is it true, as he suggests in connection with his analysis of Chinese intellectuals, that bureaucratic connections breed formalism in philosophy?

As is well known, all Weber's works are focused, in one way or another, on the problem of the conditions which permitted the rise of capitalism. Almost needless to say, there was nothing original in this preoccupation; it stems directly from Marx, and was shared by many scholars, particularly in Germany. Marxists as well as the economists of the 'historical school' discussed it continuously, and the first edition of Werner Sombart's *Der Moderne Kapitalismus* appeared before Weber's articles in *Archiv fuer Sozialwissenschaft* (which were later incorporated into the volumes of *Religionssoziologie*). The originality of Weber's approach consisted, in the first place, in something very simple. In order to discover the causes of the rise of capitalism, other scholars studied in great detail the process of its growth, thus confining their attention to western Europe. He, on the other hand, conceived the brilliant idea of throwing light on this problem by concentrating on cases where capitalism failed to develop. This idea, it is true, would not amount to very much if he were not capable of carrying it out, but coupled with masterly execution, it gave to his works a stamp of uniqueness. The comparative point of view, moreover, saved him from pitfalls into which many others fell: unlike Sombart, for instance, he knew that neither the desire for pecuniary gain nor vast accumulations of liquid wealth were in any way peculiar to the countries where capitalism developed, and could not, therefore, be regarded as crucial factors.

Nothing contributed more to Weber's fame than his essay on

the *Protestant Ethics and the Rise of Capitalism*. Yet I must confess that I find it to be one of the least impressive of his publications; above all because it contains no structural analysis, so characteristic of the bulk of his works. Whereas in his treatment of Hinduism, Judaism and of the Chinese religions he tries to relate religious beliefs to social institutions, viewing culture and society as an integrated whole, the *Protestant Ethics and the Rise of Capitalism* contains only rather disjointed references to the social circumstances. Undoubtedly, he has the merit of widening the field of discussion by bringing to attention a hitherto neglected factor, and it must be emphasized that he nowhere claimed that Calvinist ethics were the cause of the rise of capitalism, but the one-sidedness of the essay gives some justification to the reproach that he overstated his case. In this case, as well as in what concerns the oriental religions, Weber overestimated the efficacity of religious beliefs in directly determining behaviour in economic matters but the fact that he considers both directions of influence proves that it is completely unjust to accuse him of unilateralist interpretation. As mentioned above, he explains the stultification and decay of capitalism in the ancient world in terms of structures of power, without bringing in the 'economic ethics' as an independent factor. In order to obtain a balanced view of Weber's thought, we must realize that *Agrarian Relations in Antiquity* is in no way less important than *Sociology of Religions*, and constitutes its necessary complement.

In passing judgement on Max Weber as a thinker we must remember that he died before completing his main works. The final syntheses are mostly lacking. Even so, he is the towering figure of sociology. We shall never know what he would have achieved had he lived another twenty years.

CHAPTER SIX

CONCEPTS AND REALITIES

General Considerations

IN THEIR EFFORTS to understand the surprising and unintended consequences of their collective actions, men are handicapped not only by the size and longevity, polymorphism and metamorphism of the fabrics of their social life, but also by the nature of their minds, which have been shaped through a long process of evolution so as to be able to co-ordinate physical operations which, even when they are exceedingly complicated, can be analysed into simple and discreet components. As Piaget has shown in his *Épistemologie Génétique*, symbolization of the simplest and irreducible physical operation constitutes the foundation of logic and mathematics. The human mind is scarcely provided with the means of grappling with a reality which is not only staggeringly complex but also fluid, elusive and opaque – a reality which can be apprehended only with the aid of abstractions which are so indirectly based on sense perceptions that they are always slipping into the realm of pure fancy.

The vagueness of the concepts employed in the study of social phenomena has often been blamed for its backward state, and it cannot be doubted that there is a connection between general backwardness and the vagueness of the concepts, but it is entirely wrong to imagine that we should or could clear up the terminological confusion first, and then proceed to cultivate the science. As Whewell showed a century ago the value of a term depends on whether it is 'constructed and appropriated so as to be fitted to enunciate simply and clearly true general propositions', and it follows that terminological confusion cannot be dispelled by convening committees to legislate on the matter, but only by adjusting and inventing terms whilst constructing theories which genuinely explain real events. Terminological confusion is just an aspect of the general lack of understanding, and for this reason, definitions given in dictionaries of sociological terms can inform merely about how people use these terms, without providing much guidance on how they ought to be used, because in the present state of the social sciences the current usage always leaves much to be desired.

Although the value of conceptual analysis unaccompanied by constructive theorizing must remain limited, it does not follow that such analysis must be entirely useless. On the contrary, constant attention to the meaning of the terms is indispensable in sociology because in this field powerful social forces operate which continuously create verbal confusion, much greater than what is inevitable in view of the rudimentary state of this branch of learning.

In the final analysis, the incentives to create terminological fog in the study of human affairs stem from the inescapable fact that it seldom pays (in the most literal sense of this word) to tell the truth in such matters. Playing safe, people frequently resort to ambiguity and obfuscation no matter whether they are telling the truth or deliberate lies. Obscurity, moreover, can be a source of power and income, as can be seen from the example of the legal language, which is clearly a product of striving to make it incomprehensible to the uninitiated, so as to compel them to rely on the expensive services of lawyers. Politicians and officials often deliberately couch their pronouncements in vague and ambiguous words, in order to leave themselves freedom of action to evade the issue. Even the rules and regulations of various organizations are phrased in the vaguest possible manner so as to permit the wielders of authority to evade responsibility or even to commit serious abuses. Equally common is the tendency to be mealy-mouthed, which reveals itself even in such seemingly straightforward matters as the nomenclature of administrative positions. For instance; in order not to offend susceptibilities, an incumbent of a newly instituted position of authority, instead of being called a chief or head or director, will be called a co-ordinator, and the analytically very useful distinction between co-ordination and control blurred in consequence.

The power of words to evoke emotions provides a standing and irresistible temptation to twist their original meanings in order to obtain desired reactions. Prompted by this motive, advertisers, journalists and many other kinds of writers aggravate the confusion by their incessant sensationalism which has robbed so many words of their meanings. For these reasons terminological discussion remains necessary as a kind of interminable cleaning or weeding, without which our understanding will not only not grow but will diminish with time; as, indeed, it already has in some ways. Under the impact of the aforementioned baneful influences, combined with sensationalism on the part of very many practitioners of the social sciences, desirous to pass their inept disquisitions for great discoveries, the study of human affairs has become befogged by a smoke screen of nebulous and pretentious verbiage.

As suggested earlier, some notion of a possible theoretical hypothesis must underlie a terminological analysis, if it is to be really creative, and to amount to more than routine cleansing. However, there are some very general criteria which all concepts ought to satisfy, if they are to be fitted into sociological theories such as can be envisaged at present. The first is that types should be preferably defined in a way that permits inclusion of several cases: in other words, very narrow as well as very wide definitions should be avoided unless some important considerations make them imperative. The concept of feudalism, for instance, can be made so narrow as to apply only to, say, northern France in the 13th century, whilst it can also be defined so widely that it will fit all pre-industrial states. Neither of these extremes lends itself to subtle theorizing, which calls for a definition which helps to classify pre-industrial polities. Or take 'totalitarianism'. Many definitions have been proposed which fit only Nazi Germany or Soviet Russia, and not even both, whereas it might be more illuminating to have a definition which distils the common features of these régimes without pre-judging the question of compatibility or concatenation of these features with other perhaps equally important characteristics.

In contrast to zoological and botanical taxonomy, no sociological classification can place every social entity in one category and no other. A genetic classification into non-intersecting classes is possible in biology and impossible in sociology because diversification of biotic species proceeded only by divergence, whereas social evolution exhibits divergence, convergence, permutation and various combinations of these. The methodological conclusion which can be drawn therefrom is that there is no point in trying to work out an exhaustive and non-intersecting classification of societies in their entirety, and it might be better to devise a scheme of classifying societies in terms of specific combinations of several characteristics, each of which might also occur in other combinations. This means that types should be defined in terms of simpler characteristics which would normally occur in other combinations as well. For this reason, in contrast to the situation in biology, a sociological taxonomy cannot be depicted by a tree-like figure on a plane: in fact, it is very unlikely that it could be pictorially represented at all because it would require several dimensions; although this does not mean that a classification referring only to a certain aspect of various social entities could not be pictorially represented.

The absence of fixity of type among social entities – their capacity to merge, split and transform themselves in multifarious ways – makes it almost impossible to found the concepts of social pathology on an objective basis. In medicine the notion of the pathological is based on the assumption – which, though not absolutely correct, constitutes a workable approximation – that what deviates widely from the norm constitutes an impediment to survival of the individual or of his progeny. In spite of mental diversity, we are very stereotyped in physiological functions, and it is a sobering thought that even a most radical non-conformist wishes to conform as far as bodily temperature is concerned. So when a physician sees a large growth on somebody's nose, he can safely assume that it is a malignant tumour, and rule out a possibility that the patient is turning into a perfectly healthy rhinoceros. Not so in sociology: even phenomena generally regarded as pathological, such as crime and commotion, may be inevitable accompaniments of a social metamorphosis which will bring forth a new social order, just as viable as the old, and perhaps even stronger and more desirable in many ways.

It may be worth remarking, incidentally, that the advent of atomic bombs, which made a suicide of the human species quite probable, has reduced to absurdity the religion of conformity propagated by the psychologists, who not only made adaptation to a society in which one lives (irrespectively of its qualities) into the decisive criterion of mental health, but even erected it into the highest goal of human endeavour; thus implicitly condemning all intellectual and moral pioneers, and lumping together as 'unadjusted' the thief and the sage. It is quite possible that a juxtaposition of mechanical ingenuity with evil and ungovernable proclivities amounts to a biological failure, and that unless men infuse more reason and kindness into their dealings, the days of humanity are numbered. So, being adapted to a crowd incapable of assuring their survival can hardly constitute a proof of sanity or fitness.

Biological taxonomists are often perplexed by intermediate forms which fit into none of their pigeon-holes. In sociology, however, the difficulties stemming from the shading-off of types assume staggering dimensions: everything is a matter of degree and of vague estimates thereof. In consequence, we have to operate with polar distinctions, concentrating on cases which approach either pole, never forgetting that with very many cases assignation to any type must remain arbitrary. Not many sophisticated classifications can be found in sociology and the related disciplines. The study of social structures based on kinship has advanced furthest in this respect; no doubt because in this field possibilities are particularly limited, and configurations consist of permutations of a fairly small number of basic relations, so that the anthropologists can depict most complicated networks of kinship with the aid of only four symbols: namely, those for a male, a female, an offspring and a spouse. Radcliffe-Brown's *Introduction to African Systems of Kinship and Marriage* offers a synthesis of the achievements in this field.

The few analyses which follow, not being embedded in expositions of theories, cannot amount to more than a preliminary cleaning up of pieces of ground. They are intended as examples of how well-worn, more than ambiguous and long-abused words, heavily loaded with emotion and prejudice, can be analysed and defined so as to facilitate rather than hinder rational thought.

Examples

Autocracy

Autocracy can be defined as a structure of power characterized by: (1) a clear ascendancy of one person at the top of its administrative hierarchy; (2) lack of any laws or customs in virtue of which the ruler might be called upon to account for his actions; (3) absence of any legal or customary limitations on the exercise of authority by the ruler. The last of these criteria does not imply that auto-cracy and totalitarianism are identical, as the absence of institu-tional limitations on the ruler's authority does not necessarily lead to the establishment of systematic governmental control over the totality of social life of the subjects. While an autocracy may be based primarily on the loyalty of the subjects or on the fear of punishment, usually both ingredients are present, with great variations in their relative importance. For instance, Tsar Nicolas I or Hitler could rely on the loyalty of their subjects (apart from conquered nations and persecuted minorities) to a greater extent than could Stalin or Chang-tso-lin.

The proposed definition leaves equally open the question of whether the supreme authority is bestowed in accordance with pre-established norms or whether it is conquered (be it merely through a threat of violence). In the former case we have a legitimate autocracy (hereditary or co-optative); in the latter a dictatorship.

Monocracy can be distinguished from autocracy as an over-lapping, but not co-extensive, type of authority, characterized only by our criterion No 1, that is to say by a clear ascendancy of one person at the top of an administrative hierarchy (as distin-guished from collective authority), leaving open the questions of accountability and scope.

Authoritarianism

'Authoritarianism' has at least three distinct meanings. In the psychological sense – when we speak, for instance, of authoritarian character – it connotes a disposition uniting zealous obedience to one's hierarchical superiors, and obsequiousness and sycophancy towards the stronger in general, with overbearing and scornful demeanour towards those who are in one's power. Secondly, the term 'authoritarianism' can also be used to describe the manner of conducting administration, characterized by reliance on apo-dictic orders and threats of punishment, averse to employing either consultation or persuasion. Finally, 'authoritarianism' can desig-nate an ideology advocating the propagation, or applauding the prevalence of authoritarian administrative procedures, and extolling the paragon of authoritarian character. The relationship between authoritarian propensities, procedures and ideologies is that of mutual facilitation. Persons with authoritarian propensities naturally tend to resort to authoritarian administrative procedures, and espouse authoritarian ideologies, while the prevalence of authoritarian procedures forms authoritarian characters, and increases the number of people who have vested interest in authoritarian ideologies – in addition to making these ideologies seem more 'natural'. In view of this, we might be justified in using the word 'authoritarianism' without further qualifications as a description of a condition of a social entity, when we wish to refer to a concurrence of authoritarian propensities, procedures and ideologies – provided that we remember that we are abstracting from the variations in the proportions of these ingredients. From the point of view of social dynamics the latter might be of utmost importance.

The assessment of the degree of authoritarianism meets with further difficulties. In the first place, various aspects of social life may not be equally pervaded by it, even if on the whole there is a trend towards consistency. For example, the American business organizations are more authoritarian than their British counterparts, whereas the reverse is true of family patterns. Secondly, there may be great differences in this respect between various parts of social structure. Thus, for instance, in medieval Europe the manor was a very authoritarian entity, whereas the feudal hierarchy was in fact comparatively unauthoritarian.

Militarism

Like most sociological terms 'militarism' is used in several distinct senses which must be examined in turn.

1. 'Militarism' is sometimes taken to mean militancy or aggressive foreign policy involving the readiness to resort to war. It does not seem profitable to adopt this usage, as the words 'militancy' and 'combativeness' adequately describe these features.

2. In other contexts 'militarism' means preponderance of the military in the state. Such a preponderance implies a differentiation of civil and military spheres of authority, and of civil and military administrative personnel. It would be improper, therefore, to apply the term 'militarism' in this sense to situations where such differentiations are absent, as was the case in all primitive

states such as, for instance, the Zulu and Ankole Kingdoms in Africa, or the Polish kingdom under the early Piasts, or even the enormous empire of Genghis Khan. Whereas the differentiation of the roles of the chief priest and of the war leader occurs even in small tribes, the first trace of a distinction between military and civil (to be exact – financial) spheres of authority, exercised over the same subjects, appears in the Persian Empire in the fifth century BC. Although some American Indian tribes had war chiefs as well as peace chiefs, this arrangement constituted neither a division of authority over the same persons nor an allocation of the population to permanent units; it could be best described as alternation of types of authority.

This usage is perfectly reasonable, yet much could be said for employing the term in a somewhat different sense.

An important feature distinguishing different kinds of military preponderance is the extent to which the rank and file share the privileges of those at the top of the hierarchy. Variations in this respect depend on the military participation ratio, which has been defined as 'the proportion of militarily utilized individuals in the total population of the state' (*Military Organization and Society*, p. 33 Int. Lbr. Soc., Routledge & Kegan, Paul, London 1954, Grove Press, New York 1954). Obviously, if the military participation ratio is very high the privileges of the rank and file have to be diluted to the point of non-existence. Germany under Wilhelm II and Poland under Pilsudski exemplify a variant where political preponderance and economic favours were restricted to the officer corps. The late Roman Empire, on the other hand, is an instance of the more inclusive variant, the distinctive feature of which is the inclusion of all soldiers in the privileged body. The connection between the preponderance of the military and bureaucracy depends on the type of military organization.

Contrary to widespread opinion, this preponderance is not necessarily accompanied by external militancy: Tokugawa Shogunate in Japan, as well as a number of Latin American military dictatorships, are examples to the point.

3. 'Militarism' can also be interpreted as connoting the extensive control by the military over social life, coupled with the subservience of the whole society to the needs of the army. This leads usually to a recasting of various parts of the social life in accordance with the pattern of military organization. It seems,

however, that we might reduce the danger of ambiguity if we use the term 'militarization' instead of 'militarism' to describe this phenomenon.

Militarization can occur without the preponderance of the military as can be seen from the examples of Britain and the US during the Second World War: nevertheless, it seems that this can be so only in the short run. On the other hand, many cases show – a number of Latin American dictatorships, for instance – that preponderance of the army can endure without producing a wholesale militarization.

4. It has been proposed by some writers that by 'militarism' we should mean the pointless, or even harmful from the point of view of efficiency, addiction to drill and ceremonies, and adulation of trappings. But the tendency towards a shift of valuations from ends to means, and from content to form, is a ubiquitous social phenomenon; and 'militarism' in this sense is thus merely a manifestation of this tendency in the military field. This usage seems to be unprofitably restricted.

5. Sometimes the word 'militarism' is used to refer not to an institutional arrangement but to an ideology propagating military ideals. Such an ideology often accompanies preponderance of the army (eg Germany under the Hohenzollerns, Japan under Tojo), yet the latter can occur without it (eg Cuba under Batista, where the soldiers ruled but were despised). Furthermore, an ideology extolling the soldier and the military virtues may flourish even where the army is weak (eg Germany at the time of Weimar Republic). For the sake of clarity, it would be better to speak of 'militaristic ideology' than of 'militarism' in this sense.

6. There is an interesting phenomenon which, however, it would be inappropriate to call 'militarism': namely, the inclination to imitate military demeanour and paraphernalia in the walks of life entirely unconnected with war. The example of the Salvation Army shows that such a 'militarism' can flourish even where militarism in other senses is not prominent.

7. Sociological analysis would probably be facilitated by defining militarism as the compound of militancy, preponderance of the army in the state, adulation of military virtues and militarization. Where all four components are present to a high degree (eg Japan under Tojo), we have a clear case of militarism. Where only two or three are in evidence we might speak of partial militarism.

Different types of militarism could be distinguished in accordance with the relative strength of the components.

Dictatorship

In contexts referring to ancient Rome 'dictatorship' is usually employed as equivalent to the Latin *'dictatura'*. In times of exceptional stress the Roman senate often decided that for a period of six months absolute power be vested in one man, whereupon one of the consuls designated the incumbent. A 'dictator' could be impeached after the expiry of his tenure of office. It is plain, then, that in its classical form Roman dictatorship was a form of legitimate authority. Only towards the end of the republic was the title of dictator assumed by generals who seized power by illegal means.

Sometimes the word dictatorship is used in what might be called a mythical sense: as, for instance, in the expression 'dictatorship of the proletariat'. For whereas it might happen that a dictatorship would be exercised in the interests and with the support of the proletariat, it is inconceivable that those actually wielding supreme authority should continue to belong to the proletariat, that is to say, remain manual workers.

Most commonly by dictatorship is meant the type of authority characterized by at least some of the following features: (1) lack of laws or customs by virtue of which the ruler (or rulers) could be called upon to account for their actions or be removed; (2) lack of limitations on the scope of authority; (3) acquisition of supreme authority by contravention of pre-existing laws; (4) absence of provision for orderly succession; (5) use of authority for the benefit of a restricted group only; (6) obedience of the subjects being due solely to fear; (7) concentration of power in the hands of one man; (8) employment of terror (terror can be distinguished from severe punishments by its unpredictability). As the term 'dictatorship' is indiscriminately applied to various incomplete combinations of these features, the question arises: which of them should we adopt as constitutive criteria? Even the case which is reputed to have been a dictatorship *par excellence* – that of Hitler's régime – fails to exhibit all of these features: for Hitler reached the headship without breaking the constitution. Moreover, there are many borderline cases: usurpers of thrones, for instance, such as many of the Roman emperors, would have to be included among dictators if we adopted criterion No 3 as decisive.

It seems that the most useful heuristically would be this definition: dictatorship is the type of government exhibiting the following features: (1) the supreme authority is absolute; (2) the headship of the state was acquired by conquest, that is to say not in virtue of pre-existing laws; (3) there is no rule of succession which can be regarded as established. Other features enumerated would then be regarded as contingent – including criterion No 7, so that we could speak of personal as well as collective dictatorships.

Tyranny

In contexts referring to the history of ancient Greece 'tyranny' is used in its original sense: it signifies the type of authority to whose more recent exemplifications the name of dictatorship is given. To be exact, a tyrant is a man who holds kingly authority in a polity where there is no king by law. As the Greek writers sometimes speak of 'good tyrants', it is evident that the word was not entirely derogatory.

In other contexts 'tyranny' usually means oppressive and cruel treatment. Often, however, any government of which the speaker disapproves is dubbed a tyranny. As there is no universal agreement on the proper way of governing we could not derive from this epithet much information about the behaviour of the government in question without knowledge of the preferences of the speaker. Further confusion stems from the indiscriminate application of the word tyranny to the manner of exercising authority, to the body of persons who practise it, and to the state in which this takes place. In any case the word is strongly evocative of opprobrium.

The postulate of non-valuation (also known as 'value-freedom', *Wertfreiheit* or ethical neutrality) requires that only such terms be employed in sociological analysis whose denotation does not in principle depend on the ethical convictions or desires of the speaker. Its primary justification is that it enables persons of differing ethical convictions, loyalties and desires to engage in fruitful discussion and thus permits the accumulation of knowledge. Moreover, it is recommended as a prophylactic measure against 'wishful thinking' and 'thinking with blood'. But it is an error to imagine that it forbids students of society to have firm ethical convictions, or strong feelings, or to engage in collective action. It concerns solely the classifications of statements and the choice of concepts to be employed in analysing social processes.

One way of making 'tyranny' into a general concept satisfying the postulate of non-valuation would be to define it as a régime which is felt by a substantial part of its subjects to be cruel and oppressive. Alternatively, we might define 'tyranny' as 'the type of government which secures obedience mainly or entirely through the fear of punishment'. Most useful heuristically seems to be the following definition: 'tyranny is the manner of exercising authority which involves very frequent recourse to punishments of utmost severity'. This criterion entails the two preceding. A tyranny, as thus defined, can be regular or erratic, according to whether the punishments follow some rules laid down beforehand, or whether they are meted out whimsically. 'Terror' can be described as a special kind of tyranny. Its characteristics are: (1) that no observance of commands – no matter how punctilious – on the part of prospective victims can ensure their safety; (2) that punishments are inflicted indiscriminately with the deliberate aim of creating an atmosphere of fear and paralysing resistance. These features distinguish terror from policies of extermination. Moreover, terror must be distinguished from robbery and indulgence in sadism, although it is always accompanied by them.

Tyranny is compatible with various types of government: autocratic – whether of revolutionary (eg Robespierre) or traditional (eg Ivan the Terrible) variety – oligarchic (eg Sparta), and even democratic, where a minority may be tyrannized by the majority (eg the treatment of sinners and dissenters by Savonarola's democratic and levelling régime in Florence). This is true not only of states but also of smaller social aggregates.

In diagnosing tyranny we must bear in mind not only that this is a matter of degree, but also that conditions prevailing in various parts of any social aggregate may differ. To illustrate this point, in Russia Peter I tyrannized the nobles and the nobles tyrannized the serfs, whereas in the Poland of that time a royal tyranny over the nobles was out of the question, but the way in which the latter ruled the peasants was undoubtedly tyrannous. On the whole, the governance of the British Isles in the early 19th century could not be described as a tyranny, yet we can say with justification that the urban poor as well as the Irish peasantry lived at that time under a tyranny.

Despotism does not absolutely necessitate tyranny, although it undoubtedly tends to be accompanied by it. Despotism without tyranny may occur if the despot is of benevolent disposition and his authority unchallenged. The reign of Marcus Aurelius seems to prove that this unlikely conjunction is not impossible.

In his *Historical Essays* published in the 1870's Edward Freeman says: 'Tyrants may perhaps be divided into three classes. There are some whose cruelty is simple military or judicial severity carried too far, whose blows smite men who really deserve to be smitten only not with so heavy a stroke. A tyranny of this kind is not inconsistent with many personal virtues, and it of itself implies a real zeal for the public good. Again, there are some tyrants whose cruelty has a definite object, who strike in order to destroy or to weaken some hostile party, who are ready to inflict any amount of suffering which suits their own ends, but who take no pleasure in oppression, and who are capable of becoming mild and beneficent rulers as soon as opposition ends. Such were the authors of both the first and the second proscription. Sulla and Augustus alike shed blood without mercy as long as anything was to be gained by shedding it; but neither of them had any appetite for slaughter and confiscation when the need for them had passed by. Lastly, there are the tyrants whose tyranny is utterly reckless and capricious, and in whom the frequent practice of cruelty seems at last to create a sort of enjoyment in cruelty for its own sake. Such was the cruelty of Caius and Nero. The second and third classes are distinguished from each other by the fact that tyrants of the second class commonly get better, while tyrants of the third class commonly get worse. The horrors of the second proscription were followed in due course by the long paternal reign of Augustus. On the other hand, both Caius and Nero began with a professed hatred of cruelty of every kind, which we have no right to assume was mere acting. The one form of tyranny is the cruelty of statesmen, reckless as to the means by which an end is to be compassed; the other is the cruelty of men in whom weakness and frivolity are united with a childish delight in the mere exercise of power. But the tyranny of Domitian was something which stands quite by itself. He may be said to have begun with a tyranny of the first type, which gradually changed into one of the third.'

National Character

People untouched by psychological or sociological sophistication do not hesitate to attribute character to nations, and in doing so usually make rash and palpably untrue assertions. As this notion, moreover, is often used for propagating chauvinism and racialism, it is small wonder that the very term 'national character' fell into disrepute among scholars. Nevertheless, here as on many other issues, common sense seems to be partly but not entirely wrong: one finds, to be sure, people of all kinds of character everywhere, but nobody who has lived in the midst of different nations can escape the impression that there are national differences in this respect, particularly as the national origins of a person can often be guessed at sight in spite of the lack of distinctive dress.

When an eminent psychologist dismisses the issue by declaring that 'science knows nothing about national characters' he is guilty of pseudo-scientific dogmatism, for he confuses a declaration of ignorance with a proof of non-existence. It must never be forgotten that a rejection of an idea without conclusive grounds is no more scientific than its acceptance without evidence: credulity and dogmatism assume both affirmative and negative forms. We must not be like the author of an ethnographic study of the Somali tribes written about eighty years ago who wrote: 'ignorant natives believe that malaria is caused by mosquito bites'. Let us then refine the popular concept of national character in order to free it from naïve or propagandist superfluities.

At the outset it must be made clear that an assertion that a certain nation exhibits certain characteristics need not imply that it always did so: we can accept the view that there are national characters, and at the same time reject the idea that they are unchangeable. In other words, the question of existence must not be confused with that of persistence. We can, moreover, employ this concept without assuming that national character is in any way biologically determined. Thus we free our concept from implications which would render it illegitimate, and restrict the problem to ascertainment of actual characteristics of a nation, without making our findings dependent on our knowledge of antecedent conditions or causes.

In order to be able to discuss profitably the problem of national character, we must make clear what we mean by 'nation', because, obviously it is not a matter of legal nationality. I propose the following definition: a nation is a population located within a certain territory, characterized by some features of culture which distinguish it from other similar populations, and whose members conceive of themselves as forming a community which aspires to political unity and independence (in the sense of not being governed by outsiders). In a way this definition pre-judges the issue because if a population exhibits a feature of culture which differentiates it from other populations, then it can be said to have a distinctive character. Such an interpretation, however, would be too simple and therefore useless. Nobody denies that the Hungarians are characterized by speaking Hungarian and eating more paprika than the Germans or the Poles. People who question the validity of the concept of national character have something else in mind: they do not deny that there are great differences in customs but they doubt whether members of different nations differ in psychological characteristics. But what is the difference between a cultural (or social) and a psychological characteristic? The solution which I suggest is to modify somewhat Durkheim's definition of social fact, and define residually as psychological those traits in respect of which people differ from each other irrespectively of their membership of large groups: thus the inhabitants of any country or members of any social class differ from each other in respect of kindness, cruelty, honesty, courage and so on, in spite of speaking the same language, having the same religion, wearing similar dress, eating similar things and so on. Obversely, those features which members of social groups have in common would be considered as cultural (or social) traits.

The proposed distinction between psychological and cultural traits pre-judges at least one aspect of the concept of national character. Differences between groups in respect of features which are neither general nor absent within any group can be only statistical. It implies, moreover, that the concept of national character is interpreted distributively and not collectively: that is to say, that it refers to characteristics of individuals composing a nation and not to characteristics of a nation as a whole. The latter are in fact subsumed under the concepts of culture and social structure. The differences between cultures and social structures cannot, of course, be described in purely psychological terms. It does not seem advisable to use the term 'national character' to denote the structure of the national community because such a usage lends itself to hypostatization by insinuating that a nation possesses attributes pertaining to persons.

Even if we assume that there are no significant statistical differences between members of different nations in respect of basic biologically determined traits such as general intelligence, it cannot be denied that there are marked differences in features of great social importance such as courtesy, honesty, gaiety, talkativeness and so on. Only a traveller who is deaf and blind could fail to notice that the Spaniards are on the whole more talkative than the Scotsmen, or that the Germans are more obedient than the Poles.

Apart from simple differences in frequency of traits, national character may be described in terms of human types which, though by no means prevalent in the midst of a given nation, and perhaps even fairly rare, are peculiar to it in the sense that they are much more common within it than anywhere else. These are the types which appear in caricatures, comedies and jokes. Apart from purely symbolic figures which appear in political cartoons, these images contain a grain of truth: the proof is that if they are transposed they cease to be funny. A person who is considered as typical is not frequently found, and he represents the peculiarity of his nation by combining the extremes of qualities in respect of which his nation deviates from averages for other groups. He represents a quintessance of peculiarities.

There are many rather elusive traits which give rise neither to any particular organizations nor to any specific institutions but pervade the workings of all institutions and organizations existing in a given nation. Take, for instance, the famous English reserve.

To illustrate his concept of unsocial sociability, Schopenhauer likened human beings to lonely hedgehogs who are unhappy when separated but prick each other when they get together. This simile well illustrates the inescapable dilemma of social life. By being open and frank one can make true friends more easily but one is also likely to get into arguments, and the best way to avoid them is to keep silence. As friction is a necessary concomitant of lack of reserve in intercourse among persons who have not chosen each other for compatibility, social life within unselected groups can be either smooth and superficial or deeper and more tempestuous. The English reserve exemplifies the first option, the so-called 'Slav soul' the second.

It seems that this divergence is connected with differences in class structure which in England has been fluid and blurred for a much longer time than on the Continent, and particularly in eastern Europe. In a caste society one cannot lose one's status even if one gets drunk with a valet, whereas in a society with fluid and blurred class divisions there are many people who might lose status by making an inappropriate friendship. It is quite possible that the English reserve is the product of a long-standing abundance of individuals whose status could not be ascertained at sight.

Nations differ greatly in homogeneity: some communities which it is customary to call nations are so heterogeneous in customs and outlook that we cannot attribute to them any definite character. For example: there is no justification for speaking of national characters in west Africa because the populations encompassed by the new states are extremely heterogeneous and the tribal solidarities are much stronger than the feeling of belonging to the 'nations' arbitrarily created by the European governments who carved up Africa without regard to ethnic divisions. When Poland was revived as an independent state in 1919 the differences in the mode of life and outlook between regions were so great that it was hardly legitimate to speak of the national character of the Poles. These differences were mainly due to the impact of different conditions of existence under the Russian, German and Austrian rules. Furthermore, whereas in ex-German Poland the class divisions were rather weak, in the other parts of the country there was a well-nigh impassable barrier between the upper and the middle class on the one hand, and the peasants and workers on the other, to which corresponded radical differences in typical characters. These examples show that crystallization of national character is a matter of degree.

BOOK TWO

Problems of Substantive Theory

PART ONE

VIOLENCE AND SOCIETY

CHAPTER SEVEN

FEROCITY AND CONVENTIONS

WE CAN DEFINE war as organized fighting between groups of individuals belonging to the same species but occupying distinct territories, thus distinguishing war from fights between isolated individuals as well as from struggles between groups living inter-mingled within the same territory, which can be classified as rebellions, revolutions, riots and so on.

The custom of blood-feud, whereby members of a clan or another kinship group avenge the death of their kinsman by killing any member of the group to which the killer belongs, gives rise to forms of fighting which are often difficult to classify. Sometimes blood-feud leads to proper battles which can be con-sidered as constituting warfare, but more often it produces a sequence of individual killings which do not amount to war as defined above.

Many thinkers have pondered about why there are wars, but before we can form an intelligent opinion on this matter we must consider whether war is something universal or something which can be found only among certain peoples and on certain levels of civilization. We must also enquire whether anything resembling human wars occurs in the animal kingdom.

Individual animals commonly fight duels for possession of mates. The horns of the stag are used solely for this purpose; he fights with his hooves when he defends himself from beasts of prey. But there are no organized battles between groups of stags.

Many animals fight with members of their own species for territories which they appropriate, but these are fights between individuals – not between groups. Violence is executed on the prey by the predator, but this resembles the behaviour of the hunter rather than the warrior. Groups of social animals will often attack a member of their own species of unusual shape or colour, but the nearest human parallel to such behaviour is lynching not war. However, with very few exceptions, ants of any given colony will engage in collective struggles against other ant communities, even those of their own species. As these struggles follow definite patterns we can without exaggeration describe them as wars. The ants of the tropical genus Asteca which nest in the hollow twigs of trees form clusters of communities which, if they are of more or less the same age and strength, may live for a long time in peace, until with the growth of the tree the equilibrium is disturbed, and one of the communities begins to increase in numbers disproportionately, owing to a more favourable position with regard to food supplies. Eventually it perforates the wall of its nest and invades its neighbour. The vanquished colony is expelled from its site, leaving many of its offspring to swell the ranks as well as the larders of the conqueror. Similar strife usually goes on in other parts of the tree. A succession of eliminatory fights eventually leaves only one victor which comes to dominate the entire tree, and henceforth pursues a peaceful existence until the tree dies.

The wars of Asteca ants appear insignificant in comparison with the activity of *pheidole megacephala*, a small yellow myrmecine ant from Madagascar, which is known to have colonized the Old World and much of the West Indies within the last fifty years, making use of human transport, and liquidating many apparently superior species *en route*. Pheidole has since been exterminated in many places by *iredemyomax humilis*, a fragile and weaponless ant, which began a campaign of expansion from Argentina a few years ago. Both of these species conquered by superiority of organization and scale of attack, thus overcoming heavily armed but more loosely organized colonies of much larger individuals. Was it thus, we may ask, that *homo neanderthalis* fell before the smaller and weaker but better organized *homo sapiens*?

Many nations and tribes loved war, and regarded courage and skill at fighting as the highest of virtues. The Norsemen, to take one of the more extreme examples, imagined heaven as a place where warriors never cease to fight, where wounds heal instantaneously and those who would normally be killed rise up immediately to fight again. Many peoples were more peaceful but all nations and tribes of whom there are records, are known to have engaged in warfare. Even the small bands of hunters and plant-gatherers, who lead an isolated existence in the depths of bogs and forests surrounding the river Amazon, fight each other occasionally. The Pygmies did not wage wars on a substantial scale, but they have been known to fight, and in any case were continuously on the run, fleeing from large tribes of bigger and better armed men, who often robbed or enslaved them. In the long records of history and ethnography we can find only one case of a people who know no organized violence: namely the Polar Eskimo. And here it was simply the lack of opportunity that prevented wars, because, obtaining their sustenance in widely dispersed family units, the Polar Eskimos never gather in sufficient numbers and in sufficient proximity to other groups to engage in organized fighting. Sporadic fights between individuals do occur among the Eskimos, and sometimes even lead to killing.

As far as prehistoric peoples are concerned, we can infer their habits only from the remains of their tools and weapons; and this evidence, together with that of finds of skulls crushed by clubs and axes, shows that war began very early. We may legitimately conclude, therefore, that war has been a permanent feature of the social life of human beings ever since they emerged from an anthropoid stage.

When we examine the records of history we find considerable variation (both in time and in space) in the frequency and ferocity of warfare. The Indians of the North American Plains waged wars continuously, particularly after they obtained horses from the Spaniards. Their brethren farther north, living in greater dispersion in thickly wooded areas where rapid movements were more difficult, appear to have devoted a somewhat lesser part of their time to war. If we take the history of Europe, we find that the 17th century was the age of endemic warfare whereas the 18th and the 19th constituted eras of relative peace, notwithstanding the wars of Napoleon. Our own century, with its world wars, has so far been much more warlike than its predecessor. If we look at the history of humanity as a whole we can find no permanent trend either towards intensification or towards abatement of warfare. Naturally, with the progress of technology, the growth of population and the replacement of small tribes and principalities by large states, the wars came to be waged with larger armies, and the number of victims of each big war exceeded that of the preceding.

In proportion, however, to the numbers engaged the losses in recent wars were no larger than those of ancient campaigns.

During the Middle Ages, and the same applies to the tribal mode of existence, it often happened that warriors fought for a few hours and then went home; but they were continuously harassed and seldom a month or even a week passed without some fighting somewhere in the vicinity. During the most recent wars the fighting never stopped for several years, but, on the other hand, the populations of many states have enjoyed peace for decades. So, what really has happened is that instead of a multitude of small wars as of old we have had in this century a few big wars.

Wars have varied not only in the frequency and intensity of the effort put into them but also in the ferocity with which they were conducted – that is to say, in the degree to which the behaviour of the combatants was restrained by rules and conventions. Often unlimited wars were waged: wars in which every possible means of destroying the enemy was used. In other wars the opponents behaved in accordance with a commonly accepted code which prescribed what was permissible and what was not. Indeed some wars appeared to be lethal sporting matches. We may call a conventional war one in which the opponents do not have recourse to all the means of destroying the enemy which are available. In such a war the opponents do not even seek to destroy each other but only to obtain some limited advantage.

When we look at the history of mankind we find no persistent trend towards either conventional or unlimited warfare; and even among very primitive peoples we find both kinds. Some of the small tribes who live in the forests of the Amazon basin are believed to kill any stranger who strays into their territory. They appear to maintain no regular relations with their neighbours, whom they fight with poisoned arrows propelled by blow-gun. The Australian aborigines, on the other hand, usually wage war in a highly conventional manner: they declare a war formally, giving the enemy due notice, fight battles at prearranged times and places, without attempting to exterminate the foes, and stopping the fight by mutual agreement when they feel that enough blood has been spilled. Occasionally, however, when they feel that the injury is too deep for the account to be settled in a normal way, they decide upon 'a war to end wars', whereupon they try to assault the enemy camp by surprise and exterminate its inmates, sometimes even including women and children. The usual conduct of war by the Indians of the North American Plains comprised a formal declaration of war, but once the enemy had been warned that the war was on, no holds were barred and every effort would be made to attack the enemy by surprise.

At the height of the medieval civilization the wars were almost sporting matches: bloody, to be sure, but just as restricted by conventions. Let us look at one of many examples of such a spirit. At the beginning of the 15th century Jagiello, the king of Poland and Lithuania, was fighting the Order of the Teutonic Knights. On one occasion he found their army when it was crossing a river, and, although many of his warriors were eager to pounce upon the enemy, he restrained them because he thought that it was unworthy of a knight to attack the enemy who was not ready. When both armies finally met upon a fair ground they first engaged in parleys, during which the envoys of the Teutonic knights gave Jagiello two swords, thus mocking the inferior armament of his troops. Having slept overnight, each side celebrated a mass in its camp. When both sides were ready they signalled to each other by trumpeting, and then rushed into battle.

As a rule, the medieval knights considered it unworthy of their honour to attack by surprise or pursue the defeated enemy. The knights who fell from their horses were usually spared and released for ransom.

In Italy at the time of the Renaissance warfare assumed an extraordinarily limited and conventional character, when wandering mercenaries came to constitute the mainstay of the armed forces of the small city-states into which that country was then divided. These mercenaries, who had no roots anywhere and offered their services to anybody who wished to employ them, never fought out of conviction, and for this reason worked out a technique of mock warfare. Sometimes in the battles between armies numbering thousands of soldiers only a few were killed and these mainly through accidents. In one famous battle only one soldier died, having been kicked by a horse. Often the battles were decided by bribing enemy soldiers to come over. Never, either before or since, has war been rendered so harmless.

Another period of highly limited warfare in Europe was the 18th century, during which there were many wars but they consisted of innumerable marches and sieges whilst the battles were few and not very ferocious. How far the respect for conventions of war could go was shown by the famous battle of Fontenoy which started with an invitation by the French commander to the English soldiers to fire first.

Up till the Second World War conventions were on the whole observed in warfare. During all the wars of Napoleon not a single town was destroyed deliberately by his troops. When the Prussian army besieged Paris in 1870 it refrained from indiscriminate shelling of the city. During the First World War cities were destroyed but neither the prisoners nor civilians massacred. Such massacres became commonplace during the Second World War.

It must not be inferred, however, that restraint in war was normal until the recent times. On the contrary, the periods of restraint were exceptional. The Romans and the Greeks, for instance, waged war in a brutal and entirely unchivalrous manner: attacks by stealth, without declaration of war, were common, and in order to weaken the enemy his crops were burned, wells poisoned and buildings destroyed. The Assyrians and the Mongols exterminated entire populations in order to instil fear in prospective victims and thus weaken their will to resist.

Whether a war is limited by conventions or not depends largely on against whom it is fought: when the enemy is of different culture, language and race the war is normally unrestricted. The Galla tribes of eastern Africa, for instance, distinguish clearly two types of war, for which they have different words: first, a war against other Galla tribes which is fought according to rules, and in which the vanquished are either not touched at all or taken into the tribe of the victors; second, a war against those who do not speak Galla – the 'dumb ones' – waged without regard to any rules, and which in case of victory leads to an extermination of the entire enemy population.

Similar connection between the strangeness of the enemy and the ferocity of warfare has been observed in many other cases. The wars between the Christians and the Turks were notoriously more ferocious than those between various Christian kingdoms. Also the wars which occurred in Europe when political conflicts coincided with religious differences were worse than those of the previous centuries. The ferocity of the last war was connected with the rejection of the heritage of the Christian civilization by Hitler and his followers. We must not exaggerate, however, the importance of this factor: people give vent most readily to their pugnacity and cruelty when the enemy differs in race, language and creed, but often enough they are utterly ruthless even with those with whom they are united by a common language, culture and religion. Unity in these respects creates a possibility of limiting war through conventions but in no way ensures that such conventions will develop and acquire a force sufficient to curb the evil propensities of human nature.

Restraint in the choice of the methods of fighting is linked with the expectations about the consequences of a defeat: if to be defeated means to be butchered or enslaved for life then no such restraint can be expected.

In the treatment of the vanquished we find extreme differences. Genghis Khan and other Mongol rulers used to celebrate their victories by tying up the defeated chieftains, laying them side by side, putting boards on them, and feasting on the top whilst their victims were being gradually crushed to death; finding, as a Mongol saga puts it, that 'the groans of the vanquished foes are the sweetest music'. When Timur, the emperor of central Asia, caught sultan Bayazid, he kept him until death in a golden cage in which he could neither stand nor sit nor lie down. It was only in Europe towards the end of the Middle Ages that the princes began to treat their defeated opposite numbers with some consideration. This courtesy did not necessarily extend to the lower ranks of the soldiery and civilian population, although even they were treated better than heretofore. Since that period until the Second World War the populations of Europe have suffered pillage and vexations, but they have never been exterminated or enslaved or driven from their lands, which was a common fate of the defeated in antiquity. Transfer of a region from one state to another involved during that era little change for the civilian population: all it usually meant was that they would have to pay taxes to a different sovereign. The Second World War brought a tragic reversal to barbarism: deportations and massacres of civilian populations, including women and children, killings of prisoners of war, and indiscriminate bombing of cities.

In view of the atrocities committed during the last war we might well doubt whether humanity has progressed very far. Perhaps the only ground for hope is the fact that the perpetrators of these recent crimes were after all ashamed of them and tried to conceal them, whereas in earlier times cruelty was a ground for boasting: on the tombs of Assyrian kings, for instance, there are descriptions of how many defeated and helpless enemies they slew, blinded and mutilated.

The most outstanding features of the history of mankind are the accumulation of technical knowledge and the increase in the scale of societies. The examples of how war stimulated inventions range from the improvements in early metallurgy to the construction of interplanetary rockets, but on the other hand, by causing wholesale destructions and retrogressions of civilizations, war has often acted as a brake upon rather than a stimulant of technical progress and evolution towards increasing complexity and scale.

It is an unpleasant truth that, human nature being what it is, without war civilization would never have arisen and mankind would still be divided into small bands wandering in the forests and jungles. Advanced civilization with extensive division of labour can only arise within a large and fairly dense population engaged in peaceful exchange of goods and services. Such a condition requires an extension of the control of a single government over a considerable area. There could be only one way in which small tribes could be welded into states and small states into large ones: namely, conquest. All noted cases of emergence of a state out of stateless tribes fall into this pattern. There have been a few instances of tribes forming a confederation like the famous league of the Iroquois, but as they had no strong central governments, these polities cannot be regarded as states. All such unions, moreover, were founded for the purpose of waging war.

In Africa we can find a number of examples of how a state emerges from a fusion of tribes. The kingdoms of Ankole, Baganda, Ruanda and several others came into existence through conquest of various tribes of agriculturists by tribes of pastoralists who became the nobility whilst reducing the agriculturists to serfdom, and whose war leaders became kings.

Fusion of small states into larger ones also takes place through or under the influence of war. Egypt, China, France, England, Russia came into existence through being conquered by one prince. Even when a union occurred through a dynastic intermarriage as was the case, for instance, with Poland and Lithuania or Castille and Aragon – an alliance in war usually underlay the arrangement. We can see similar process taking place today: the European

Common Market and the gradually emerging confederation of Western Europe are based in a large measure upon a military alliance, and only because they feel threatened are the member states inclined to surrender some of their sovereignty. As a larger state has a greater chance of winning, war has fostered the process of the swallowing of smaller states by the larger. This tendency, however, was limited by the fact that without modern means of transport a large state could not always mobilize armies corresponding to their size.

Apart from being an instrument of political unification, war has promoted technical progress in other ways too. Firstly, it often gave a direct stimulus to invention: at all times the weapons were the most advanced gadgets which any civilization has possessed. Secondly, it produced the expansion of technically more advanced societies at the expense of the more backward in this respect. However, we must remember that very often superiority in military technique was not accompanied by all-round technical superiority. Thus the nomads were for a very long time stronger than the settled agricultural peoples, who exceeded them greatly in the development of arts and crafts but were not equally mobile. The nomad's everyday existence naturally prepared him for war on horseback. As the weapons were still very rudimentary – sabres, spears, bows and arrows – they could be produced by semi-primitive peoples just as well as by the more advanced.

The invention of firearms constituted a turning point, because it gave unquestionable military superiority to the urban civilizations, capable of mustering skilled craftsmen, mathematicians and workshops, and made nomad invasions impossible.

If we look at the spread of industrial civilization throughout the world, we find that its chief cause was the overwhelming military superiority of the industrialized over unindustrialized states. The peoples of Asia and Africa would have in any case imitated certain features of European civilization, but they showed no inclination to abandon their traditions entirely. Nevertheless, in the face of the superiority of European arms, even a tradition-loving people like the Japanese had to modify profoundly their way of life, and to adopt those features of European civilization which were indispensable for industrialization and efficient administration, without which no modern army could exist. The peoples who could not (or had no time to) transform their cultures so as to be able to have modern armies were conquered, and their traditional ways of life dislocated.

Until very recent times war was the only kind of collective action undertaken on a truly large scale. There were armies of hundreds of thousands when production was carried on only in small farms and workshops. Only during the last century did large-scale organizations come into existence which were devoted to peaceful activities; and even now the largest private corporation is small in comparison with an army of a sizeable state. For this reason, it was in the armies and the navies that the art of organizing and directing large bodies of men was evolved.

The most obvious effect of a war is that it produces a slowing down of the growth of the population or even a decline in numbers. Moreover, as young men are usually more exposed to the dangers than the rest of the population, one of the usual consequences of a war is numerical predominance of women over men, which may lead to widespread spinsterhood unless polygyny is practised. Indeed, polygyny was an institution which was almost indispensable to warlike peoples because it enabled them to maintain their military strength by preventing the scarcity of men from affecting the numbers in the next generation.

Even very severe losses sustained in a war can be compensated quickly if the birth rate is high. Where the birth rate is lower (as is the case in more civilized societies) the consequences may be more enduring. For instance, in France after the First World War (in which more than two million French soldiers fell) there was a serious lack of young men, in consequence of which leadership in most fields remained in the hands of the old, with the result that activity in all domains was sluggish, timid and backward-looking, and French economy and culture stagnated.

It has been argued that in addition to purely quantitative losses, a war may cause a qualitative deterioration of the population: healthy, courageous and patriotic young men are most likely to be killed, whereas those with physical defects or a lesser sense of duty, combined with skill at malingering, have a much greater chance of surviving. However, we cannot be sure what really happens because biological selection and genetic transmission of mental characteristics are exceedingly complex processes; and, on the other hand, physical and moral deterioration which has been noticed after some wars can be attributed to impoverishment, disorder, ideological disorientation and other circumstances of a similar nature. In so far as qualitative biological selection does take place, it must depend on the character of warfare. If civilian populations are slaughtered, then the soldiers incur no greater risks than the rest. Also, famine and pestilence which followed in its wake often caused far more deaths than the fighting itself; and these scourges afflicted the heroes and the shirkers alike. Moreover, biological selection affected by wars could not have been very important when armies contained a very small proportion of the population. It can also be argued with some plausibility that when fighting is done by professionals, society benefits by getting rid of individuals particularly attracted to violence.

As far as the physical quality is concerned, fighting with swords must have produced a very different selection from that affected by combat with firearms, where survival is almost entirely a matter of chance, and bigness a handicap rather than advantage.

Destruction of wealth occasioned by war has often been so terrible that countries were unable to recapture their former prosperity for many generations. The Thirty Years' War, for instance, wrought such a havoc in Germany that its population diminished by a half, and more than a century elapsed before the country regained its former economic and cultural level. When the Mongols invaded Iraq in the 12th century they destroyed the essential parts of the system of irrigation which had been built up gradually during the preceding three thousand years; and the country has not recovered to this day, as its cultivated area is less extensive now than it was in the days of Babylon.

The more complex the economy, the more vulnerable it is to dislocations. We might expect, therefore, that highly industrialized states would suffer more from war damage than more primitive communities. However, up till now this has not been so because, until the invention of nuclear bombs, capacity to construct kept pace with capacity to destroy. True, having climbed higher, industrialized societies have further to fall before they reach the depths of misery; and for this reason the difference between the state of Germany in 1939 and its condition six years later could have no equivalent on the lower level of complexity. But, on the other hand, the capacity of modern large-scale production enabled the countries which lay in ruins at the end of the last war to recover with an astonishing speed. In a way the destruction which they suffered gave them even a certain advantage over the victors because it forced them to renew their industrial equipment, while the victorious nations were satisfied with older machines.

Civil disorders followed many wars. Often, the aggravating factor was the presence of large numbers of disbanded soldiers who could find no place in the civil society, who were accustomed to violence and disdained work. Instances of such a predicament range from ancient Rome to Germany and Italy after the First World War where unemployed ex-soldiers provided the core of the Fascist and Nazi movements.

Efficiency in war requires unreflecting courage, rigid discipline and unquestioning loyalty to the group. Bushido (the code of the Japanese samurai) included the following command: 'Do not think! Thinking makes cowards'. Such an outlook is incompatible with cultural creativity which requires independence of thought and a critical attitude to generally accepted views. It is not surprising, therefore, that nations whose entire culture was oriented towards war made few contributions to science, philosophy and the arts. The cultural heritage which the ancient Greeks have left was entirely the product of the commercial cities. The Spartans, whose social life centred around military training, contributed nothing. Actually, in order to prevent any possible contamination of the martial spirit they banned philosophy and art. Other military nations – like the Romans or the Mongols – were equally unproductive. In Germany, literature and philosophy were produced not by the military nobility but by the non-military *bourgeoisie*; and the bulk of cultural contributions came not from militaristic Prussia but from less warlike principalities.

New weapons always had profound effects upon social life. One of the chief causes of the fall of the Roman Empire was the seemingly trifling invention of the stirrup which was made somewhere in central Asia during the second century AD. Until then the Roman legions – superbly well organized units of infantry – had nothing to fear from horsemen insecurely perched on their mounts. With stirrups horsemen could carry heavier armour and weapons and fight much better, with the result that horse-breeding nomads became strong enough to invade the surrounding agrarian empires and defeat their more numerous and better organized armies.

Taking a broad view of the history of the world we find that there have been periods when small states were being swallowed by the larger – the periods of political unification, such as those when the Roman or the British Empires were built – and also periods of political disintegration when large empires were falling apart, and were being replaced by a multitude of independent states, as was the case when the Roman Empire fell. Liquidation of the European overseas empires, which is now reaching its final stage, provides another example of a process of this kind. Such processes are caused by conjunctions of many factors among which changes in military techniques occupy a prominent place.

A situation becomes very propitious for empire-building when one nation suddenly develops, or acquires in some way, weapons or tactics or forms of military organization which are better than those of the surrounding peoples. The Romans, for instance, were able to conquer so many lands because of their superior organization and tactics, without having weapons better than those of their neighbours. In contrast, modern Europeans were able to acquire colonies in America, Asia and Africa chiefly because, owing to the development of industry in Europe, their arms were much better than those of the peoples of other continents. Once the inhabitants of these colonies learned how to organize themselves and how to handle modern weapons, the task of keeping them in subjection became hardly worthwhile, with the result that they were given independence. It must be added that the decreasing warlikeness of European peoples – itself the fruit of prosperity – has undoubtedly accelerated this process.

Another military factor which greatly affects political evolution is the relationship between the techniques of attack and the techniques of defence. When fortifications can be built which cannot be stormed, conquest becomes difficult. It becomes easier when siegecraft catches up with or overtakes the art of fortification, and makes defences more vulnerable.

The rise of the earliest large states was connected with advances in siegecraft. The Assyrians were the first to develop an effective method of assaulting strongholds with the aid of battering rams. They also created the first cavalry in the Near East. These novelties enabled the Assyrians to found an empire larger than any hitherto seen.

Until Philip of Macedon introduced into his armies the artillery of catapults and balistas, the Greeks knew of no other means of reducing fortified places than starving them out. Thus by tipping the balance in favour of attack, Philip was able to weld the Greek cities into one empire. A converse example is provided by the disintegration of the Roman Empire which was accompanied by a change in favour of defence since the barbarians who conquered it were too uneducated to build or handle complicated siege engines.

Although the art of siege revived in later centuries with the general progress of arts and crafts, it was unable to catch up with the art of fortification. The baronial castles which came into existence enabled the barons to defy the kings, for such castles were impregnable. Unlike fortified cities the castles were built on sites chosen solely for their military advantages, and, being manned only by small garrisons, they could withstand blockade for a very long time.

Towards the end of the Middle Ages kings began to subjugate petty principalities, and to gather more and more power into their hands. Besides the economic factors involved, this process of monarchic centralization was greatly assisted by the invention of the cannon, with the aid of which castles of rebellious barons could be reduced.

Whenever an improvement in the technique of transport and communication occurs which is not counterbalanced by a rise in the effectiveness of defence, conquests will be facilitated, and the size of political units will tend to grow. Thus the domestication of the horse stimulated empire building in antiquity. The Hyksos, who spread the use of horses into Syria and Egypt, created an empire wider than any hitherto seen; and when the Egyptians acquired horses they in turn embarked upon conquests abroad. Horses were at that time used solely for drawing war-chariots. The Assyrians increased the mobility of their armies by using horses for riding, thus forming the first cavalry we know of, and creating with its aid an empire wider than any that had existed previously. An even greater empire was built by the Persians, who were a nation of horsemen, having been originally pastoral nomads.

In India the introduction of the horse coincided, roughly speaking, with the domestication of the elephant, and this increase in mobility enabled great kingdoms to swallow a multitude of small independent principalities. Similarly, the introduction of the compass, and improvements in the art of sailing, enabled the Europeans to build their colonial empires.

Most recent developments in transport and communication have brought into existence super-states which are dividing the world between them.

Groups of people which have to cope with emergencies – like crews of ships and squads of firemen – require a single leader, while bodies such as municipal corporations or trade guilds which need not undertake speedy action can be efficiently run by committees. War is an emergency which requires more efficient and speedy co-ordination of effort than any other activity, and for this reason, it has always fostered concentration of power in the hands of one man. Even very primitive tribes which have no headmen in times of peace have them in war. It follows that the more serious and frequent are the wars in which a state engages the more autocratic will be the form of its government.

The earliest prehistoric cultures of Europe were apparently relatively peaceful, judging from the lack of elaborate weapons and fortifications among their remains. They also left no traces of powerful chieftains in the shape of distinguished abodes and graves. But where we find elaborate weapons and fortifications we also discover remains of palaces and tombs of kings. Also among contemporary primitive peoples, ethnographers have noticed that the ones without chieftains are the peaceably inclined.

The Romans in the days of the Republic were so suspicious of personal authority that they divided the command of the army between two generals (whom they called consuls) who led it on alternate days. But at times of great danger, when everything had to be done in order to ensure victory, the Romans used to suspend this arrangement and give unlimited authority to one man for the duration of the emergency.

The needs of warfare create habits of command and obedience which continue in times of peace; and so, if wars are frequent and intense and peace is rare, then peacetime political organization will resemble that necessary for waging war. Not only actual war, but even the threat of it, induces societies to organize themselves in such a way as to give preponderant power to one man, for preparedness means being organized so that war could be waged at once, without the long process of rearranging the form of government to meet the emergency.

Representative government came into existence in England which, being an island, did not need for its defence large armies. The navy, on which it relied for its security, could not be used for seizing power or suppressing the civilian population. The parliamentary system of government was successfully transplanted, and functioned without interruptions, only in countries which were likewise exempted from the necessity of maintaining large armies. This was the case of all English-speaking former English colonies. Even in these countries, where the traditions of parliamentary government are so strong, the two World Wars brought about a considerable concentration of power: the chief executives (president in the USA, prime ministers in the British Commonwealth) have acquired great additional powers in wartime, many of which they have retained. The present tension in international affairs diminishes in many ways the influence of the peoples on the actions of their governments.

It is not a matter of mere coincidence that the exceptionally peaceful period which lasted in Europe from the Napoleonic wars till the First World War, saw the spread of ideologies and political systems which emphasized the freedom and the rights of the individual. Conversely, there is a close connection between comprehensive mobilization of men and resources, first put into practice during the First World War, and the rise of totalitarian systems characterized by complete regimentation of the population, and their indoctrination with the martial spirit. The incessant propaganda is also understandable in the light of the needs of the war machine. In contrast to earlier times, when soldiers led a relatively easy life only occasionally interrupted by short battles, and had opportunities of enriching themselves with booty, the recent wars have been uninterruptedly gruelling and entirely unprofitable to the fighting men even on the victorious side. Elaborate propaganda is, therefore, required to instil into them the will to fight.

In small-scale societies all men are warriors. When hunting constitutes the main activity apart from war, the discrepancy between peacetime and wartime roles is not great. Owing to the smallness of the scale, wars are short, and there are no permanently organized armed forces.

The professional warrior appeared on the scene only when

agriculture progressed sufficiently to enable the cultivators to produce more than they needed for subsistence, so that they could be forced to feed the soldiers. Availability of the surplus made conquests possible and profitable; and for this reason the spread of settled and intensive agriculture was followed by the appearance of large states.

Wars ending in conquest increase, or cause, social inequalities. In the first place they create a division between the conquerors and the conquered. Secondly, they bring into existence larger social units which can only be ruled by stricter subordination. But since social inequalities also have foundations which are not military – such as wealth and magical and religious prestige – what often happens is that existing class inequalities acquire through war a military 'flavour', and that military distinctions gain in relative importance.

Sometimes wars not only do not exacerbate social inequalities but on the contrary have a levelling effect. It is unprofitable to allow the soldiers to starve, and they must often be kept in a fighting mood by offers of shares in the booty or other advantages of victory. Their morale normally is better if good service brings reward, and if they are generally respected. Moreover, if the struggle is very serious and calls for the utmost exertion, military talent must be utilized in full, which means that candidates for command must be sought in all ranks, for talent is not confined to any single class. In other words, under certain circumstances the impact of war undermines hereditary privileges which lower the efficiency of the armed forces, and thus diminishes inequality between classes.

Another possible cause of diminution of social inequality is the tendency for the sense of solidarity to grow among people who fight together. And this applies not only to armies but to whole nations in time of peril. The sense of solidarity inspired by common danger may make the wealthy and the privileged more willing to share a little of these boons with their less fortunate countrymen.

The influence of war upon social inequalities within the contending nations depends largely on the extent to which the mass of the population is needed to take part in the war effort. If the fighting is done by a small professional army without collaboration of the civilians, then the attitude of the general population does not matter very much, and therefore, no inducements need to be offered to the lower classes. On the other side, when all able-bodied men (and even women) are needed either for fighting or for armaments production, they must be persuaded by propaganda as well as palpable concessions that they have a stake in the country.

The extent to which the population takes part in the war effort depends on the state of military art and on the productive capacity of the economy, which was often insufficient to arm more than a fraction of the population. The equipment of a medieval knight would be nowadays considered very cheap in comparison with contemporary armaments, but in the Middle Ages it was impossible to provide a large portion of any country's inhabitants with the equipment of a heavily armed horseman. Thus the best way to organize a country for war was to have a small number of warriors, equipped and supported by the rest of the population. This kind of military organization produced a division of the population into the privileged warrior nobility and the defenceless and poor peasantry. The weapons of the knights were equally useful for defending the country from external foes as for defending the privileges and wealth of the military nobility. For this reason none of the many peasant rebellions which broke out in the Middle Ages could succeed.

In the 15th century the introduction of firearms ended the predominance of the heavily armoured horseman; whilst the development of commerce and of monetary circulation enabled kings to replace feudal levies by soldiers paid and equipped from the royal coffers. This change spelled the end of feudalism and the advent of centralized monarchies, but it did not affect social inequalities very much because military service was still restricted to a small section of the population. In contrast, universal conscription, first introduced in France during the Great Revolution – and later adopted by all the countries of continental Europe – prompted an abolition, or at least a substantial diminution, of many inequalities. In France it coincided with the Revolution which, at least in principle, made all the citizens equal before the law, and gave the land to the peasants. In Prussia the introduction of general military service led to the abolition of serfdom; later to the establishment of a parliament, and eventually to the setting up of the first scheme of industrial insurance in the world. A similar connection between a widening of military service and a diminution of social inequalities could be observed in a number of other countries.

In the cases mentioned above the trend towards a certain levelling of social inequalities affected political rights – that is to say, it included a trend towards democracy. This, however, is not inevitable. Modern totalitarian régimes (particularly in their Communist varieties) have demonstrated that a considerable diminution of economic inequalities, and a radical reduction of barriers to conviviality, can be combined with a more thorough subordination of the masses to the will of the rulers.

War has been blamed on human nature, and it is perfectly true that if all men were kind and wise there would be no wars. It is clear that the capacity for cruelty is required for war, and the proneness to collective follies always facilitates wars and other kinds of social conflicts. Fortunately however, there are reasons for doubting whether war is an absolutely necessary consequence of human nature being what it is. If human beings were in fact endowed with an innate proclivity for war, it would not be necessary to indoctrinate them with warlike virtues; and the mere fact that in so many societies past and present so much time has been devoted to such an indoctrination proves that there is no instinct for war. Moreover, if men had an innate propensity towards war, similar to their desire for food or sexual satisfaction, then there could be no instances of numerous nations remaining at peace for more than a generation. Nor can war be regarded as an inevitable consequence of national sovereignty because there are examples of sovereign states which have waged no wars for more than a century – these are Switzerland, Sweden, Norway and Denmark. One could say that with Switzerland, surrounded as it is by much more powerful neighbours, peacefulness is a matter of necessity rather than choice, but as far as the Scandinavian countries are concerned, it is clear that although they were too weak to attack their neighbours to the South, they could have fought among themselves, as many other small states did. There are a few other examples of peacefulness when a conquest would be very easy. The United States, for instance, could conquer Canada without much effort or fear of reprisals, but nevertheless, the Canadians have no fear of such a possibility. In spite of being exceptional, these examples do show that truly peaceful co-existence is possible. The question is: under which circumstances?

Wars have been fought for land, cattle, buildings, gold, women, slaves, trading rights, raw materials, and all other kinds of possessions, but also for sheer power and glory. They have also been fought for the sake of ideologies, but there is not a single case of war waged for ideological motives alone, without regard to more personal benefits.

Rulers who embark upon aggression at their own initiative are prompted chiefly by their desire for more power and glory – by the wish to be above their opposite numbers, and directing a war can be fun for a callous despot. Louis XIV – to mention one of innumerable possible examples – used to start a war whenever he was bored, without, of course, exposing himself to any dangers or privations. Unlike contemporary despots, he was quite frank about it. It follows that one condition of abolition of war is an elimination of situations which permit rulers to amuse themselves in this way at the expense of frightful suffering of their subjects: in other words, elimination of despotism. It is quite clear, unfortunately, that existent despotic states cannot be transformed from outside, and our only hope is that they might gradually evolve into more humane forms of government.

As far as ordinary people are concerned, who have to endure all the sufferings, their most important motives in supporting aggression are: (1) collective frenzy or (2) simple obedience combined with the herd spirit or (3) a sense of desperate frustration which makes them covet other people's goods, and welcome all adventures. Usually these factors are intertwined. Mass movements assume forms of collective mania chiefly in response to extreme frustration of elementary needs, including the need to have a secure place in the social order. Such frustration is most commonly the consequence of poverty, or at least impoverishment in relation to customary standards. If that is so, we need not be surprised that war was a permanent and universal institution, for poverty was everywhere – and still is in most parts of the world – a permanent condition of the great majority. Only in very recent times, and only in the few fortunate countries bordering the north Atlantic has grinding poverty become rare.

In conditions of misery, life, whether one's own or somebody else's, is not valued, and this greatly facilitates warlike propaganda.

In an industrial society unemployment not only brings poverty but also breaks up social bonds and creates a large mass of uprooted men, whose frustrated desire for a place in society may lead them to favour measures of mass regimentation. Moreover, when there is not enough to satisfy the elementary needs of the population, the struggle for the good things of life becomes so bitter that democratic government, which always requires self-restraint and tolerance, becomes impossible, and despotism remains the only kind of government that can function at all. But absolute power creates the danger that a despot may push his country into war for the sake of satisfying his craving for power and glory. It is generally imagined that the only remedy against war is to institute a world government, but this view can be easily refuted. In the first place, political unification often merely means that instead of inter-state wars, civil wars take place which can be just as bad or even worse. To mention one of very many possible examples: as soon as the Romans defeated their dangerous enemies, they started fighting among themselves, thus bringing the lands which they 'pacified' into a much worse condition than they were in when they were divided into a multitude of independent and warring states. During the last hundred years the countries which waged fewest wars – Spain, Portugal and the republics of Latin America – had the longest record of internecine strife and revolutions. For this reason we cannot assume that we could eliminate bloodshed simply by instituting a world government, because the outcome would depend on whether the sources of strife and violence would be eliminated. It must be remembered that wars against rebels have constituted, next to external wars, the chief occupation of governments throughout history. On the other hand, the only really peaceful area of the world – Scandinavia – has no supreme authority, the real cause of its peacefulness being that it is free from poverty and despotism. The same is true about internal peace: only countries where there is neither poverty nor despotism do not suffer from internal violence.

Prosperity cannot be maintained over a long period unless the growth of population is well below its biological maximum, which means that some limitation of the growth of population is a necessary condition of abolition of war.

The remedies of signing treaties of eternal peace, convening congresses and preaching condemnation of wars, have been tried innumerable times and without much effect. They may be needed but in themselves are clearly insufficient. Elimination of poverty has not yet been tried except in very restricted areas, where it has, in fact, had the result of instilling a pacific disposition. For this reason, a determined attempt to bring the majority of the population of the world out of its present condition of misery, offers the best hope of abolishing war.

CHAPTER EIGHT

THE ARMIES AND THE PRIVILEGED STRATA

THE MAJORITY of European critics of the traditional social order have taken it as self-evident that military officers were bound to be conservative by the very nature of their profession, that is to say, always inclined to throw their weight on the side of the established social order and the privileged classes. The idea that an army could become a chief engine of social revolution would seem to them absurd. This opinion was not – and is not – without foundations, yet it cannot claim absolute validity. In the Near East we recently saw social revolutions carried out by army officers. In Ancient Rome the traditional aristocracy was decimated and despoiled by the soldiers on more than one occasion. This poses the question of the factors which determine whether the influence of the army will be conservative or radical, or even subversive.

Subversiveness is a rather loose and emotive term, and for this reason some terminological clarification might be useful. An established order of privileges may be altered in three possible ways. The first is a transformation which changes the whole nature of the privileges besides producing vertical mobility on a large scale. A thorough industrialization of a rural society, or a replacement of private by state ownership of the means of production are examples to the point. The second type of change is a process of levelling. Almost needless to say, this means that the inequalities diminish – not that they disappear altogether – for no case of complete abolition of all privileges has so far been noted. The third possibility is the replacement of the incumbents without any profound changes in either the nature of the privileges or in their span. We can safely leave out of consideration profound transformations for the simple reason that in no case have they been produced by an army's intervention in politics. The social reforms which ensued from the recent military revolutions in the Near East do not really amount to basic transformations. The Meiji reforms in Japan, though precipitated by a show of military helplessness, were a complex and comprehensive process, and cannot be cited as a case in point. We are left, then, with the processes of levelling of privileges and of displacement of the incumbents. By subversiveness I mean the inclination to bring about either of these modifications of social circumstances. Our judgement on the ethical value of subversiveness as thus defined will depend on how we evaluate the established order and the alternatives.

An army may be employed against the enemies outside, or against their own civilian population. Both of these modes of employment produce modifications of the social structure, but they do it in entirely different ways. A war, particularly when the very survival of the state is at stake, produces an adaptation to the requirements of bellic efficiency, whose nature depends on the technique of warfare. The need for efficiency may impose considerable levelling of social inequalities, as well as an increase in vertical mobility, but it may also have an opposite effect. In the cases of adaptation to bellic efficiency the impact of the army does not consist of sheer compulsion, and in the extreme cases may even be backed by the enthusiasm pervading the whole population. This mode of influence of the armed forces on society might be called consociative. The other mode of influence is coercive and the essence of it is the forcing of an unwanted social order upon the civilian population by the use or the threat of violence. Almost needless to say any concrete case presents an intermixture of both, though in widely differing proportions. Both modes of influence are largely determined by the military participation ratio, which I have defined as the ratio of militarily utilized individuals to the total adult masculine population.*

Where the armed forces constitute the ruling class there can be no question of their subversiveness. Neither in medieval Europe, nor in the Ottoman Empire, nor in any other society of similar type, did the warriors menace the social order, in spite of their frequent rebellions. They scrapped among themselves for spoils and glory, but never took the side of the humble against the

* On the influence of this factor on social structure see *Military Organization and Society*.

rich. The possibility of an assault upon the social order (as distinguished from an attack on the incumbents of authority) arises only when there is a differentiation between the civilian and the military sectors.

Gaetano Mosca considered the subordination of the armed forces to the civilian authority to have been one of the most distinctive and crucial features of the European civilization. Although many military dictatorships have arisen since he wrote *Elementi di Scienza Politica*, there can be little doubt that ever since the end of the Middle Ages European armies have on the whole been very obedient. The number of European monarchs who have been killed by their troops is negligible in comparison with what went on in other parts of the world. In spite (or perhaps because) of its antimilitaristic ideology, China suffered a number of military rebellions on a scale unparalleled in Europe: the revolt of An Lu Shan during the reign of the T'ang Dynasty was a social cataclysm of the first magnitude. Mosca's explanation of this peculiarity of the Occident is that it was due to the integration of the armed forces in the body politic, and particularly to the integration of the officers' corps with the ruling class. Let us for the moment disregard the other ranks and examine the validity of Mosca's thesis in so far as it concerns the officers. In a way it seems paradoxical to explain somebody's subordination by the fact that he belongs to the ruling class. Moreover, the commanders of armies have, everywhere and always, enjoyed opulence and other privileges, and in this sense they belonged to the top layer of society. The question is whether in addition to this they were united with the rest of the ruling stratum by the bonds of kinship, common outlook and habits, and of common economic interest.

Mosca's explanation does appear to hold if we compare Europe with Asia. Naturally, one must be very careful when speaking of the whole of Asia, for the circumstances varied enormously in time and space, but it does seem that, unlike Europe, Asia was not free from the phenomenon which might be described as the alienation of officers. In Europe the monarchy and the nobility found on the whole a *modus vivendi*, and created a code of rights and obligations which was fairly well observed, whereas in the Orient (with the partial exception of China) a violent struggle went on continuously between the rulers and the magnates. I cannot attempt to give here an explanation of the causes of this difference, for which I must refer the reader to my *Military Organization and Society*. What is important for the present argument is that in the deadly struggle against the magnates, the rulers often employed slaves and mercenaries recruited from the lowest strata. These troops revolted frequently and on some occasions deposed the rulers, decimated and despoiled the nobility, and put themselves in their place. In this way, even before the Ottoman conquest the Turks replaced the Arabs as the ruling ethnic element in the Near East. By a similar process the Slave dynasty established its rule in northern India, and the Mamluks in Egypt. Such a thing has never occurred in Europe since the time of ancient Rome. What did occur in Rome fits perfectly Mosca's thesis – which is not surprising in view of the high standard of his classical scholarship. So long as the senatorial nobility furnished officers it was secure. Marius and his soldiers were proletarians, or at least of proletarian origins. The generals and the soldiers who exterminated the Roman nobility in the third century AD began their lives as sons of peasants in the outlying provinces. Here, however, it was not so much the rulers' tactics which excluded the nobles from the higher military posts as their own ineptitude and preference for more pleasant ways of life. It must be remembered that ancient wars were much harder and more dangerous than the wars waged in modern Europe until 1914.

Unless an army is too weak to be able to impose its will on the civilian population, as in the US in the last century, the integration of the officers' corps in the ruling layer appears to be a necessary condition of some measure of its political neutralization. The evidence from Latin America shows that it is not a sufficient condition, for there pretorianism flourished notwithstanding the monopolization of the higher military posts by the land-owning families. This was due in the first place to the uncrystallized character of the political order, to the lack of any accepted code of behaviour in political matters, to disorderly administration and the absence of well-organized political parties, which made violence inevitable. In Chile, where the ruling class was cohesive and more orderly, the military remained at the back of the stage. The second cause of the predominance of the military in Latin American politics has been the bitter class warfare raging there ever since the days of the conquest. A very important factor here was the absence of the necessity of united effort in a common struggle against foreigners, which did so much to infuse a strong dose of supra-class solidarity into the European nations. It is sad to find that the absence of concern for the common good might be the result of a relatively unwarlike existence. Apart from warranting the foregoing qualification, the data on Latin America do not contradict Mosca's thesis: the armies did not remain in the background of politics, but they were very far from being subversive. On the contrary, they invariably intervened in the class struggle when the ruling classes were losing their grip on the masses. The exceptions to this rule also fit Mosca's thesis. The very few attempts at some levelling of social inequalities made by the military were initiated or led by officers who were not closely related to the very rich; and who were, moreover, below the rank of the general. 'The social identification with the urban groups where he originated was probably the fundamental cause of the junior-officer uprising that occurred in Latin America's armies in the second quarter of the twentieth century'.[1]

The case of Egypt fits perfectly Mosca's thesis. Nasser and his colleagues did not belong to the hereditary rich who shunned the military service. The honorific as well as economic position of an army officer was low, so that the officers shared, and later canalized, popular discontent. The Iraqi revolution was headed by Kassem, a general and a man of somewhat more substantial family background than Nasser, and yet his government was more radical than the Egyptian in the way in which it attacked the old ruling class. However it is well known that social determination of attitudes has only a statistical validity, and always admits individual exceptions. The social origins of the majority of Kassem's assistants seem to have been more demotic than those of Nasser's.

'Almost invariably, Latin America's popular revolutions of this century were led by the young officers. They became the sponsors of fundamental change and reform, the underminers of traditional institutions, the proponents of public-welfare measures. . . . These young officers thought of themselves as enlightened members of a new, modern generation. Regarding the generals as unimaginative and behind the times, they sought to bring the armed forces into more sympathetic relations with the rest of the society. They were also interested in power, which could be had by gaining popular support, by playing the role of saviours of the

[1] Edwin Lieuwen, *Arms and Politics in Latin America* (Praeger, N.Y., 1960).

downtrodden masses.'[1] There are examples from other areas of the world (The Young Turks, Decembrists in Russia, Nasser's team) which show that on the whole political interventions of younger officers tend to be less on the conservative side than those of their seniors. This may be due to the natural conservatism of old age, or to greater satiety induced by having reached the summit of hierarchy. However, there are good grounds to believe that youth as such infuses a certain rashness and extremism into political action, but does not decide whether it will be carried out for the benefit of the privileged or of the hampered. Young men are, no doubt, not only more rebellious, but also more susceptible to the appeal of impersonal ideals, than their elders, yet they can very well rebel against social equality, and the ideals which they uphold may be élitarian in the extreme. In Japan, in the thirties, the young officers terrorized their seniors as well as the civilian politicians into adopting a policy of aggression outside coupled with the repression of liberal and pro-labour elements at home. The differences in rank and age are particularly likely to foster socially subversive ideas when accompanied by differences in class affiliations, especially if demotic affiliations constitute an impediment to promotion. Apart from the cases mentioned above this was the situation of Napoleon Bonaparte and of a considerable number of other officers of the French army on the eve of the Great Revolution.

Integration or alienation may determine the attitudes of the officers, but for effective action they must have control over their men. There are examples of *coups d'état* which failed because the soldiers did not obey orders, and remained loyal to the existing government. This was notably the case with the Generals' Revolt against Hitler in 1944. The second danger is that, by ordering the soldiers to disobey the established authority, the commanders may provoke a general rebellion which might turn against them as well. There were examples of this during the Wars of Independence in Latin America. Let us examine the circumstances which make either of these dangers more or less imminent.

The first factor to be considered is the strength of the factors binding the soldiers to the civilian society. Other things being equal, the weaker they are, the more absolute is the control of the officers over the men in political matters. The alienation of the soldiers from the civilian society may be the result of long-term

[1] Lieuwen op. cit., pp. 128-9.

service, or of foreign origins, or of methods of recruitment which select special psychological types, or of posting in distant lands or in the midst of a cultural environment with a distinctive ethos. One or more of these features characterized all military formations renowned for incursions into politics: the Roman pretorians, the mercenaries of the Islamic monarchs, the French parachutists in Algeria. In ancient Rome military revolts began when the army acquired these characteristics. Psychologically unselected short-term conscripts can be used for this purpose when either the whole population is ignorant or politically apathetic, or when they are drawn from an unassimilated ethnic minority. The troops which Pilsudski used for destroying the constitutional government in Poland came from the eastern territories which were not ethnically Polish; the troops which opposed him came from western Poland where there was only a German minority which was able to evade the military service. In Latin America the lowest ranks are either mercenary (as they were in Cuba) or recruited among illiterate peasants. In Peru, Colombia and other *mestizo* countries these peasants have the further advantage of being Indians who have to be taught Spanish.

The alienation of the army largely determines whether it can serve as an instrument of rebellion without the danger of a chain reaction which would spread into the civilian population. The same applies to the internal struggles within the army. When in 1934 the NCO's and privates of the Cuban army, led by sergeant Fulgencio Batista, imprisoned or killed their seniors, and replaced them as the rulers of Cuba, the civilian population stood aside: the affairs of the mercenaries were of no concern to them.

The strength of any social body depends on its solidarity, which is not fostered by extreme inequalities and the absence of upward mobility. That the latter circumstances weaken the nations was noticed long ago. At the beginning of the last century a Polish historian Joachim Lelewel attributed the fall of Poland to this cause (without, of course, using these terms). It was a proof of Mosca's genius that, diverging from all current opinions, he put forth the view that the relative docility of the European armies depended on the rigidity of class divisions in their midst. He reached this conclusion by comparing them to the armies of the Roman Empire. Military commanders of modern Europe could not easily defy their rulers because, being divided from their men by an impassable economic and cultural abyss, they did not enjoy the popularity of their Roman counterparts. To put it into psychological parlance, there was no basis for projective identification. The uniting force of common hopes of enrichment was lacking too.

To the foregoing arguments a proviso must be added that the internal horizontal chasm only hampers the armed forces' intrusions into politics, but it does not make them altogether impossible. In the same way the integration of the rank and file in civilian society makes them less suitable as an instrument of *coups d'état*, yet they can be used in this way if the issues do not arouse strong passions among the population. Other factors which neutralize the importance of the soldiers' convictions are the discipline, the efficiency of the organization and the unanimity among their commanders.

An important question which must be considered is whether wars or preparations for them foster or impede military intrusions into politics. The chief difficulty in answering this question stems from the ways in which the impact of war is connected with other factors such as the growth and vertical unification of the armed forces, which strengthen an army's internal position irrespectively of whether a war is being waged or not. Thus it frequently happens that when a war ends, the balance of power between the military and the civilian authorities finds itself severely tilted in favour of the former. Moreover, the after-glow of the apotheosis of the military chiefs which normally takes place during a war, endows them with political prestige which they could not acquire in time of peace. This is the origin of the father-figures of Hindenburg, Wellington, Eisenhower, de Gaulle. If a defeat has undermined the standing of the rulers, or if the country is infested by ex-combatant desperadoes who can find no satisfactory place in civilian life, an aftermath of war might generate disorders which would automatically bring the armed forces into the arena. In these ways, then, wars stimulate military intervention in politics. On the other hand, however, 'the devil finds work for idle hands': soldiers who have no wars to fight or prepare for will be tempted to interfere in politics. Taking a long term view, it seems that there is an inverse connection between strenuous warfare and pretorianism. In Rome the civil wars began when

Carthage – the last enemy who could threaten the very existence of the empire – had been destroyed.

In modern Europe the country which was most plagued by revolutions – Spain – did not take part in any major war since the time of Napoleon. What is even more telling is that it acquired this propensity only when it ceased to conquer and to send colonial expeditions. On the other hand, in Russia, which was nearly always at war and conquering, the army remained remarkably obedient. The Japanese, who remained confined to their islands throughout most of their history by the overweening might of the Chinese Empire, have an unrivalled record of civil wars. Latin America, where very few wars were fought, experienced more military revolts during the last century and a half than the rest of the world put together. The inverse connection between outward militancy and proneness to revolts, which the foregoing evidence suggests, is explained, apart from the factors discussed above, by the fact that external and civil wars are alternative releases of the pressure of population on resources.

CHAPTER NINE

NUCLEAR WEAPONS AND THE NEW MARTIAL VIRTUES

POLITICAL RÉGIMES have always been decisively influenced by the requirements of military technique, and one may view totalitarianism as an adaptation to the needs of mass warfare which requires all-pervading regimentation and incessant and unopposed propaganda. The question now is: how does the military technique based on nuclear weapons and missiles affect the structures of the societies which employ it? In trying to give a tentative answer to it, I shall deal only with certain aspects of this problem. It is hardly worthwhile to discuss what might happen to mankind in consequence of an all-out nuclear war consisting of indiscriminate mutual destruction. The most likely outcome of such an eventuality – the extinction of humanity – does not lend itself to further sociological speculation. The possibility that the social evolution of mankind might begin anew from the level of primitive existence, if there are some survivors, is more interesting; although the chances seem to be that, owing to the exhaustion of the ores which could be mined with the aid of primitive techniques, mankind would never again be able to transcend the level of the Stone Age, apart from the well-known possibility that radioactivity might cause biological degeneration of the species.

The shrinking of the world and the fantastic and still increasing deadliness of the weapons rule out the possibility that the present arms race may go on for a very long time, which leaves two possibilities: conquest or general and genuine agreement.

The prospects of a genuine agreement are not encouraging. Human nature is such that bickering comes naturally, and nothing is more common than examples of the propensity to 'cut off one's nose to spite one's face'. This general human frailty is dangerous enough, and the discrepancy between mechanical ingenuity and moral backwardness may very well prove fatal to mankind. This situation is connected with the fact that whereas the technical level is fixed by the achievements of the most gifted inventors, the ethical level is determined less by the most benevolent of men than by their opposites, because of the way in which the processes of selection for positions of authority favour ruthless power-seekers. This seems to have always been so, but it is worth noting that the diminution of the role played by inheritance has brought no improvement in this respect. When thrones and dignities were hereditary they often fell to imbeciles or bloodthirsty madmen, but on occasion they came into the hands of benevolent men or women. When the posts of command are thrown open to competition, idlers and imbeciles have no chance but neither have the gentle nor those with too many scruples, whilst bloodthirsty madmen are by no means excluded. A sociological generalization can be proposed that the less determined is the selection by factors other than the sheer ability to manipulate men, the more ruthless and astute will be the rulers. This sociological theorem explains why American presidents and British prime ministers could be outmanoeuvred by Soviet rulers. It also explains the relative mildness of European kings as compared with the monarchs of the East, bred in polygamous households, amongst numerous half-brothers whom they had to kill in order to mount the throne. To win a competitive prize one must desire it very strongly, and therefore, nobody is likely to have power who does not crave it. For this reason, the issues on which the survival of humanity depends will in all likelihood continue to be treated as gambits in the game of power seeking.

Imposition of hegemony puts fewer demands on human nature, as it could result from a free play of very common propensities. Whether an attempt in this direction would in fact lead to the establishment of a world government or to a holocaust would depend on the situation in military technology and on chance. I shall say nothing about the latter element, and only a few words about the former – solely in order to dispel the common preconception that a victory in a future war is out of the question. It is true that as things stand now an all-out war can benefit nobody, but we must not assume that this state of affairs is immutable. Some startling inventions might make indiscriminate blasting with hydrogen bombs futile or even impossible. Some combination of radar and television might enable people to see any point on the globe or even inside it. Some rays might be invented which kill or paralyse living creatures within the area on which they are directed, or even impede the functioning of mechanisms by creating magnetic fields, using anti-matter or something else that cannot yet be imagined. The argument that such things can never be done carries little conviction because it has been found to be wrong so many times before. It is clear, however, that a victory in a future war can only be the fruit of superior technical inventiveness, and could never result from the mere multiplication of the armaments existing at present.

Before proceeding to examine the social implications of a race in military technology, I should like to make an aside and point out that there are few reasons for believing that a world government – an ideal earnestly desired by generations of humanitarian political thinkers – would in fact be so ideal, even if it came into existence through negotiation instead of conquest. Experience with existing international organizations demonstrates the law of the least common denominator, which Gustave Le Bon formulated in order to account for the frequently observed fact that people behave worse in crowds than individually. The level of probity, efficiency and enlightenment in an international organization is about the same as in the administrative machines of its member states with the lowest scores on these points. This is in no way surprising because probity and efficiency can be attained only if at least the persons in key positions act in accordance with commonly accepted principles, and how can this occur in an organization whose personnel have no common convictions – whose declared purposes are merely declared but not seriously felt. It might be said that these features are the consequences of the extremely federalist – nay, amorphous and acephalous – character of the present international organizations, and that they would disappear in a real world government. Even if we concede this point – which in fact carries little conviction outside the possibility of universal hegemony – two indelible vices of a world government would remain. The first would be its size, because largeness (as has been known since Plato and Aristotle) renders any form of control from below less effective and favours abuse of power. The second indelible vice of any world government would stem from the mere fact that it would be the only sovereign government – a government from which there would be no escape. To appreciate the portent of this fact we must remember the enormous importance which possibilities of escaping had not only for alleviating suffering but also for encouraging resistance to tyrannies. We must also bear in mind the prominent role of exiles in spreading the spirit of freedom and, in particular, the spirit of free thought. Living under a despotism has been the normal fate of mankind ever since large states arose, and intellectual and moral progress has been possible only because from time to time little evanescent islands of freedom emerged which gave to a few generations of their favoured sons the opportunity to think and speak freely. Even if it avoided excesses of tyranny, an effective world government would most likely suffocate the germs of intellectual and moral progress by the dead weight of bureaucratic conformity. This prospect might be better than that of a holocaust but is hardly very entrancing. It must be remembered, moreover, that in the past governments showed concern for their subjects mainly when they needed their cooperation in fighting foreigners. In a world state there would be no threats from outside to countervail the normal tendency of rulers to segregate themselves from the ruled, and to ill-treat them.

In order to be militarily decisive an invention (or rather a series of inventions) must be kept secret. In this respect the advantages of totalitarian régimes are obvious. In the USA even the army is not very good at safeguarding secret information. The craving for publicity is so deeply embedded in the American tradition, that it could not be extirpated without radical changes in the constitution and in the mentality of the people. The executive might have to be freed from supervision by Congress, so as to prevent investigating committees from compelling generals and officials to make public the information which spies could obtain only with a good deal of work. Freedom not only to travel abroad but even to move without restrictions within the boundaries of the state facilitates spying enormously, and makes it quite impossible to keep secret the location of sizeable installations. The security of tenure of official posts, the adherence to the principle of treating a person as innocent until his guilt is proved, and the rule of law in general, all constitute serious handicaps in counter-espionage. It does not follow, of course, that these handicaps cannot be sources of strength in other ways, but the fact remains that they give a very substantial advantage to the totalitarian state in the race in military technology.

Until the appearance of the sputniks it was commonly believed that freedom guarantees technical superiority, in spite of the evident fact that primacy in the field of rocketry belonged to Nazi Germany before it passed to Russia. Reasoning on the basis of this fact I wrote in 1951 in my *Military Organization and Society* (p. 166) the following passage, for which I was severely criticized by at least two reviewers.

'It has been said that liberal régimes are in a stronger position than their totalitarian rivals because, in virtue of the freedom of thought which their citizens enjoy, they will always have technical superiority. But this argument is far from convincing. Freedom of thought was a condition of the rise of science, when the latter's utility was not evident. But now, when even the most obscurantist government appreciates the utility of natural sciences, scientific research may be fostered even in the most despotic state. There is no reason why research in physics and chemistry should require the freedom to doubt the basic tenets of social creeds; particularly in view of the ability of human mind to keep bits of knowledge in watertight compartments. A critical and inventive attitude in one's speciality may be accompanied by unbounded credulity in other fields.'

Liberal states labour under another serious disadvantage in the contemporary technological race. In any of them a scientist who undertakes to work on a military project has to forgo freedoms which all the other civilians enjoy: unlike his colleagues who are occupied with pure science and teaching, he is under continuous observation, his private past is open to inspection, he has to be careful about the friends he makes and so on. In contrast, his counterpart in Russia or China loses nothing by taking up military work because he would be subject to all these restrictions in any walk of life. He may even gain some freedom because, being a valuable worker, he is less likely to be thrown into prison for a fictitious or insignificant shortcoming. This means that a totalitarian state has much less difficulty in attracting the best brains to military technology. Another advantage stems not so much from the totalitarian character of the Russian and Chinese régimes as from the poverty of their subjects: the difficulty of attaining a fairly comfortable existence ensures that everybody is extremely susceptible to material inducements, and thus facilitates the direction of brain power, which in any case is easier in an authoritarian than in a libertarian state.

The requirements of secrecy and direction of brain power foster certain features normally included in the concept of totalitarianism. This does not mean, however, that all the features of totalitarianism as we know it enhance the chances of obtaining technico-military preponderance. The old-fashioned totalitarianism of Hitler and Stalin was perfectly adapted to the needs of mass warfare. Cannon-fodder, as well as man-power needed for production, had to be harangued, doped by rituals, and terrorized at the same time. Now that the military usefulness of the masses diminishes, the need to control them so stringently decreases too. It would seem, therefore, that obligatory enthusiasm, mammoth parades and other related features of the rules of Stalin, Mussolini and Hitler have outlived their military usefulness, though the possibility still remains that they might survive for other reasons.

Social inequalities are influenced by the factor which in *Military Organization and Society* I called 'facility of suppression' – that is to say by the ease with which an unorganized mass can be defeated by an organized armed force. In spite of their frightfulness, nuclear weapons so far do not seem to have influenced this factor very much because they cannot be used for street fighting or guerrilla warfare. In any case modern non-atomic weapons alone preclude the possibility of a victorious revolution without defections in the army and police.[1]

On the whole it seems that nuclear weapons favour a kind of moderate and rationalized totalitarianism: without extravagant regimentation of the masses and ritual follies, without absurd incursions by the rulers into the realms of natural sciences, without

---

[1] Practically none of Batista's soldiers went over to Castro, but the rebels could win because, owing to extreme and general corruption and cowardice, the army disintegrated. In contrast, in Algeria the French army dominated the situation militarily till the end, and was physically capable of exterminating the entire Algerian nation. The Algerians were given independence because many Frenchmen, including de Gaulle, realized that continuation of the war would transform the French republic into a brutal totalitarian dictatorship. The other factors involved were the prosperity of France which made long-term military service very unpopular, international pressure and the net economic disadvantage to metropolitan France of holding Algeria with the aid of a large army.

crazy doctrinarianism, but with thorough and systematic control over the movements and work of the inhabitants, and absence of freedom to form associations, let alone to criticize the régime.

There is another very general aspect of the impact of nuclear weapons on social life: I do not mean the often noted phenomenon of the widespread feeling of futility of existence, induced in many imaginative persons by the imminence of the holocaust, but the fact that the introduction of these weapons constituted the last step in the devaluation of martial virtues which began with the invention of gun-powder. When firearms first appeared they were generally condemned on the ground that they permitted a dastardly weakling to kill a man of strength and valour. Now we reach the stage when a sickly woman scientist suffering from an anxiety neurosis may constitute a far greater military asset than thousands of tough and fearless soldiers.

The chief military virtue is nowadays neither physical endurance nor pugnacity but technical inventiveness; and in view of the fact that military virtues are usually extolled, we should expect the spread of the cult of this quality. The ideal which is most useful from the military point of view is that of a man or woman who invents what is demanded without asking why, and in fact this ideal is energetically inculcated throughout the breadth of the Soviet Empire. On the other hand in the West (above all in the USA) we find the opposite: cheap literature as well as mass media propagate the cult of brainless toughness combined with disdain for 'egg-heads'. There are two possible explanations (which do not exclude each other) of this trend which may well prove fatal to the West. One is that it is simply engineered by the advertisers, who dislike people who think too much and do not buy without asking why, and for this reason foist upon the public the ideal of a brainless tough and a dumb doll. The other explanation of the present cult of male toughness is that it is a spurious compensation for lost reality. When men carried swords and used them habitually, and when life was altogether dangerous, they found nothing repugnant in powdering themselves, wearing frills and observing the punctilia of courtesy. In contrast the young men of today, pampered at home, protected by the police, prepared by their teachers to be smooth organization men, live in dread of being taken for 'chickens' and find in rudeness and 'tough speech' the only opportunities of proving their manhood. There is a curious historical parallel of this phenomenon. In ancient Sparta the training in endurance, designed to produce future warriors, became extravagantly cruel when it lost its usefulness – when Sparta came to be just one of many little towns of the Roman Empire. Just as the contemporary cult of toughness, this example shows how a feature of character may come to be stressed most when it entirely loses its original function.

The use of mass media of communication in such a way as to foster the cult of violence, selfishness and stupidity, instead of teaching civic virtues, may very well become the chief cause of the defeat of the West, which may take place even without an outright war; because whatever the evils of doctrinarian propaganda, it must be admitted that in the Communist states mass media are not used for the purpose of extirpating all the virtues which are necessary for the strength of any state.

Nuclear weapons might bring mankind to its doom or they might turn out to be a boon, but they certainly prevent mankind from continuing on its normal course of customary brutality: men will have to treat each other better or they will all perish. By making war suicidal even for the rulers, atomic weapons took away from them the opportunities of pushing others into carnage for the sake of their own amusement and glorification. Despotism still represents a great danger to peace because of the possibility that a madman might reach the position in which he could not be restrained from bringing everybody to destruction. A rational despot, however, cannot nowadays be excessively bellicose.

Countless covenants of peace and condemnations of war have proved to be of no avail against the evil propensities of rulers, but there is a slight chance that the immediate danger to their lives might be more effective. It all hinges, however, on whether they will behave rationally.

Apart from general impediments to rational behaviour stemming from the apparently ineradicable waywardness of human nature, irrationality has been assiduously cultivated by various institutions, above all the armies. Inculcation of blind obedience and of readiness to die without asking why, and elevation of these habits to the status of the highest virtues, cannot fail to propagate irrationality. With the devaluation of the traditional martial virtues, rationality may come to be more appreciated. To be exact, this process has been going on for a very long time – in fact at least since the invention of firearms – but until now its pace has been exceedingly slow and there have been numerous relapses. In contrast, the change in this respect wrought by the advent of atomic weapons promises to be quick and radical. It will probably diminish the chances of irrational types attaining positions of power, and thus reduce the risks of war. Bureaucratization also acts in the same direction, as it favours the ascent of calculating manipulators rather than of fiery demagogues or strong-arm men. It was not good will towards the capitalists but cold calculation of consequences which has persuaded the Soviet rulers of the advantages of coexistence. There is some assurance of peace in the fact that in the struggle for promotion within the Soviet system calculating manipulators have an advantage over fanatics.

PART TWO

TYPES OF POLITY

CHAPTER TEN

FEUDALISM

IN MEDIEVAL DOCUMENTS we find the words *feudalis* and *feudum*, derived, it is believed, from the words *fehu* and *od*, which in Old High German mean cattle and wealth. It was only in the 18th century, however, that the term feudal began to be used to describe the general condition of European society during the Middle Ages. Soon afterwards, European travellers, struck by the resemblances between what they read about the history of their countries and what they saw in the East, began to apply this term to the institutional arrangements of non-European countries. When Saint-Simon, Auguste Comte and Marx put forth their evolutionary schemes, they included feudalism as one of the necessary stages through which humanity must pass. This gave rise to a long-drawn-out debate on whether feudalism was something peculiar to Europe, or whether it was a phenomenon of a more generic nature. Historiographers (owing, no doubt, to their love of detail and dislike of generalities) favoured, on the whole, the former view. Their tendency was to restrict the denotation of the term to western Europe. Even Poland and Sweden were considered not to have passed through feudalism, because in Poland the nobles held the land as hereditary property (ie the tenure was allodial – not feudal), and in Sweden the nobles never acquired judicial authority over the peasants. On the other hand, in historical sociology, and above all in political debates, the meaning of feudalism was becoming very wide. The Marxists were and are always determined to call feudal every society which is neither capitalist nor socialist nor tribal. As is well known, Marx envisaged social evolution as going through the stages of tribalism, slave-owning, feudalism and capitalism in order to arrive at the ultimate goal of socialism. The vested interest which the Marxists have in

WAYNESBURG COLLEGE LIBRARY
WAYNESBURG, PA.

finding feudalism everywhere stems from the fear that, if we admit the possibility that one of the intermediary stages is not really necessary, we may begin to doubt the inevitability of the final goal. Altogether, owing to the strong emotional loading of this word, many debates about the definitions of feudalism were prompted by considerations of propaganda rather than of heuristic usefulness. Often it is used simply as a term of opprobrium, implying the evils of inequality, exploitation and traditionalism. The value of most discussions among historians, on the other hand, has been impaired by the neglect of three rather obvious truths: first, that the denotation of any concept depends on its connotation; second, that in the realm of social phenomena the presence or absence of a feature is mostly a matter of degree; third, that in dealing with clusters of imperfectly correlated traits, we are faced with variations in the relative degrees in which the constituent features are present in different cases. In order to form a rational opinion on whether the concept of feudalism is of any use in the study of oriental societies, we must carefully analyse its most important semantic variations, bearing always in mind that definition cannot be true or false, but only more or less useful as an analytical tool.

Not uncommonly, by feudalism is meant simply the rule of hereditary nobility. Conceived thus, this term would cover numerous polities, widely different in many respects, ranging from the tribal kingdom of the Barotse in southern Africa, and Ireland at the time of St Patrick, to Venice in the 18th century and Saudi Arabia of the present day. As such a polity can be adequately described as aristocratic or nobiliary, it seems superfluous and wasteful to call it feudal as well.

Another fairly common interpretation of our term is such that a society is called feudal if it is dominated by the owners of large estates. In strict logic, this criterion does not imply the preceding, because we can imagine a society where owners of large estates dominate the rest of the population, but where the turnover among them is so great that they do not form a hereditary stratum. In reality, however, ownership of landed estates tends to remain in the hands of the same families for considerable periods, and for this reason domination by owners of large estates implies domination by a hereditary stratum. True, in some agrarian societies the turnover of the incumbents of highest dignities was remarkably rapid, but there social position depended on rank in the administrative and military hierarchy – not on ownership of land. According to Bernier and other European travellers, the position of a high dignitary in the Mughal Empire in India was very unsafe. Frequently, poor adventurers were elevated to the rank of *jagirdar* and equally frequently, prominent *jagirdars* were deprived of their power and riches, and relegated to the lower classes. The *jagirdars* did not own the lands which they held; these were assigned to them as reward for military and administrative services, were forfeited with demotion or transfer, and could be neither bequeathed nor sold. Notwithstanding the exclusion of the Mughal and the Ottoman Empires, and of a number of other oriental states, the criterion of domination by owners of large estates would give 'feudalism' a very wide denotation which would cover early Rome as well as medieval Hungary and Virginia on the eve of the American Civil War. As the essential characteristics of this type of society can be designated by the word 'latifundiarist', it is better to keep the term 'feudal' for another purpose. It remains to be noted that latifundiarism, as thus understood, is compatible with a republican constitution, as well as with an absolute monarchy. Republican Rome and Spain under the Hapsburgs and the Bourbons are examples to the point.

Taking the mode of production as the basis of classification, we might choose manorial economy as a criterion of feudalism, and call feudal every polity whose subsistence is provided by manors. A manor can be defined as a large estate entirely or nearly self-sufficient, a substantial part of which is cultivated for the benefit of its master by peasants, who are rewarded with strips of land, the fruits of which they can retain in the main part. The principal objection against adopting a definition of feudalism based on this criterion is that it seems needless to apply the term feudal to a type of society which is unambiguously designated by the word 'manorial'. Moreover, manorial economy can coexist with many variants of juridical relations between lords and peasants. In medieval France and England a serf enjoyed a substantial security of tenure, and even the right of inheritance, whilst his dues were fixed by custom. In Russia in the 18th century he could be evicted at any time and even sold. In the areas of Latin America which have not yet been transformed by urban influences, manorial economy survives, although legally the peons are free citizens. A manor must not be equated with a *latifundium*, of which it is a sub-category. A plantation, working for export, and manned by slaves or hired labourers also belongs to the category of *latifundium*. In the medieval Occident the manor provided the economic basis for a feudal hierarchy, but elsewhere it existed under other forms of 'top government' (to use an expression coined by writers on management): in Byzantium the manor constituted the predominant form of rural life even at the time when the top government was a highly centralized bureaucratic despotism. The Spanish Empire in America provides another example: the Spaniards transplanted the manorial economy, nevertheless the government of the empire was very far from feudal – its essential features were rapid rotation of officials, subject to minute control by the central government. On the other hand, in medieval Japan, whose form of government resembled most closely the classical feudalism of western Europe, there were no manors. The Japanese *sho* did not constitute a unit of cultivation, but was simply a collection of peasants' households from which a lord levied tribute in kind. The same is true of Islamic *itqta* which resembled the European fief in being land held on condition of rendering military service; its holder, however, in no way directed production, which was carried on independently by peasants, but merely collected dues. The conclusion which emerges is that, in view of the fact that manorial economy may or may not accompany the features of political structure which are regarded as constituting the essence of feudalism, it is preferable not to take manorial economy as a criterion of feudalism. It seems needless, moreover, to qualify as feudal a type of society which can be adequately described as manorial.

Some writers have suggested that we might regard feudalism as essentially the custom of rewarding administrative and military services by grants of land. The difficulty here is that this custom can be found in all agrarian states with undeveloped commerce, and therefore, some further specification is required. In the first place, security of tenure varies widely. If a grant of land can be withdrawn at will, it is usually called a benefice; a fief differs from it by the greater security of tenure based on mutual agreement. Max Weber's distinction between *Pfründenfeudalismus* and *Lehenfeudalismus* refers precisely to this difference. Let us postpone, however, for a while the examination of the question of security of tenure, and consider another point: namely, that the criterion of conditional tenure of land excludes some cases which satisfy other possible criteria of feudalism. Medieval Poland, for instance, resembled coeval western Europe very closely – there was manorial economy, seignorial immunities, hereditary nobility and so on – but the nobles owned their land, though their ownership was not free from obligations to the crown and restrictions stemming from the solidarity of the clan. They owed military service, but failure in this respect constituted a crime, not a breach of contract.

A further specification as to the use of this criterion is necessary because of the possibility that feudal tenure of land may constitute only a very subsidiary element in a structure built on entirely different lines. In Ptolemaic Egypt, for instance, many soldiers received grants of land as their reward, and for this reason were called '*kleruchoi*'; nevertheless they lived on the margin of an economy which could, without much inexactitude, be described as planned or centrally controlled, or as state socialism. The kingdom of Hammurrabi was in the main a bureaucratic despotism of a primitive kind with a fairly developed commerce; it contained feudal elements in its military organization, but they were peripheral. In contrast, in medieval Europe and Japan grants of land on condition of service constituted the sole economic foundation of the machinery of government, such as there was. If we accept the practice of rewarding military and administrative services by conditional grants of land as a criterion of feudalism, we must make sure that we speak of the latter only in cases where this type of land tenure is a central – not merely peripheral – element in the structure of the state. It must be noted that in some cases a part of the income had to be transmitted to the ruler, so that this arrangement bordered on tax-farming; or the services rendered might become nominal, so that benefices would become appanages. There are also many examples of how land which was originally held on feudal tenure becomes full private property.

The scholars who argue that feudalism existed only in western Europe insist on treating the element or contract as decisive. At the apogee of Occidental feudalism suzerains entered with their vassals into formal contracts which specified minutely rights and duties of both parties, and even recognized the vassal's right to rebel in case of a breach of the stipulations by his suzerain. Acceptance of this criterion would in fact reduce drastically the denotation of 'feudalism', by excluding all oriental and even eastern

European states. The procedure of enfeoffment was fully developed in Japan, but even here the contractual element was much weaker and decisively tilted in favour of the overlord. There is evidence that in Muscovy feudal contracts were occasionally made, but they were a marginal and irregular feature. In post-medieval Poland the kings made contractual agreements with the nobles on a number of occasions, but these were rather in the nature of treaties sealing collective bargaining – similar to the English Magna Carta – not individual enfeoffment. In the Islamic Orient there were no contracts between rulers and their subjects.

On the other hand, the contractual element figured prominently in the Mohammedan emirates of what is now northern Nigeria. There the reciprocal rights and duties of the emirs and their vassals were clearly delimited and the power of the emir restricted by a council consisting of the principal magnates. Provided it obtained the approval of the overlord, the Sultan of Sokoto, the council could even depose an emir who violated the rights of his vassals. It may interest Marxists that these emirates fit nowhere into their evolutionary scheme: their political structure was entirely feudal but their economies were based on slavery, and the slaves constituted between one third and two thirds of their population.

In the Ottoman Empire the greater part of the land was distributed to warriors as benefices. Economically, the Ottoman *timar* in the western part of the empire was very much like the fief of western Europe, and unlike the Japanese *sho*, although with respect to security of tenure the European fief and the *sho* resembled each other much more closely than either of them resembled the *timar*. A holder of a *timar* could be deprived of it instantaneously if he displeased the sultan or the pasha in any way. The Mughal *jagir* resembled the Japanese *sho* as far as the organization of production was concerned, whilst its tenure was very similar to that of the *timar*. If we wish to retain 'feudalism' as a concept which can be applied to a number of cases, we must not insist on the criterion of a formal contract, and must be prepared to call feudal any type of tenure under which land is held on condition of rendering military service. We could distinguish contractual feudalism as a sub-species of feudalism in general.

If we interpret the meaning of 'feudal tenure' in this sense we are faced with the question whether we should not, nevertheless, restrict it in some other way, because we find beneficiaries of such a tenure whose position in their societies resemble very little that of medieval knights or of Japanese samurai. The *kleruchoi* of Ptolemaic Egypt, the *limitanei* of the Late Roman Empire or the Byzantine *stratioi* were soldier-farmers, rendering military service in person instead of paying taxes – very much like the Tzarist Cossacks (not to be confused with the original independent Cossacks of the Dnieper). I think that it is advisable to describe this kind of tenure of land as semi-feudal, and reserve the term feudal only for the type of tenure which entailed seignorial jurisdiction. The latter feature calls now for some comment.

We can speak of seignorial jurisdiction when a person who enjoys the economic benefits of a territory (whether on feudal or allodial tenure) exercises full administrative and judicial authority over its inhabitants. As with all other institutions, in this respect too there are often great discrepancies between nominal and real situations. In contemporary Peru, for instance, notwithstanding that according to the law all the inhabitants are free citizens, an owner of an estate in the backlands exercises (with the connivance of the agents of the government) unlimited authority over his peons, which includes the power to punish by death, as well as to enjoy *ius primae noctis*. In medieval Europe seignorial jurisdiction was safeguarded by what were called immunities. These were exemptions from service and taxes, and (what matters most in the present context) from interventions on the part of the overlord into relations between a lord and his vassals or serfs. In other words, an overlord would promise solemnly not to interfere with his vassals' dealings with their subordinates. It amounted to a renunciation by the sovereign of direct authority over his humbler subjects. Such formal renunciations were not common in world history. A holder of a Turkish *timar* exercised unlimited authority over the peasants; nevertheless, the sultan or the pasha could at any time reverse his orders, or even punish him for acts which displeased them. Extent of seignorial immunities varied inversely with the power of the ruler over the magnates. It reached its absolute maximum in post-medieval Poland, where the kings relinquished even the slightest vestiges of direct authority over the peasants. This example makes it clear, incidentally, that seignorial immunities can flourish without feudal tenure of land; for, as said earlier, tenure of land in Poland was allodial. We find, moreover, seignorial immunities even in semi-pastoral hamitic kingdoms in Africa, which shows that they need not go together with manorial economy. If we wish to retain 'feudalism' as a sociological category of a fairly wide denotation, we ought not to insist on full and absolute character of seignorial immunities, and we should be content with extensive *de facto* authority, irrespectively whether subject to a review by a higher instance or not. Seignorial authority in this wide sense has been very common throughout the world, and can still be found in many areas.

Seignorial jurisdiction is not always linked to military service. In Russia and Poland it attained its apogee in the 18th century when the nobility had entirely lost their military character. This raises the problem whether we ought to call such societies feudal. Personally, I am against it. The character of the ruling class is of such decisive importance, and military orientation has such a pervasive influence on all aspects of social life, that it seems highly advisable to speak of feudalism only where the ruling nobility is composed of warriors. At this juncture, however, we are obliged to clarify what we mean by 'warriors'; for if we laid down a rule that every society which is dominated by military men is to be called feudal, then we should have to include in this category Poland under Pilsudski and Cuba under Batista – to mention two out of many available examples. Fortunately this presents no great difficulty, and etymology suggests a solution: the word soldier came into use in order to distinguish fighting men who were paid from those who presented themselves with their own arms and equipment in fulfilment of an obligation attached to their tenure of land. This difference in the method of equipping and remunerating armed forces influences the structure of a polity in so many ways that it must be taken into account in any sociological classification. We should speak of feudalism, therefore, only where fighting men are warriors not soldiers – that is to say, where they provide their own equipment and sustenance, not where they are armed, paid and mustered. Once again, however, we must make another qualification. Reliance on warriors instead of soldiers cannot be elected as a sufficient criterion of feudalism, because then it would cover all primitive tribes. Monopolization of military function by a privileged class must be regarded as an essential feature of feudalism.

A dichotomous division of a society into ruling warriors and peasants precluded from bearing arms, does not in itself necessitate hereditary devolution of status. The widespread idea that the strata of the medieval society were absolutely closed does not bear scrutiny. Strong and daring men, by joining various war bands, often succeeded in entering the ranks of the nobility. There was, for instance, a whole category of knights raised from serfs, whom medieval documents call *ministeriales*. Similar phenomena occurred in Japan. Hidyoshi, for instance, the man who became a supreme ruler of Japan, and laid the foundations of the Tokugawa *shogunate*, started his life as a peasant. Nevertheless, it is true, on the whole, that neither medieval Europe nor Japan were characterized by intensive vertical mobility. There are, however, examples of societies with very pronounced vertical mobility, which nevertheless satisfied other criteria of feudalism; the most extraordinary of them is that of the Mamluks of Egypt – a collectivity of warriors, whose position in society, and the manner of living, resembled that of a feudal nobility, but who replenished themselves by co-opting slaves bought on the markets of Caucasia. Mughal *jagirdars*, mentioned earlier, did not form a hereditary caste either. In contrast, in ancient Sparta, in Sassanid Persia, in medieval Europe towards the end of the Middle Ages, in the Ankole and Ruanda kingdoms in central Africa one could become a warrior only by birth. I think that by introducing the consideration of social mobility we should make the difficulty of defining feudalism even greater than it inevitably must be. I suggest, therefore, that we refrain from including any reference to it in the definition, and take as one of the criteria the mere division of a society into ruling warriors and disarmed peasants, irrespectively of how the ruling stratum is recruited.

The existence of a dichotomous division referred to above by no means determines all the important features of the social situation. The warriors may be nomads or semi-nomads, like the ruling tribes of Bakitara or Ankole in central Africa, who lived among their herds, and did not interfere with the village communities of their subjects except to collect tribute. Or they may, like the Spartans, live in their city on the produce brought by their serfs. Owing to the crucial role which the warrior-peasant dichotomy played in the life of the Spartan state, some writers describe it as feudal: Max Weber in his earlier writings, and Alexander Rüstow, for instance, speak of *Polisfeudalismus*. Some

Russian writers use an equivalent phrase with reference to the Kievan principality. Curiously, the towns of early Kievan Russia resembled in some ways the city-states of Greece before the era of the efflorescence of its civilization. The Varangians – the ruling race of Kievan Russia – lived concentrated in towns on the Dnieper. They were warriors and traders who collected tribute from the village communities of the surrounding Slavonic tribes, which they partly traded for the wares of Byzantium. Unlike the early Greeks, however, they were united by submission to one ruling clan and its head. Whatever might be said about Kievan Russia, the social institutions of Sparta, and of other Greek states, had so little in common with those of medieval Europe, that we might very well doubt whether the term feudalism ought to be applied to them. It seems better to reserve this term for societies where the nobles live dispersed throughout the territory, and rule the peasants singly, not collectively; so that every peasant has only one immediate seigneur, and the latter dwells in the vicinity. Another reason why the Spartan constitution should not be called feudal is that Sparta was a *de facto* republic – proverbially egalitarian as far as the collectivity of warriors was concerned – whereas 'feudalism' suggests a hierarchy. The word hierarchy brings us to the next point.

It is advisable to insist on the hierarchic structure of the stratum of warriors as the necessary ingredient of feudalism. This formulation, however, requires further elaboration, because there are hierarchies which nobody would dream of calling feudal.

When we compare the feudal hierarchies of medieval Europe (and others of similar kind) with hierarchies which are commonly called bureaucratic, the feature of the former which obtrudes itself upon our attention is their embryonic character: above all, the simplicity of their structure. Whereas in a bureaucratic hierarchy there are intersecting networks of authority, a feudal hierarchy can be depicted by an inverted tree symbol; there is no functional division of authority, and everyone has only one chief. In Germany, France and the Low Countries there were, it is true, some exceptions to the principle of undivided allegiance, but they were products of confusion and lack of order – not of divisions of the sphere of authority based on some principle. Another basic feature of feudal government is the inability of the ruler to control the actions of local potentates effectively; in other words, extreme dispersion of power. Dispersion of power alone is not sufficient to distinguish feudalism from other forms of government: in the Roman republic, for instance, at a certain moment the Senate ceased to be able to control the activities of proconsuls, but the constitution of the republic could not be depicted by an inverted tree.

Feudal dispersion of power is a cause as well as a consequence of the lack of functional division of authority. Separation of fiscal from military authority has always been an essential condition of effective central control over the local agents. This step was first taken in the ancient Persian Empire. All the other early attempts at instituting functional division of authority were also motivated by the desire of the rulers to curtail the independence of their vassals – it was, in fact, an application of the principle 'divide and rule' to administrative organization.

Dispersion of power is, of course, a matter of degree. When it becomes extreme it amounts to a disintegration of a polity – the fate which befell many an empire. At the other extreme, a process of centralization may replace feudalism by bureaucratic despotism. The example of Tokugawa Japan shows that a process of centralization can reach an advanced stage by tightening the discipline among the vassals, whilst the feudal framework and the outward forms are preserved. Notwithstanding many feudal characteristics, the Ottoman Empire was semi-feudal rather than feudal mainly because of the strength of the sultan's authority. Like the Mughal Empire at its zenith it could be described more exactly as a feudaloid despotism.

In view of the fluidity of the phenomena with which we are dealing, and of prevalent discrepancies between *de facto* and *de jure* situations, we should not be too formalistic; like the historians who questioned the reality of feudalism in England because the Norman kings (unlike the Capetians in France and the Hohenstaufen in Germany) never relinquished their claims to direct command over their sub-vassals, who had to swear an oath of loyalty to the king as well as one to their immediate overlord. If we wish to have any general categories which can be applied to more than one case, we must allow for inessential variations. Norman England had no doubt a more centralized régime than coeval France or the Holy Roman Empire; nevertheless, in comparison with T'ang China or the Abbasside caliphate, Norman

England was a very loosely held state, and therefore, satisfied this criterion of feudalism.

Dispersion of power and simplicity of the hierarchy did not always coincide with the criteria of feudalism discussed earlier. In the Mongol Khanates the hierarchies were simple and decentralized; nevertheless, in the areas of nomadism (that is to say, apart from the states which the Mongols founded by conquering sedentary populations) the element of seignorialism was absent: there was no dichotomous division into peasants and warriors, for all men were warriors. I think it is better to call such political formations feudaloid rather than feudal.

Considerable diagnostic difficulties stem from two complications. Firstly, a central region often is governed with the aid of a patrimonial bureaucracy, like the area round Paris under the Capetians, or the area round Delhi under the Mughals, while the provinces are held by a feudal hierarchy. Secondly, feudal relations can be inserted as a part of the lower reaches of a bureaucratic structure – the position of Byzantine *stratiotai* provides an example of such an arrangement. Inversely, a hierarchy might have a feudal character only on its upper rungs as was the case in China towards the end of the Chou dynasty, where the relationships between the emperor and the princes exhibited pronounced feudal features, whilst the inner administration of most principalities was embryonically but unmistakably bureaucratic. Furthermore, no society forms a system constructed consistently on one principle. In medieval Europe, for instance, the Church, although it was interwoven with the feudal hierarchy, remained a foreign body as far as the principles of its organization were concerned. In the same way the towns constituted a cancerous growth which ate through feudalism.

It might have been noticed that I said nothing about the genesis of feudalism, but this was not by oversight. I think that it is an unprofitable method to define a type of social structure by reference to its genesis, because we pre-judge thereby the question of how can it in fact come into existence – or to put it in medical terms, we confound diagnosis with etiology. Such a confusion may not matter in more developed sciences which deal with more palpable entities, but in sociology – where we have to grapple with tantalizingly elusive phenomena – it can be very harmful. This error hamstrings the very meritorious disquisition of

Rushton Coulborn, in his book *Feudalism in History* (Princeton, 1956).

Notwithstanding the approximative nature of the foregoing findings, this analysis must inevitably be brought to an arbitrary conclusion: a choice must be made, based on an assessment of the heuristic utility of various possible definitions. Trying to avoid meanings which are either very wide or very narrow, I propose the following definition.

Feudalism is a type of social structure characterized by the following features:

1 A division of the population into noblemen-warriors and peasants normally excluded from military service.

2 Relative unimportance of classes other than the said nobles and peasants.

3 Individual authority of nobles over peasants.

4 The custom of rewarding military and administrative services by grants of land held on condition of continuing these services.

5 Combination of such a tenure of land with jurisdiction over its inhabitants.

6 Administrative positions forming a simple hierarchy, which implies fusion of military, fiscal, judicial and general administrative authority.

7 Pronounced dispersion of power, which in extreme cases might verge on complete independence of local potentates.

A number of other features are necessary concomitants of those included in this definition: this type of structure occurs only in agrarian states with undeveloped commerce and monetary circulation, and rudimentary means of transport. It is favoured by illiteracy of the ruling class, low level of administrative skill, and a territory which is large relative to the means of administration. The example of the Inca Empire, however, shows that even a preliterate society can support a highly centralized political structure.

Preferably we ought to call a polity feudal only if its structure exhibits all the characteristics specified above. When dealing with cases where only incomplete combinations of these features are present we might use the words semi-feudal and feudaloid. French writers often speak of feudalism when they refer to the erosion of the official government's power by pressure groups, and the building up of extra-legal networks of relations of dependence between individuals and organizations, which resemble feudal bonds because they are based on the exchange of adherence for protection. For the sake of exactitude, we should call such phenomena quasi-feudal rather than feudal.

CHAPTER ELEVEN

ORIENTAL DESPOTISM OR AGRARIAN BUREAUCRACY

THE VIEW THAT despotism was the normal condition of oriental states dates back to the ancient Greeks who were very conscious of the uniqueness of their political systems. Equally aware of the contrast between their institutions and the oriental monarchies were the defenders of the republican constitution of ancient Rome: the murder of Caesar was justified on the ground that he tried to impose oriental despotism on the Romans.

The political philosophers of the Era of Enlightenment clearly understood that the absolute monarchies to the west of Russia were not really absolute in comparison with their oriental counterparts. In Montesquieu's scheme the absolutist kingdoms of Europe were classified as monarchies, and the monarchies of Asia as despotisms. Montesquieu related his political typology to what the American anthropologists nowadays call 'basic personality structure', to the climate, the position of women and several other features of social life. Montesquieu's classification became the stock-in-trade of political writers of the 18th century; but on the whole they treated the form of government in isolation from other aspects of social life, as the concept of social structure had not yet been formulated. However, David Hume made a remarkable sociological discovery in one of his essays by pointing out that whereas the European nobilities were stabilized and organized into corporations, the magnates under oriental despotisms enjoyed neither security of tenure nor the right to form a corporation. Without using these terms, of course, he argued that a high turnover in the ruling *élite* was a necessary correlate of despotism. The next step along this line of thought was Tocqueville's thesis that aristocracy constitutes the chief rampart against despotism.

Tocqueville derived this idea not from comparing the Occident with the Orient but from his study of the process and consequences of the French Revolution.

Several earlier writers referred to the fact that control over a system of irrigation enhances the power of a ruler over his subjects, but Marx seems to have been the first to formulate explicitly the thesis that Oriental despotism was the consequence of dependence on large-scale irrigation. Emphasizing the structural concatenation between the economic and political aspects, he gave currency to the term 'Oriental society'; though by recognizing it as a sociological type *sui generis* he implicitly undermined the validity of his scheme of unilinear evolution which specified five stages: tribal, slave-owning, feudal, capitalist and communist. Although he was never very concerned about logical consistency, it was no doubt for this reason that he did not develop his concept of 'Oriental society' further, and that this topic failed to attract the attention of his disciples until it was taken up by Karl August Wittfogel, who after three decades of intensive work (and an ideological re-orientation) has now presented us with the first extensive analysis of oriental despotism as a sociological type.

Wittfogel's *Oriental Despotism* is an important book and absolutely indispensable to sociologists interested in comparative studies. It is not a historical survey of the various régimes which existed in Oriental lands, but an attempt to construct and analyse a type of social structure. One of its merits is that it tries to show how the strictly political institutions were related to other features of the social structure such as methods of cultivation, land tenure, security of property, taxation, vertical mobility and so on. By providing data on these topics the author has rendered a great service to historiography and comparative sociology, for there is no other work which supplies this type of information on non-Western societies. The older works on Oriental history and comparative sociology furnished many details on political events, beliefs and customs, but never even raised many of the questions to which Wittfogel's book provides at least partial answers. The only writer who made a detailed comparative study of the structures of Oriental societies was Max Weber. Though theoretically much less sophisticated than Weber's works, as far as factual information is concerned, Wittfogel's study constitutes an important step forward in many respects: his data are more reliable, as they embody the results of recent research and the fruits of his own study of the sources which Weber could not use; they bear, moreover, upon at least one aspect of social life – namely, vertical mobility – to which Weber paid very little attention, as he does not seem to have been acquainted with Pareto's theory of the circulation of elites.

With a long array of fascinating data Wittfogel confirms the view that a speedy turnover within the ruling *élite* constitutes an essential condition of despotism, and that it was in fact characteristic of most Oriental societies in contrast to their European counterparts. The idea that permanent purge is an indispensable means of maintaining absolute sway is not new, and can be traced as shown in greater detail in my *Military Organization and Society* to Aristotle and Shang Yang. Wittfogel's book, however, greatly adds to our factual information on this point.

The central thesis of Wittfogel's work is of almost disarming simplicity. Whereas in Europe agriculture always depended on rainfall and did not necessitate irrigation, in the Orient natural conditions were such that the bulk of the land could not be cultivated without large-scale irrigational works. As only a centralized administration could organize the building and maintenance of large-scale systems of irrigation, the need for such systems made bureaucratic despotism inevitable in Oriental lands. The inclination towards geographical determinism dominates Wittfogel's thinking so much that he speaks of 'hydraulic societies', using this term interchangeably with 'Oriental despotism'.

A great weakness of Wittfogel's theory (which it shares with all interpretations according to geographical determinism) is that it imputes an excessively static character to social structures. Even ancient Egypt – that 'hydraulic society' *par excellence* – went through a semi-feudal period. China too experienced several reversions to feudaloid institutions during the times when barbarian irruptions or internal troubles dislocated the bureaucratic machine. Even more pronounced oscillations between centralized despotism and feudalism can be detected in the history of India. True, it can be said that there was a tendency in all these culture-areas to revert to the type of agrarian bureaucratic despotism, but the same can be said about Byzantium, the Ottoman Empire and Russia, where this tendency could not stem from dependence on irrigation.

The basic error of Wittfogel consists in failure to distinguish between the hypotheses (1) that large-scale irrigation necessitates despotism, and (2) that all cases of despotism are products of this type of agriculture. This confusion leads him to include Russia and Turkey in the category of 'hydraulic societies' which is clearly absurd, since neither of these countries knew irrigation on a large scale. Thus the material furnished by the author himself exposes the falsity of his assertions. Other relevant examples could be cited: the Late Roman Empire, which could hardly be called oriental as it stretched over the whole of western Europe, exhibited all the traits of oriental despotism, although its agricultural basis was essentially the same as it was later under feudalism. The very well organized despotic empire of the Incas stretched over areas which could not even today be encompassed by an irrigational system. The thesis, then, that large-scale irrigation constitutes a necessary condition of despotism can be dismissed.

The contention that large-scale irrigational works have to be accompanied by despotism is much more plausible. The argument in its favour is threefold: (1) that an extensive system of irrigation can be constructed and maintained only by a centralized government ruling the whole irrigated area; (2) that a population which depends on such a system for its livelihood cannot resist encroachments upon its liberties by the bureaucracy; (3) that the conjunction of these two circumstances inevitably produces a despotic government. An inductive examination lends some support to these arguments, provided that we restrict their applicability to the pre-industrial world. The Tennessee system distributes more water than the canals of the ancient pharaohs did, which shows that in a modern civilization water control by no means requires a despotic political régime. Wittfogel needlessly weakens his case by applying his concept to the Russian and Chinese Communist régimes. If there are economic reasons in these countries which make parliamentary government impracticable, the need for irrigation and canalization is certainly not the most important of them – not even in China.

In the pre-industrial world, owing to the meagreness of resources and the rudimentary nature of tools and techniques, the tasks of building and maintaining dams, dikes and canals were of relatively far greater magnitude than they are today; and as the populations were living on the barest subsistence level, the requisite effort could be exacted from them only with the aid of direst compulsion. As Max Weber pointed out, it was not accidental that a whip was the symbol of royal authority in ancient Egypt. Such circumstances preclude, naturally, any form of polity which requires popular consent for the exercise of authority, but it is not quite obvious why the government should assume an autocratic rather than an oligarchic character. That an oligarchic government of a 'hydraulic society' is not altogether impossible is demonstrated by the history of the archetype of such a society – Egypt – which came to be ruled during the later era of the so-called New Kingdom by a self-perpetuating corporation of priests who were even able to depose a pharaoh who tried to assert his authority over them. It must be admitted, however, that from the point of view of the long history of Egypt this was but a temporary deviation of a few hundred years from the normal condition of autocratic despotism.

One of the most important causes of the prevalence of autocratic despotism was the fact that in the pre-industrial world despotism was the only régime under which effective administration of sizeable areas was at all possible. There were, it is true, political formations comprising very wide areas and far from despotic – such as the Holy Roman (German) Empire, the kingdom of Poland and Lithuania, the feudal kingdom of France and so on – but they were loose conglomerates without effective organs of administration: they were incapable of undertaking big public works. It must be remembered that western Europe did not acquire roads as good as those which it had under the Roman Empire until the 19th century.

When we talk about oriental despotism, we must remember that from the point of view of universal history it was not the Orient that was peculiar but the Occident. Indeed, the latter constituted a deviation from the norm, having enjoyed long spells of non-despotic rule. For the rest of the world – not only in the Orient but in Africa, America and Oceania as well – despotism was the only known method of governing sizeable communities. Owing to the primitiveness of the means of transport and communication, and of the techniques of organization, despotism in the pre-industrial world never reached, and only seldom approached, the thoroughness of its modern totalitarian examples. Nevertheless, the limitations under which it operated were not juridical but purely technical: so far as he could reach, the ruler's will was unfettered. True, the traditional despots did not usually feel entitled to modify the tenets of religion and custom, or rather simply did not conceive such a possibility, but in so far as their power over individuals was concerned, it was in fact absolute. The limit of the possible was reached a long time ago: the kings of Fiji – to cite one of the most grotesque examples – used to enjoy the right to eat their subjects. Legal limitations on the ruler's authority, which give other persons the right to participate in making decisions, are fairly common only on the tribal level, and in very small polities such as the city states of the ancient Near East and Greece, ancient India and medieval Europe. There are innumerable examples, of course, of weak rulers manipulated by cliques, but this is something very different from the legally established sharing of authority.

With the exceptions noted below, all large pre-industrial states could be placed at some point of the continuum between feudalism and centralized bureaucratic despotism. Feudalism and bureaucratic despotism were the two poles around and between which the large pre-industrial political formations oscillated. There was only one relatively short-lived exception to this regularity: Rome during the last two centuries of the republic. The Roman attachment to tradition was so great that the political institutions evolved when it was still a small city-state continued to function when Rome had already become the capital of an empire. Nevertheless, as soon as the empire was conquered, the republic began to evolve in the direction of oriental despotism: by the time of Augustus it had moved half-way, and when Diocletian mounted the throne the change had already been completed. Thus the extraordinary spectacle of a large agrarian state with a republican constitution lasted about two centuries.

Carthage also remained a republic after it grew from a city-state into an empire, but its domains were never truly welded into one state, and the empire lasted only a short time.

The earliest political formations of the medieval Occident were, of course, very different from the elaborately organized Chinese bureaucracy, but from the point of view of universal history they were not particularly original and belonged to the same type as the numerous primitive patrimonial monarchies which existed at various times in Asia, Africa and South America. Europe acquired its distinctiveness only when the crystallization of contractual feudalism and the emergence of representative organs of the estates brought into existence political systems based on balance of power *de jure* as well as *de facto.*

The absolutist states of pre-industrial Europe could be placed half-way along the continuum between feudalism and bureaucratic despotism, although their movement in the direction of the latter pole was interrupted (perhaps only temporarily) by the rise of capitalism. Some of them (like the domains of the Habsburgs) were nearer to feudalism, whilst Russia exhibited all the traits of oriental despotism until the second half of the 19th century. During the 15th and the 16th centuries the feudal kingdom of Poland and Lithuania moved in the opposite direction from other European states, and transformed itself into a nobiliary republic (even though the name 'Kingdom' was preserved); but as soon as this transformation was complete effective government ceased. From the end of the 17th century the monarchic republic of Poland and Lithuania no longer functioned as a living polity, and was plunged into chaos which lasted until the country was partitioned a century later.

The United States did constitute even in their initial shape a sizeable polity which had the honour of being the first large state of a predominantly democratic character that ever existed; but it entered the industrial civilization almost as soon as it was born.

In order to obtain a better insight into the nature of despotism we should invert the problem: instead of attempting to explain the occurrence of despotism we should try in the first place to explain its non-occurrence. This inversion of the problem can be justified on the ground that despotism is the most natural form of government of large social aggregates – natural in the sense of the most probable, that is to say, requiring fewest specific conditions for its emergence and continued existence.

When we look at any example of a non-despotic system of government of a large political unit, we find that it contains an intricate mechanism of balance of power. Montesquieu's principle that despotism can be prevented only by a division of authority remains one of the greatest discoveries of sociology, and has fully withstood the test of time. As is well known, Montesquieu thought that it was the division between executive, legislative and judicial authority that made civil liberties possible in England. The writers on constitutional history usually say that he misunderstood the English system of government, but they are wrong because, although it is perfectly true that the division of authority has never been absolute in England, it was very real in comparison with the situation among Continental monarchies, let alone the despotisms of the East. Like all great discoveries, Montesquieu's idea was very simple: it amounted to the application of the old Roman maxim 'divide and rule' to the rulers themselves, thus converting it into 'divide your rulers in order not to be trod upon'. True, he formulated it in terms which were too legalistic, but as reformulated by Mosca who speaks of the balance of social forces, the principle is unassailable. However, the lack of a predominant centre of power does not need to produce a viable equilibrium: disintegration through strife or paralysis of the body politic are more probable outcomes. A political system based on an equilibrium of forces must generate conflicts, and at the same time contain them within narrow limits compatible with effective collective action. The naturalness of despotism is demonstrated by the fact that all non-despotic régimes were products of slow evolution under circumstances which can without much exaggeration be described as hot-house, and that every severe disturbance of their intricate structures caused a relapse into despotism. The movement away from despotism is long and laborious, whereas the movement towards it is quick and easy.

As suggested earlier, the thesis of Wittfogel is only partially true: in the pre-industrial world, the reliance on irrigation on a large-scale fostered despotism, but as the number of cases of 'non-hydraulic' despotism by far exceeds the number of cases of 'hydraulic' despotism, such a reliance cannot account for the prevalence of despotism, and therefore, the absence of large-scale irrigation cannot be considered as a sufficient condition of emergence of non-despotic political systems. A glance at the geographical and chronological distribution of the latter shows that indeed they all emerged in areas where agriculture relied only on rainfall, but that they also comprised only a small part of such areas – the part which was delimited by the boundaries of Western Christendom. There were embryonic developments in this direction in medieval Muscovy and India, but they soon withered.

It would be difficult to sustain that the pluralistic character of

European polities was directly inspired by the teaching of the Church, because of all ecclesiastic bodies that the world has known the Catholic Church was and is the most autocratic. The correct, though by no means novel, explanation is that it was the division between the sacerdotal and the political authority (combined with a geographical position less exposed to invasions than many other parts of the world) that made possible the emergence of non-despotic political systems – for it must never be forgotten that the division between temporal and spiritual authority is something unique to the Occident. The independence of the Church was due to a series of extraordinary coincidences such as the facts that it inherited the administrative traditions of the Roman Empire, which the invading barbarian warriors were unable to learn, that it was not confined within one realm, and therefore able to play the kings against each other, and that by enjoining celibacy upon the clergy it was able to prevent the hereditary appropriation of offices, thus maintaining the efficiency of its administrative apparatus on a level far superior to that of the feudal monarchies. The struggle between the Church and the monarchs enabled the nobility and the burghers to organize themselves into bodies of some cohesion, thus bringing into existence representative assemblies.

The second factor was the influence of commerce. All the pre-industrial states which differed radically both from feudalism and from bureaucratic despotism were commercial and maritime: Carthage, England and Holland in the 18th century, Venice (which was quite a large state at its apogee) and the Greek, Italian and Hanseatic city-states. Even in the militaristic Roman republic the merchants and capitalists had much more influence than their counterparts in oriental monarchies.

It is an interesting question why commerce fostered oligarchic rather than autocratic forms of government. It was possibly because it was difficult to control centrally, and therefore gave to its practitioners a great deal of independence from the rulers. However, the anti-authoritarian influence of commercial activities could decisively affect only the political system of a small country, because only there could the merchants acquire sufficient weight of numbers in proportion to the bulk of the population. There were many more merchants in China than in England or Holland, and before the railway age their turnover was much greater; but in proportion to the enormous mass of peasants they were few, and this was one of the reasons why they had little power.

Though ever tending to revert to bureaucratic despotism, oriental societies were not at all stable. Indeed, for reasons indicated in my *Military Organizations and Society*, they were continuously torn by armed strife and experienced more frequent violent upheavals (though not transformations) than the polities of the Occident. Their structures were characterized by a kind of convulsive homeostasis.

The complete absence of reference to the subject of revolutions in Wittfogel's *Oriental Despotism* seems to be connected with the overemphasis on the static and monolithic character of oriental societies, which in turn may have something to do with the author's anti-Marxist sallies into Marxist exegeses. The latter incidentally are a sheer waste of time because the elucidations of Marxist exegeticists are of little interest unless they can be interpreted in the light of fairly detailed knowledge of jockeying for positions between cliques inside the Communist parties. This omission is all the more curious because *Oriental Despotism* is an expansion and revision of an article published in 1937 in *Zeitschrift für Sozialforschung* under the title '*Zur Theorie der orientalischen Gesellschaft*', and one of the most interesting parts of this was the exposition of a theory of revolutions. The essence of this theory can be summarized as follows: In every dynasty the quality of the rulers inevitably declined with the passage of time. In consequence, nepotism and graft increased among the mandarins who, free from effective supervision, exploited the peasantry more and more mercilessly, seizing their lands and reducing them to debt bondage, raising taxes without passing them on to the imperial treasury. The despair and hatred among the peasants, combined with the growing inefficiency of the administrative machine, finally produced revolution which gave some capable man of humble origin an opportunity to seize the throne. The new emperor re-established order, alleviated the plight of the peasants . . . and then the cycle began anew. This cycle was combined with the cycle of nomad invasions which largely depended on the strength of the resistance, and were more likely when the empire was growing weaker.

The idea of the dynastic cycle is by no means new: on the contrary, the Chinese chroniclers dwelt with great gusto upon the theme of corruption of dynasties and their replacement by more vigorous lineages. Wittfogel, however, made an important addition: following some modern Chinese scholars, he related the oscillations in the character of the rulers to changes in taxation and land-tenure.

The theory of dynastic cycle resembles in many ways the scheme of Ibn Khaldun. This medieval Arab philosopher envisaged the following cycle. A nomadic tribe conquers a settled land; its chief becomes the monarch, and the tribesmen the nobility. Under the influence of luxury they lose their martial virtues, and the tribal solidarity vanishes. They become disloyal, factious, lazy, cowardly, and therefore unable to resist encroachments from the nomads, whose hard way of life fosters bravery, endurance and loyalty. Finally, one of the tribes overthrows the dynasty, usurps its place . . . and the cycle begins anew. Allowing for minor irregularities, the scheme of Ibn Khaldun fits the history of North Africa right up to the French conquest with surprising accuracy, and it might have suggested to Pareto his theory of the circulation of *élites*. Wittfogel's scheme fits the data of Chinese history less well, and many sinologists criticized it on this score, pointing out, for instance, that the Sung dynasty was by no means in decline when the Mongols conquered it, that military revolts were more frequently instrumental than peasant uprisings in toppling over dynasties, and that only the founders of the Han and the Ming dynasties sprang from the bottom of the social ladder. Notwithstanding these errors, Wittfogel has the merit of having drawn the attention of sinologists to hitherto neglected social processes. From the theoretical point of view, Wittfogel's scheme constitutes a contribution to the study of what might be termed triadic inter-hierarchic oscillations (the interplay between the constituents of the triad consisting of the ruler, the notables, the populace), which occupied a prominent place in the thought of many political philosophers, beginning with Aristotle. Machiavelli, for instance, suggests that in order to maintain his power a prince must balance the rich and the poor against each other.

Even some of the greatest figures of sociology held political views which did not harmonize with their doctrines. Marx, for instance, refused to consider the possibility that class struggles might continue in post-capitalist societies, thus unduly limiting the scope of his theory. Spencer viewed society from the point of organic analogy, which lent no support whatsoever to his individualistic liberalism, and which should have led him to espouse some form of authoritarianism, whether of socialist or conservative variety. So it is not surprising that Wittfogel's theory, which remains a form of economic determinism, contradicts his political views which are nowadays those of a militant liberal anti-communist: for if economic interdependence inevitably generates totalitarian despotism, then, in view of the inescapable growth of this interdependence, the pluralistic social order is doomed.

PART THREE

MIND AND SOCIETY

CHAPTER TWELVE

IDEAS AS FORCES

THE USUAL SCHEME for an economic interpretation of history is that changes of technology produce changes of economic structure, which in their turn transform the superstructure, which consists of political organization, religion, art, etc. In many cases this interpretation does give a satisfactory explanation of social changes. Attempts to trace social effects of changes in technology are useful and important, but they cannot be taken as final explanations because they raise another question: what caused these changes?[1]

The social conditions of technical progress may be a subject of debate, but there can be no doubt that technical and scientific invention is no more than any other activity a *deus ex machina* independent of social circumstances. The so-called 'theory of cultural lag', which really amounts to disguised Marxism, simply ignores this problem. It assumes that non-material culture must adapt itself to the progression of technology and does not envisage the possibility of technical progress being arrested by social conditions. One has only to think of many spinning and weaving machines which were invented and then destroyed during the Middle Ages, or of the steam engine of Alexandrian Greeks, the mere existence of which has been forgotten, to see that not every invention has been utilized. The cases of stagnation and decline of scientific activity, let alone of technical regression, can

[1] There has arisen an unfortunate habit of employing the term 'sociology of knowledge' to designate the study of interaction between beliefs and the condition of society. The matters treated in works on the 'sociology of knowledge' – class consciousness, pre-scientific and popular views of society, political prejudices and passions, ethnocentrism and so on – cannot be classified as knowledge in any accepted sense of that word. A proper name for this branch of learning is sociology of ideologies. In naming pursuits which claim the status of a science, words ought to be chosen with great care, and false pretensions avoided.

be explained only with reference to social factors, technology being intrinsically cumulative.

Although the introduction of new methods of production never fails to influence other aspects of life, there are many cases of profound ideological changes, and political and economic transformations, without any important modifications of technology. The rise and decline of capitalism in classical antiquity were not accompanied by any marked improvements in methods of production; there was progress not so much in technical processes as in the extension of the industry, in the number of workshops built, and the number and extension of markets opened to it. The rise and fall of the Roman Empire and the spread of Christianity occurred in the same period. No changes in methods of production corresponded to such momentous occurrences as the rise and decline of Buddhism in India, its spread to China or the conquests of Islam. Polynesian societies are very similar as far as methods of production are concerned but display profuse variety in their political and economic organization. Technology is much the same in the United States and in Soviet Russia but this similarity does not prevent profound differences in economic organization.

Even if we reject technological determinism, we can continue to consider ideologies and doctrines to be mere justifications ('rationalizations') serving to mask the pursuit of egoistic interests, as constellations of these interests are not determined solely by technology.

There is certainly a remarkable coincidence between the spread of certain ideologies and the emergence of interests for which they can serve as a useful cover. Capitalism and Calvinism, imperialistic expansion and the ideology of the 'white man's burden', advocacy of freedom of enterprise and the interests of businessmen, socialism and proletarian discontent, can be cited as examples of such connections. However, there still remains the problem of legitimacy of interpretation: if somebody asserts that he is striving to further some noble idea, while we notice that his actions curiously promote his interests, are we entitled to say that his professed enthusiasm for the cause is mere bluff? In many cases we can prove or at least presume conscious deceit, but frequently all evidence seems to indicate sincerity. It is quite obvious, for instance, that the power of the priests is not entirely due, as thought Voltaire, to their skill in deliberately deceiving the unsuspecting populace. This difficulty of interpretation can to a large extent be overcome with the aid of psychoanalysis. Clinical observation has shown that many beliefs subserve goals of which the patient is completely unconscious. But in spite of this, there are a number of reasons why the interpretation of ideas solely in terms of interests cannot provide a complete explanation.

In the first place, it is evidently possible to inculcate into human beings beliefs which are quite contrary to their egoistic interests. Nearly all nations have succeeded in instilling the idea into their members that they must be ready to offer their lives in defence of their country. Many individuals have died for abstract ideas; for Marxism, for instance, which denies the power of ideas. Furthermore, how can one's interests be advanced by believing that one is going to suffer eternal torment for one's sins?

In the second place, if it were true that ideas merely serve as justifications for interests, how would it be possible for ideological systems to spread over groups with conflicting interests? Many sects could, no doubt, express the interests of specific groups, but as soon as they became churches and imposed some kind of ethical code on all sections of the population, divergence of interests and ideologies reappeared.

Recent studies of ideas do less than justice to contributions of older writers like Taylor, Frazer and Hobhouse who stressed the importance of the ratiocinative processes. Those who maintain that interests determine the choice of beliefs, forget that ideas may be accepted or rejected simply because they carry conviction. Not all beliefs about the structure of the universe could have been determined by interests. Pasteur's theory (and the modification of medical practice consequent upon it) did not gain ground because men began to wish more ardently to be healthy. The opposition to it stemmed from deep-rooted habits and preconceptions and not from the interests of the medical profession.

Among the circumstances which decide the fate of new ideas must be included beliefs already in the field. There is some kind of intrinsic dynamics in the ideological sphere: an immanent logic of development which Cournot called *l'enchaînement des idées*. This immanent logic of development is particularly prominent in the field of scientific and technical knowledge. Social conditions may facilitate or hinder inventive activity, or even stop it altogether, but what can be invented or discovered depends on what is known already: every step presupposes the previous one. Even in the domain of religious, ethical and philosophic thought there seems to exist, as L. T. Hobhouse suggested, some similar kind of immanent logic of development: the more difficult and complex concepts can only merge gradually, after less abstruse notions have already been formulated and assimilated. The evolution of the concept of responsibility is a good example of such development. The transformations of ideas in accordance with Hegelian dialectics constitute another manifestation of their intrinsic dynamics. Marx erroneously applied the Hegelian scheme to the succession of types of society; but in the realm of intellectual production a thesis is in fact often followed by an antithesis, together with which it eventually brings forth a synthesis – which later becomes the starting-point for a new triadic sequence of this kind.

Only a small part of a culture of any given society has originated within it; but what can be imitated depends naturally on contacts with other cultures which, so far as the inner structure of a society is concerned, must be treated as accidental. The fact that China is next to India, whence it could borrow Buddhism, and not to Europe, from which Christianity might have been introduced, cannot be conceived as being dependent on the character of Chinese society and culture. True, imitation is selective, and acceptance or rejection of any trait is determined by forces operating within a society. But although conditions may be extremely propitious for the acceptance and spread of a given trait, they may not permit its independent invention and development. Northern Europe was obviously ready to adopt Christianity, but we can be sure that it could not have produced such a system independently.

Beliefs, fashions and manners may spread from one group to another without much regard to their intrinsic qualities. The group which adopts them may do so not because they satisfy some already existing need, but simply because they come from a group enjoying higher prestige. Stiff collars, long trousers and waistcoats are certainly not worn by inhabitants of the tropics because of any intrinsic merits of this attire. Religions, notions of honour and propriety, even political ideologies are often embraced regardless of their effects upon the structure of the society involved, simply because they come from a source enjoying higher prestige. Moreover, there are many cases of systems of ideas imposed by foreign conquerors, which means that they can in no way be regarded as emanations of the accepting societies.

An ideological system evolved in response to earlier conditions may persist into a later time when it could not be created. Christianity, for instance, originated from a mixture of Jewish, Hellenic and Syriac elements. After the Mohammedan conquests contacts between the Hellenic and the Syriac culture areas were well-nigh severed, and therefore this kind of syncretism would have been impossible. Nor could the Fathers of the Church have risen during the Dark Ages when the disappearance of Roman schools was followed by general ignorance. Christianity, which medieval Europe could not have produced, nevertheless pervaded every sphere of its life.

The so-called Reception of the Roman Law in early modern Europe was due mainly to the needs of developing commerce and banking and of monarchical centralization then in progress. Without these new needs Roman law would, we may presume, remain an object of interest to archivists only. But it does not follow that a legal system of the same quality could have been produced independently in Renaissance Europe. Roman law was created on the basis of legal and philosophic traditions deriving from Hellenic, Egyptian and Mesopotamian sources, the mere existence of which was not even suspected by Renaissance scholars. Besides, the number of lawyers with the requisite intellectual background was extremely small. In any case the independent creation of a legal system of such complexity would have required centuries, as it did in Rome, with the result that the nascent capitalism and absolute monarchy would have had no ready-made, appropriate legal framework. Their development would necessarily have been slowed down and perhaps, if other fostering conditions had disappeared in the meantime, permanently arrested. The body of ideas, embodied in manuscripts which lay in dusty corners of archives, constituted at that time a potential force which needed certain facilitating conditions to become effective, but which cannot be regarded as a by-product of these conditions.[1]

[1] In Britain capitalism developed without the Roman law, but the English law could not have evolved without the stimulus of acquaintance with Roman legal ideas.

Once a complex of beliefs has been embodied in a sacred book it acquires a certain rigidity and cannot easily be modified. In order to be accepted, a doctrine must satisfy some needs existing in a given society, but a number of other traits are imported accidentally without any relation between their intrinsic qualities and the circumstances already existing in this society. Christianity for example was accepted by the rulers of Eastern Europe and forced upon their subjects for a number of reasons: its clergy were the bearers of Greco-Roman cultural remains of great administrative value, such as the all-important art of writing; moreover, it inspired awe as being the religion of the more civilized and powerful countries. But it is quite clear that it was not adopted because of the attraction of its code of sexual behaviour to the converted peoples. There is not the slightest evidence that the peoples in question had been dissatisfied with their morals. Nevertheless, the Church stamped out polygyny and enforced its monogamic ideas, though only after a protracted struggle. Acceptance of an ideological system may be determined by the inner forces of a society, but once accepted it acquires a force of its own.

Innumerable examples show that every ideological system can be utterly perverted: the most noble ideals have been used to justify heinous crimes. This does not mean that ethical ideals are entirely without effects, but it does prove that ideologies and religions set no firm lower limit to conduct. Unfortunately, however, they do set an upper limit which only a few individuals can transcend. There are no examples of collective behaviour rising above the generally professed ethical standards. We can describe this phenomenon as the principle of ideological upper limit. The following two comparisons illustrate it. The Christians have often behaved more barbarously than the Moslems but it seems that Islam's upper limit of moral perfection is intrinsically below that set by the Christian Churches, chiefly because it explicitly enjoins war and the subjection of women. To take another comparison: the deeds of the Communists have been as barbarous as the Nazis' but whereas the practice of Nazism could not have lost its criminal nature without a rejection of its ideological foundation, the ideals of Communism do not altogether prevent the elimination of barbarous practices.

When it is said that a certain ideology has been fostered or generated by some social conditions, it is usually assumed that such an ideology must be a justification ('rationalization') of these conditions. But this is by no means always so. It is possible that social conditions may foster ethical notions condemning them, irrespectively of interests involved, as has happened in a way in the case of contemporary Western civilization.

We are dominated by the idea of equality of opportunity, which is so deeply ingrained in our minds that we take it for granted that this is the natural criterion of justice. We think that it is unfair that a stupid son of a prince should have an advantage over a gifted son of a pauper, although having been born clever or dull, pretty or ugly, is just as much a matter of luck as having been born a prince or a gipsy. The accident of being born poor is an unfair disadvantage to a gifted man, but the handicap of being born without gifts may bring upon the individual even worse humiliations.

The belief in the justice of equality of opportunity is a corollary of the general outlook on life called individualism, the chief characteristic of which is that it treats the individual as not organically connected with the group to which he belongs. He as such, and not his group, has rights. From this point of view customs like the blood feud or caste solidarity must appear nonsensical and reprehensible. In societies where stratification is hereditary it is families or lineages who are thought to occupy certain positions, having rights and duties. The idea that somebody should be a judge or a shoemaker simply because his father was one appears to us absurd because we think of people as individuals rather than links in the family chain. We think so because, as Simmel and Bouglé have shown, the multiplicity of intersecting social units to which an individual can belong – combined with great social mobility – makes kinship and family bonds seem less important than the character of the individual.

Social structures distinguished by multiplicity of intersecting groups and high social mobility, have been brought into being mainly by two agencies: the centralized state and the complex of economic institutions known as capitalism, which deprived smaller social units of most of their functions and authority, thus emancipating the individual from their control, enabling him to move from one group to another, and fostering ideologies of individualism, demanding equality of opportunity. But both capitalism and the centralized state facilitate concentration of power and wealth, and tend to increase social inequalities. Untrammelled capitalism with its opportunities for accumulation of wealth and with its insistence on rights of property, inevitably leads to the formation of dynasties of hereditary rich. The tension between the actual conditions generated by capitalism and the ideologies fostered by it indirectly constitutes one of the most important driving forces of contemporary social transformations. The prevalence of egalitarian ideas cannot be explained by the misery of lower classes caused by capitalism. On the contrary, the lot of the masses is far more favourable in the chief capitalist countries than in many other societies, where the poor accept their fate and no egalitarian ideas are in circulation. Among the Hindus only posthumous social ascent was regarded as desirable. Moreover, the standard of living of the lower classes is not necessarily connected with the opportunities, which in any circumstances only few can use, of rising in the social scale. Capitalism presents a clear case of an institutional complex generating an ideology which is avowedly antagonistic to it, instead of being its justification.

The crucial factors which affect the autonomous force of the immanent dynamics of ideas, seem to be the intrinsic difficulty of conceiving them and their concatenation. Ideas easily conceived emerge from obscurity, acquire and lose their influence entirely in response to changes in social circumstances. Nearly all those ideas which enter into political ideologies are of this kind, and to them Max Scheler's formulation can be applied: he maintained that all possible ideologies are always 'available' (in the storehouse of cranky circulation, as it were); their spread and influence is determined by political and, above all, economic circumstances. The relationship between ideas and interests, as conceived by Scheler, resembles somewhat the relationship between the Freudian *id* and the censor. Notwithstanding its fairly close approximation to reality, this scheme is not entirely correct, because even in this field human inventiveness has on occasions produced unexpectedly powerful concoctions. It would be difficult to sustain that the history of the world would have been the same even if Karl Marx had never lived to produce his intoxicating mixture of science, vituperation and Messianism. The relationship between an ideologue, an ideology, and social circumstances can perhaps best be conceived as similar to the relationship between the sower, the seed and the soil. Many sowers sow but their seeds wither; the seeds adapted to the soil on which they fall flourish, and their sowers become famous; on the other hand, there might be soils which are potentially receptive to a kind of seed which nobody throws on it. In other words, social circumstances might be potentially very propitious for the spread of some possible ideological concoction, but nobody propagates it. Although what is created in this field is obviously conditioned by social circumstances, the pullulation of ideologues dubbed as cranks proves that the determination of ideological production by general social circumstances is only partial. Environment limits what can be imagined, but the limits are fairly wide.

The autonomy of immanent dynamics of ideas in relation to social conditions depends also on the degree of their concatenation, coexistential as well as developmental. By coexistential concatenation I mean the strictness with which all ideas in question imply each other; that is to say, the measure in which they form a system of logically interdependent propositions. By developmental concatenation I mean the strictness with which every step requires previous steps. The clearest example of concatenation of ideas (both coexistential and developmental) is provided, of course, by the exact sciences.

In order to advance further our knowledge of the efficacity of ideas in guiding action, we should classify them. The first distinction that comes to mind is between hortative and informative ideas – in other words, between ethical recommendations and information about causal relationships and consequences of various courses of action. It is quite plain that nobody ever doubted the efficacity of knowledge and illusion in determining the choice of courses of action. Controversy exists concerning the power of moral ideas, and in particular around the question of the extent to which people can be induced to behave altruistically, or are guided by impersonal ideals other than devotion to their group and hatred of outsiders – for there can be little doubt that the last-named motive can prompt even self-immolation. People differ greatly in their responsiveness to impersonal ideals, and the question of what makes an idealist deserves the attention of psychologists; although it is very unlikely that they could discover anything worthwhile, because with their current unsophisticated and mechanized techniques, they would probably classify as idealists even the most blatant self-seekers, provided they were skilled in giving appropriate responses to questionnaires.

Reason can guide our actions and modify values in more ways than just by indicating the means to attain set goals. In the first place it can show to what extent our goals really are what we thought they were. Secondly, it can tell us about the possibility of attaining them; and thirdly, it can enlighten us about relations between them: such as instrumentality, compatibility or incompatibility, mutual facilitation or obstruction, and so on. Relative values put on future as compared with present enjoyments and attainments depend primarily on the development of the faculty of foresight. Even more important is the fact that conduct in accordance with humanitarian ethics, being based on sympathy, necessitates the ability to imagine what it feels like to be in the place of others, which depends in considerable measure on the powers of reasoning. That the faculty of sympathy need not accompany intelligence is proved by innumerable examples of astute tyrants, clever but heartless careerists, ruthless tycoons, and brilliant scientists with a defective sense of moral responsibility. Nevertheless, when reading the biographies of great thinkers one gets the impression that they were rather better morally than the common run of mankind, which cannot be said about famous men in general. It must also be said that the recognition of equitable reciprocity, as well as perception of common interest beyond the horizon of petty strife, and propensity to identify oneself with impersonal ideals, all demand a certain level of understanding. It must not be forgotten, however, that intelligence may constitute at most a necessary, but never a sufficient, condition of these characteristics, for incontrollable passions and neurotogenic complexes may nullify any beneficial influence of the powers of understanding. As a correlative argument, it must be noted that people who gravitate towards activities involving brutality (boxing, butchering, torturing, gainful ruffianism) are generally believed to have a rather low intelligence. On the basis of my own observations, I believe that this stereotype is not far from being true, although there are naturally many individual exceptions. Equally near the truth seems to be the popular image of a bully as somebody stupid. On this point we must also take into consideration another factor apart from the influence of stupidity as such: namely, the inclination to compensate for the feelings of mental inferiority by the deployment of brute force. The argument that criminals in general have a below average intelligence, which might be advanced in support of the present thesis, unfortunately carries little conviction; because what criminologists nearly always forget when they talk about typical criminal traits, is that they can only study the failures of the profession: those not clever enough to get away. It is as if we tried to assess the intelligence of businessmen by testing only those who went bankrupt, or of students by testing only those who failed their examinations. Foresight may restrain people from committing crimes, but it may also help them to commit them without being caught. Balzac maintained that behind every great fortune lies a crime, and according to Mencius the difference between a bandit and a general resides solely in the scale of operations.

Ethical progress has been intermittent and subject to severe retrocessions, but it seems unjustified to maintain that there has been none at all. The two agencies which were chiefly responsible for ethical improvements in social practices (where such improvements did take place), were the attenuation of the ferocity of the struggle for livelihood, made possible by the growth of wealth in relation to the size of the population, and the elimination of arbitrary authority, brought about by the fortuitous emergence of a balance of power. The third chief factor of ethical progress (such as there has been) was the growth of an understanding which fostered a widening of social sympathies and a greater consciousness of the consequences of actions. But as understanding can grow beyond narrow limits only in a large and complex society, we can say that ethical progress has been made possible though by no means inevitable, by the evolution of society in the direction of increasing complexity.

In the following chapter we shall examine the intricacies of the relations between bodies of ideas and social structures, on the concrete examples of Max Weber's theses concerning the connection between the growth of capitalism and the precepts of religions.

CHAPTER THIRTEEN

CAPITALISM AND RELIGION

So MANY LEARNED treatises have been written on the relation between religion and the rise of capitalism that I must give some justification for my temerity in venturing upon this ground. Not being a specialist in the history of religions, I am not competent to criticize the judgements of scholars such as Weber, Troeltsch and Tawney on points of detail. What I propose to do here is to examine the logical structure of the argument, and consider whether it is not contradicted by certain data which have not been ken into account. Furthermore, the controversy over Weber's thesis has been centred around his assertions about the role which Protestant ethics played in the development of capitalism in Europe, whilst the conjunction of his views on the impact of Eastern religions on economic life failed to attract a similar amount of attention. In what follows some comments on this wider issue are offered, but in the first place let us look at the economic impact of Protestantism within the setting of the European civilization.

Catholicism and Protestantism

There are two kinds of argument in favour of Weber's thesis: one of them can be described as the argument from harmony; the other as the argument from co-variation. Let us look at them in turn. The argument from harmony consists in showing that capitalism can be developed only by people with certain characteristics, and that a given creed inculcates such traits.

It can be admitted as self-evident that capitalism cannot grow unless there are people who accumulate capital: that is to say, who do not spend everything they earn. The argument here is that Protestantism, and especially its Calvinist variety, taught thrift, whereas Catholicism did not. No religion, of course, has ever eradicated cupidity, but the disdain for material goods professed by the Catholic Church may have encouraged spending. Cupidity, after all, is something that comes naturally, whereas thrift is not. Thrift alone, however, is not enough.

An economic system whose propelling force is private accumulation of capital will not develop very fast if people are inclined to stop working as soon as they reach a certain level of affluence. Such a system can only progress if those who have already enough for their needs should go on working and accumulating. The connection with Protestantism, particularly in its Calvinist variety, is that it taught people to regard work as a form of prayer, and the growth of possessions as evidence of the state of grace. Another important influence of Protestantism was its insistence on work as the only legitimate road to riches. Other religions, of course, also prohibit robbery and theft, but Protestant Puritanism is unique in condemning gambling. The religious ideals of work, thrift and enrichment without enjoyment and by means of work only, constitute what Weber calls 'worldly asceticism'. It is extremely plausible that a creed which preached this asceticism did in fact stimulate the growth of capitalism.

The argument that the Reformation first opened up possibilities of investment, by legitimizing interest on loans, carries less force because in reality interest-taking was very common during the late Middle Ages, and by no means limited to parasitic usury. Nevertheless, it might be claimed that by removing the need for subterfuge, the Reformation helped to direct investment into productive channels, for clandestine gains are more readily linked with parasitically exploitative than with the productive employment of capital. We can debate how much weight should be assigned to this factor, but the direction of its influence is beyond dispute.

The weakest point in the argument from harmony is the assertion linking the doctrine of predestination with the acquisitive drive. It is difficult to see how an earnest belief that one's fate is determined by something absolutely beyond one's control could stimulate anybody to exert himself. Fatalism (that is to say, belief in predestination) is generally considered to be one of the greatest obstacles to economic development in the Orient – an attitude which saps entrepreneurial energies as well as the spirit of workmanship. What seems to have happened is that Protestants took the doctrine of predestination as little to heart as they did the old injunction to expose the other cheek to an assailant. It appears therefore that this tenet of Calvin's doctrine provided neither stimulus nor obstacle to the growth of capitalism.

The general conclusion which emerges from the foregoing analysis is that, although the doctrine of predestination constituted a neutral influence, worldly asceticism ought to have stimulated the growth of capitalism. In order to obtain further light on this thesis, let us look at the argument from co-variation.

The data included in Weber's essay as well as those supplied by later investigators show clearly that in countries and regions where the Protestants and the Catholics live intermingled, the former occupy a disproportionate number of prominent business positions. In France, for instance, Protestant influence in business is astonishing in view of their small numbers. In this case the explanation that their enthusiasm for business is due to being excluded from other fields of activity cannot be sustained because we would have to go right back to the *ancien régime* to find bars against the entry of Protestants into official posts. There remains a possibility that the mere fact of being in a minority had a bracing effect upon them, but the predominance of the Protestants over the Catholics in the economic life of a country like Germany, with a more or less evenly balanced population, cannot be accounted for in this way. Only in the cases of Ireland and Prussian Poland can the economic inferiority of the Catholics be possibly explained by the fetters imposed upon them by their Protestant rulers. For this reason, these cases lend no support to Weber's thesis, but they do not contradict it either. It could be said that Protestant predominance in American business is due to the fact that they descend mainly from the old-established population, whereas the Catholics came more recently as poor immigrants, but for Canada and Holland this explanation plainly does not hold. The case of Holland is particularly significant because there the Catholics were a minority relegated to a politically subordinate position but with ample opportunities for business activities. In some ways their position resembled that of the Protestants in France after the end of legal discrimination. Nevertheless they furnished far fewer successful businessmen than either the Protestants or the Jews. Thus, even if we allow for the influence of other factors, the data unambiguously suggest that Protestantism is more conducive to business activity than Catholicism.

We can adduce another argument from co-variation in support of Weber's thesis, using as our units of comparison states instead of sections of populations located within the boundaries of one state, and pointing out that capitalism developed furthest and fastest in predominantly Protestant countries. In the world of today only the first part of this statement is true: the economies of English-speaking countries, dominated by Protestants, continue to represent the furthest stage in the evolution of capitalism, but their rates of growth are exceeded by those of France, Italy and Western Germany. The latter fact, however, does not invalidate the thesis of Weber, but only demands that we make explicit what is implicit: namely, that this thesis applies in full only to a situation where accumulation by private individuals constitutes the driving force of economic development. Once giant concerns and trusts enter upon the scene, and the 'ploughing back' of their undistributed profits becomes (jointly with state financing) the chief form of investment, worldly asceticism loses its importance because most of the saving then becomes in a sense 'forced'. It must be remembered, moreover, that Weber's analysis referred to an epoch when the margin of affluence was very much smaller than it is in the industrial countries of today, and as saving is more difficult for the less opulent, worldly asceticism sanctioned by religion was necessary for the rapid accumulation and productive investment of capital.* The important point here is that capitalist enterprise of a non-predatory kind was developed by persons who did not have very much money. There have always been large accumulations of liquid and real wealth in the hands of the economically parasitic individuals and of corporations, but they contributed little to industrial growth, at least in its early stages. With the proviso, then, that it refers without qualifications only to economies consisting of small firms, the arguments from approximative co-variation support Weber's thesis. Nevertheless, owing to the bewildering complexity of this problem, these comparative data lend themselves to other interpretations as well.

In his *Materialistische Geschichtsauffassung* (perhaps the greatest

---

* Another important qualification is that religious beliefs cannot affect economic behaviour decisively unless they are taken very seriously – not practised as a tranquilising make believe, as commonly happens nowadays.

work of Marxist historiography) Karl Kautsky attempted to invert Weber's argument in accordance with the Marxist view that religion is a mere epiphenomenon without any causal efficacity – a view which is contradicted by Marx's statement that religion is the opium of the masses, for one cannot deny the power of opium. Narrating the spread of various heresies during the later Middle Ages, Kautsky shows how the class of artisans and petty business-men provided a fertile ground for the conception and dissemination of ideas which found their final embodiment in Calvinism. For artisans and petty traders, fairly safe behind their walls from the depredations of feudal lords, hard work and saving were unique means of improving or even merely maintaining their positions. These conditions generated, according to Kautsky, the mentality which found its final sanction in Calvinism. This argument has considerable force: the evidence adduced by Kautsky and other writers does show that Calvinism struck roots above all in the cities where commerce and handicrafts prospered. The chief protagonists of Calvinism in German cities belonged to circles connected with business. Notwithstanding these new data, the thesis on the epiphenomenal character of Calvinism cannot be sustained because it fails to account for its spread among the Hungarian nobility, and above all, for the conversion of Scotland. At the time of John Knox, the Scotsmen, who later came to dominate English finance, were semi-tribal rustics famous for their dissolute habits. Knox and his followers made them into the most perfect examples of worldly asceticism. Here then the causation appears to have worked in the direction opposite to that suggested by Kautsky.

In Scotland Calvinism came to prevail without capitalism; in Italy capitalism failed to bring about religious schism of any kind. The case of Italy is particularly interesting because it contradicts not only Kautsky's thesis, but the extreme formulations of Weber's thesis as well: in Italy capitalism was born and prospered without any aid from Protestant ethics, and in fact the Papal See was one of the greatest centres of banking operations in the world. The Italians invented techniques essential to capitalism as the bill of exchange and double-entry book-keeping, and they controlled banking in northern Europe until the 17th century: the main London street for headquarters of banks is still called Lombard Street. At the time of Calvin and John Knox capitalism was much more developed in Florence and Venice than in Geneva or Edinburgh. Presumably one of the reasons why Protestantism had so little appeal for the Italian *bourgeoisie* was the close connection of Italian bankers with the tributary machinery of the Church – a fact which might have had something to do with the external manifestations of piety for which Florence (the seat of high finance) was renowned. The second reason might have been the Italians' disinclination to fight for their religious convictions: Machiavelli maintained that the nearer a place was to Rome the less truly pious were its inhabitants. Be that as it may, the fact remains that the example of Italy shows that neither Protestantism in general, nor Calvinism in particular can be regarded as mere epiphenomena of capitalism.

The thesis of Weber is affected only in the extreme formulations of some of its interpreters: for although the case of Italy proves that Calvinism could not have been a necessary condition of the emergence of capitalism, it does not rule out the possibility that Calvinism, had it been able to strike roots, could have given greater impetus to Italian capitalism. Indeed the evidence from Italy supports the less extreme interpretation of this thesis because Italian capitalism ceased to grow after the end of the 16th century, and indeed began to decline thereafter. The cause for this withering of economic impetus is very difficult to unravel: there were a number of factors involved, such as the diminishing importance of the Mediterranean as a trade route, foreign invasions and wars between the Italian states, and so on. The spirit of enterprise had waned but as it had religious backing at no time, there is little reason to attribute this to the changes in religious outlook – religion may have had something to do with it but in an indirect way.

When we look at the geographical distribution of Catholic and Protestant populations, it seems so arbitrary that it is difficult to imagine that it could be the product of any such constant trend as the development of capitalism. A closer inspection of the process of the Reformation confirms this impression: a single battle often decided whether a country or a region were to remain Catholic or to become Protestant – and as is well known the outcomes of battles often depend on accidents. The princes' power of imposing the creed of their choice upon their subjects – proclaimed in the sinister principle of *'cuius regio eius religio'* – enlarged the scope of chance, because actions of single individuals exhibit less regularity than the joint actions of large numbers.

Although in his writings on oriental religions Weber takes into account the indirect effects of religious beliefs, the explicit stress throughout his *Religionssoziologie* is on what he calls 'economic ethics', that is to say, on the influence of the religious code of behaviour upon business attitudes. But it might be argued that the influence of the ecclesiastical organization upon the distribution of power was of greater consequence for the development of the economy. Some writers have argued that the most far-reaching impact of the Reformation consisted in replacing an autocratic ecclesiastic organization by a looser one, thus weakening the conservative forces of society. Moreover, the Reformation furthered the growth of capitalism by effecting the confiscation of the gold possessed by the churches and monasteries, and putting it into circulation, thus eliminating the greatest source of thesaurization, which must have acted as a brake upon productive investment.

There is another way in which Protestantism may have stimulated the growth of capitalism. A perfectly capitalist society is not viable: when the sole motive of individual actions is the unbridled pursuit of gain, the administration of the state becomes disorderly and corrupt, and the growth of capitalism is therefore impeded. This is not a purely deductive argument because we can see that the countries where capitalism developed furthest and fastest, are blessed with more than average share of civic virtues. In the United States the great captains of capitalism may have been utterly ruthless and even dishonest, but on the whole the civic communal spirit is very strong there even today, and was much stronger when capitalism began to develop. England, Holland and lately Sweden have long been famous as examples (relative, of course) of orderliness and civic virtues, and for their adherence to the principle that honesty is the best policy. The same can be said about the Germans, in spite of their authoritarian proclivities. The case of Japan also shows how civic virtues are useful to capitalism, but this case is irrelevant when comparing Catholicism with Protestantism. It must be noted, on the other hand, that all the so-called under-developed countries are conspicuous for their lack of public spirit.

If we accept as valid the assumption that capitalism requires a good measure of civic virtues if it is to prosper, we face the questions of whether this has anything to do with Protestantism, and of whether it is not entirely a matter of circular causation: for it might be argued that widespread poverty undermines civic virtues, and the lack of them makes poverty difficult to eliminate. It is a fact, however, that if we compare Protestant with Catholic countries, the difference in the prevalence of civic virtues is striking. Without going into the intricacies of the possible causes, we must note the possibility that Protestantism might have stimulated the growth of capitalism indirectly, by fostering the civic virtues required for the smooth functioning of the state.

The contention that Protestantism stimulated the growth of capitalism in indirect ways which cannot be subsumed under Weber's concept of economic ethics, far from disproving Weber's thesis merely amplifies it.

Some weight must be assigned to the complete lack of arguments in favour of the contrary thesis that Catholicism is or was more propitious than Protestantism to the development of capitalism. At most it might be argued that under certain circumstances Calvinism fails to produce much spirit of capitalist enterprise. Among the examples which might be cited to this point the most conspicuous are the Calvinist Hungarian nobility and the Boers of South Africa – although the Boers do show somewhat more inclination towards 'worldly asceticism' and business activity than the people in economically analogous positions in Catholic countries. On the whole, then, if we bear in mind that Weber regarded Protestantism as a factor which fostered the development of capitalism, but was not its sole cause, we can accept his thesis as valid.

Judaism

The volume of *Religionssoziologie* devoted to Judaism is unquestioningly a great work, full of illuminating insights and brilliant suggestions; nevertheless, its central theme sheds little light on the relation between religion and the rise of capitalism, simply because as an economic force Judaism was negligible during its formative period and long afterwards. The Jews were a very small nation, leading a precarious interstitial existence, oppressed and pushed around by mighty nations and empires, and finding consolation in religious contemplation. As far as the evolution of ancient capitalism was concerned the nature of their religion was of no consequence: no matter how conducive to capitalist activity it might have been, the shaping of the economy (even of their own little country) was not in their hands.

During the earlier parts of the Middle Ages the primitive condition of society ruled out any development of capitalist enterprise regardless of whether the tenets of religion fostered 'the spirit of capitalism' or not. As soon as it became materially possible, the Jews began to play a prominent role in commerce and banking but as they were under residential restrictions and not allowed to own land, they were not in a position to take part in the development of industry.

As soon as the restrictions imposed upon them ceased to be crippling, the Jews proved to be at least as successful in business as the Calvinists, and as the successful Jewish businessmen were as a rule just as pious as their Calvinist counterparts, there is no reason to think that the economic ethics of Judaism is in any way less propitious to capitalist activity than that of Calvinism. Indeed it would be strange if it were so, because the teachings of Protestantism (particularly of its Puritanical varieties) consisted mainly of the precepts of ancient Judaism.

Weber believed that the Jews could not have become the principal promoters of the nascent capitalism because they were incapacitated for this role by their 'double ethics' which made their commercial transactions insufficiently predictable. It is clear, however, that this bias does not belong to the core of Judaism and is perfectly explicable as a response to persecution and disdain. Where the Jews were not harassed and achieved opulence, they usually conducted business just as respectably as anybody else.

In his famous book *The Jews and Modern Capitalism*, Werner Sombart argued that the Jews were the true creators of capitalism. He based his contention on a number of instances in which an arrival of Jews in substantial numbers was followed by an efflorescence of business activity and a rapid growth of wealth. This was the case with Holland, Venice, the city of Frankfurt and many others. Contrariwise, expulsions of the Jews were in several instances followed by the economic decline of a city or even a whole country, as was the case with Spain. However, Sombart does not take into account the data which do not fit his thesis, such as the fact that in England the foundations of capitalism were laid during the period between the expulsion of the Jews and their return. It could even be argued that the presence of a very large number of Jews was fatal to the development of capitalism as the Jews were much more numerous in the economically backward eastern Europe than in the countries with a developed capitalist system. The causation here is extremely involved.

Originally it was the economic backwardness which caused the influx of the Jews into eastern Europe: objects of animosity from their Gentile competitors in more highly urbanized lands in western Europe, they were welcomed in countries without a native trading class. However, their presence in large numbers acted subsequently as a brake upon commercial development because as soon as trade came to be monopolized by the Jews it became a depressed occupation. Being isolated from the surrounding population, the Jews were in a much weaker position than the *bourgeoisie* integrated with the rest of the society, and therefore they were unable to resist the encroachments of the nobility; which was the reason why the Polish and Hungarian nobles preferred them.

In spite of the startling achievements of its adherents in the field of business, Judaism could never become a decisive factor in the development of capitalism because it was a religion of a minority of strangers which could never mould the character of any European nation. The Jews neither wished nor had the chance to convert to their faith the Christian majority; and it was out of the question that they should attain a truly dominating position in any country of the diaspora. In consequence, the Jews could use their aptitude for capitalist enterprise when the circumstances were propitious but were powerless to create them.

Weber was partly right: Judaism was not a crucial factor in the rise of capitalism; but he was wrong in imputing this to its economic ethics. These ethics were extremely favourable to capitalism but their influence was always severely limited by the non-proselytic character of Judaism.

Confucianism

Weber's volume on China constitutes an even greater contribution to sociology than his volume on Judaism, but nevertheless its general thesis seems to be wrong. True, everything influences everything in social life, and there can be little doubt that by contributing in some way to the maintenance of the structure of traditional Chinese society, Confucianism somehow acted as an indirect brake upon the development of capitalism; but as far as the direct influence via economic ethics is concerned, it does not appear that Confucianism impeded capitalist activity in any way. Analysing this problem along the lines similar to the foregoing treatment of Protestantism above, let us first examine the argument from harmony – or rather disharmony.

In spite of what Weber says, I think that it is difficult to find among the tenets of Confucianism anything directly opposed to capitalist activity. Filial piety, patriarchalism and family solidarity do not hamper business very much, and were by no means absent from European civilization at the time of the rise of capitalism. Ritualism (which is the factor stressed by Weber) was, it is true, very marked in traditional China, but it concerned personal relations – not economic activities. The general outlook of Confucianism was practical and rationalist. I think that Weber was wrong in maintaining that Christianity contributed to the 'demagicalization' (*Entzauberung*) of the view of the world any more than Confucianism did.

The fact that Confucianist literature assigned a low status to merchants cannot be regarded as an important factor for two reasons: firstly, because it was not uncommon in the ideological literature of the countries where capitalism was rising; and secondly, because it was an effect rather than a determining factor of the existing distribution of power, as can be seen from the fact that the equally low status assigned to soldiers in Confucianist writings did not prevent them from attaining very high positions, and at times dominating the society.

Although many of its pre-conditions – such as well-developed transport and currency, a wide area of peaceful commerce, and a very high level of handicrafts – existed in China, capitalist industry could not develop there because of the fetters imposed upon business enterprise by the bureaucratic state. Officials always regarded businessmen with resentment and employed many means to keep them down. Fiscal extortion prevented if not accumulation of profits, at least their regular investment in productive establishments, which was in any case difficult owing to the official regulation of location and methods of production. That these factors, and not economic ethics, were responsible for the arrest of capitalism in traditional China is demonstrated by the behaviour of the Chinese emigrants to British and Dutch colonies, most of whom continued to adhere strictly to their traditional religion: within the institutional framework of these colonies, their religion did not impede capitalist enterprise, in which the Chinese immigrants were phenomenally successful.

Confucianism, then, did constitute a serious obstacle to the development of capitalism, but it did so not through the influence of its economic ethics upon the behaviour of those engaged in commerce and industry but in virtue of its fitness to serve as a political formula cementing the omnipotent bureaucratic state.

Hinduism

The central theme of Weber's volume on Hinduism – which like its companions could alone constitute a worthy achievement of life-long work – is less open to criticism. In reality, Hinduism did constitute a formidable obstacle to the rise of capitalism, owing to its numerous taboos prohibiting utilization of resources, and impeding collaboration in production by enjoining avoidance between persons of different castes. Although usury had flourished in India since time immemorial, and large-scale financial operations were by no means unknown, the capitalist mode of production together with large-scale trade, was first introduced by the British, and began to strike root as a native growth only when the hold of Hinduism became less astringent, owing to the spread of Laicism.

The esoteric mysticism of the Brahmins had, no doubt, something to do with the withering of the early buds of Hindu science, but as far as the shaping of the economy was concerned, more important was the support which Hinduism lent to social parasitism by making the toiling masses listless and utterly servile. As Weber rightly pointed out, with its promise of reincarnation into a higher caste as the reward for keeping dutifully to one's station in life, Hinduism functioned as the most powerful 'opium of the people' ever invented. Other factors too fortified parasitism in India: frequent conquests, the instability of political order, and the ruthless fiscal extortion which diverted energies and wealth from production.

Notwithstanding these qualifications, Weber's thesis stands: Hinduism was effective in vpreenting the rise of capitalism in India, not only indirectly via its influence on the structure of power, but also directly via its economic ethics.

Weber's *Religionssoziologie* illustrates how a work can be truly great but nevertheless mistaken in some of its assertions; which only goes to show that science proceeds by successive approximations. So, having discovered some of his errors we should resist the temptation of assuming an air of superiority. Given the novelty, magnitude and complexity of the problems, to have insisted on more conclusive verification, and logically more rigorous formulation, would in all likelihood have prevented Weber from producing his works: the first outline had to be rough. It is not our merit but merely luck to be able to see certain points better by standing on his shoulders.

CHAPTER FOURTEEN

FREEDOM, INFLUENCE AND PRESTIGE
OF THE INTELLECTUALS

THE LACK OF agreement on what is an 'intellectual' makes it necessary to begin with a definition, which must, moreover, be free from the laudatory or pejorative undertones implicit in the many current uses of this word. Let us define an intellectual as a person whose energies are devoted to the creation, elaboration, critical examination or interpretative dissemination of ideas of general importance – of ideas, that is to say, which do not bear solely upon the actions of their propounders, or of those whom they advise. As thus defined, the 'intellectuals' would form a subset of the 'brain-workers': the latter being defined as people whose work requires high intelligence and extensive knowledge. This distinction refers solely to the difference in the type of activity, and implies no evaluation. It is a much greater achievement to win a battle against the odds than to write a mediocre treatise on strategy, yet only the latter activity qualifies one as an intellectual.

As always with sociological definitions, we have a large number of borderline cases. Take, for instance, the criterion of interpretative dissemination. It cannot be doubted that the author of *Relativity Theory for the Layman* is an intellectual, whereas an ordinary printer or typist is not. But what about a translator? Obviously, a translator of a Babylonian text on mathematics is an intellectual, whereas a business correspondent is not; but the spectrum between them is continuous. Or take the phrase 'whose energies are devoted'. Clearly, Kant, who spent nearly every hour of his life on thinking about philosophy, satisfied this criterion. So did John Stuart Mill, whose duties at the India Office were anything but exacting. It is less easy to classify people like Walter

Rathenau or Trotsky. We must admit that there are part-time as well as full-time, and temporary as well as life-long intellectuals. This, of course, has nothing to do with the excellence of their contributions: Leibniz was a part-time intellectual.

The proposed definition cuts across main occupations. Thus a scientist would be classified as an intellectual if he deals with general problems – be they problems of applicability – but not if his sole concern is the application of his knowledge to particular tasks. A novelist or a playwright who tries to put across his vision or judgement of some aspects of life, would come under our category, whereas a writer whose sole aim is to amuse or distract, would not. Journalists are likewise divided: a serious commentator is an intellectual, a crime reporter is not.

The expression 'critical examination' does not imply any questioning of the basic assumption of one's belief: such a criterion would leave very few individuals within the set. We shall classify exegeticists as intellectuals, as long as their cerebrations contain an ingredient of elaboration or original interpretation.

Intellectuals can be classified according to the ways in which they obtain a livelihood. Some earn their living by intellectual work, others do not. We have, then, professional as well as non-professional intellectuals, with the usual shadings off. Montaigne, Copernicus, Montesquieu, Cavendish and Darwin belonged among the latter. The former are divided into employees and the freelancers who live by selling their products. The non-professionals can be either holders of sinecures (John Stuart Mill, Mendel) or men of means (Lavoisier, Herbert Spencer, Darwin). From the same point of view it is useful to classify the employee-intellectuals according to their security of tenure, and the extent to which they are directed and supervised in their work. As these divisions intersect, we obtain four sets of employee-intellectuals:

1 Insecure tenure and detailed direction: most research fellows, associates, etc who can be classed as intellectuals come under this heading.

2 Secure tenure and detailed direction: for example, some research officers in the British Civil Service.

3 Insecure tenure and no direction. This variant is not often found nowadays, but it was quite common in the days when the patronage of kings and magnates was the intellectuals' chief source

of a living. In the hey-day of Islamic civilization, for example, considerable numbers of scholars were kept at the courts primarily for adornment. Usually they were allowed to busy themselves with whatever they liked but they could lose their positions at a whim of their benefactors.

4 Secure tenure and no direction: this has been the traditional condition of university professors in Europe.

In preparation for further analysis I should like to introduce another distinction: namely, between the intellectuals who deal mainly with judgements of value, and those primarily concerned with judgements of fact. I know that there are philosophical difficulties with this dichotomy, that most utterances contain admixtures of both, and that our judgements of value affect our judgements of fact, and vice versa. Nevertheless, it is fairly clear that Newton's *Optiks* contains almost exclusively judgements of fact, whereas the opposite is true of the Sermon on the Mount. On the other hand, Aristotle's *Politics* is a more or less evenly balanced mixture of both kinds of judgements. We have, then, two types of intellectuals, whom we might call inquirers and exhorters. An inquirer devotes himself to finding what happens, when, how and why; an exhorter tells us how we ought to act and feel. These types represent, naturally, the extremes of a continuum: Einstein and Champolion should undoubtedly be counted as inquirers, Buddha and Goebbels as exhorters, and Aristotle and Marx were mixtures of both. These distinctions cut across the economic classification.

Freedom

The process of adding to the stock of ideas has two phases: production and dissemination. Freedom of thought, therefore, has also two aspects. The freedom of production is perfect if every intellectual can chose the objectives and the methods of his work in accordance with his own judgement. Dissemination is perfectly free if every intellectual is able to make his ideas available to all who might be interested.

Freedom of thought is not equivalent to intellectual opportunity. Perfect intellectual opportunity means that every person of requisite ability and diligence can embark upon intellectual pursuits. A situation can arise such that those who are intellectuals

WAYNESBURG COLLEGE LIBRARY
WAYNESBURG, PA.

enjoy well-nigh perfect freedom, though the opportunities for becoming an intellectual are open only to a minority of potential candidates. England in the 19th century with its gentlemen scholars approached such a state of affairs. On the other hand, in Poland today everybody who has sufficient ability and is prepared to conform can become an intellectual, but no intellectual can escape close supervision. An important point which emerges here is that a high level of conformity can be secured by selective allocation of opportunity without recourse to repressive restrictions on the freedom of thought. This explains, for instance, why the great freedom and security of tenure enjoyed by English dons and German professors did not engender much iconoclasm in their midst. Obversely, the close supervision exercised over their counterparts in the Communist countries of eastern Europe has been partly due to the impossibility of selecting for loyalty when there was a shortage of competent candidates; particularly as during a social upheaval the outward clues to a person's character lose their reliability. In contrast, in a stable society, with well crystallized social types, certain mannerisms can be safely taken as symptoms of definite attitudes, because (apart from talented imitators) nobody can acquire them without undergoing rigorous indoctrination of a strictly determined type. For this reason, it is possible that, at least in the Soviet Union, as the régime lasts, more effective selection will replace conspicuous supervision. Such a change has already taken place in the army to some extent: the officers are not being watched in the way they were in the early days of the régime.

In order to induce people to do what they would not do spontaneously, we can punish or reward them. It is the old story of the carrot and the stick; although this distinction is not so clear as it looks, for one can punish by withholding an expected reward, and reward by staying an impending punishment. Let us overlook, however, these complications: the unsophisticated usage is adequate for the present purpose. The important inference from this trite statement is the simple but often forgotten truth that outright punishment is not under all circumstances the only method of imposing conformity. Furthermore, it seems that, given the bounds of conformity, the recourse to penal repression varies inversely with the amount of prizes distributed to the intellectuals by the government, or the institutions acting in concert with it, relatively to the number of aspirants. When many intellectuals in the United States faced considerable difficulties in making a living, the hostility towards the social order was much more widespread among them than it is now. The predominance of neo-conservative ideology came with prosperity and full employment among the intellectuals; active persecution (even at the time of McCarthy) played a negligible part in extirpating subversive tendencies in their midst.

In Tzarist Russia many intellectuals were condemned to penury and drudgery whether they conformed or not, but they were seldom forcibly restrained from pursuing their interests. Now the conformists are well paid, and the others excluded altogether. The difference in docility between Polish and Soviet intellectuals may possibly not be entirely due to Polish nationalism and more ruthless repression in the USSR, but may also be connected with the much greater financial rewards given in the latter country to the doctrinally pure.

Among the factors which complicate the relationship we are discussing, the most obvious is the narrowness of conformity. Other things being equal, the more rigid the conformity exacted, the stronger must be the pressure. Moreover, the susceptibility to material inducements varies in accordance with the principle of diminishing marginal utility. It depends, above all, on whether the alternatives make a difference to the satisfaction of bodily needs; and also on the strength of hedonistic proclivities, and on the extent to which wealth confers status.

To make it clear: in an opulent society with full employment like Britain in 1960, an impecunious intellectual, who because of his iconoclasm has been blacklisted by the academic appointment boards, the BBC, the newspaper editors etc, need not suffer poverty if he is prepared to take up a menial job; and owing to the relative shortness of hours of work, he may even be able to cultivate his interests, if he has a strong will. In contrast, in countries like most of the new states in Africa, with much unemployment and in which the workers toil long hours for small pay, but where academic and civil service appointments are well paid, an intellectual without private wealth has only two alternatives: well rewarded compliance with the official views, or misery.

Given the alternatives, their power to determine behaviour

depends on the value put on material as compared with other satisfactions. And naturally, the efficacity of material inducements is enhanced if possessions determine the respect which a person enjoys.

Scarcity of wealth does not entail its high valuation. Indeed, these factors often work in opposite directions. According to the perceptive study of the Indian intellectual by Edward Shils (*The Intellectual Between Tradition and Modernity*, The Hague 1961, p. 40): 'Aesthetic indifference, poverty, respect for the woman's sphere, all enter into the domestic standard of living of the Indian intellectual, and help to explain the bareness and ugliness which is frequently experienced there. But when we discuss the economic situation of the Indian intellectual, it is also appropriate to refer to his quite easily borne asceticism . . . his own needs, his own demands for material things, are narrow and they are not intense. One does not hear him in undignified complaints about the material deficiencies of his household, or about his own small income.' The profusion of wealth, however, need not dull the sensitivity to pecuniary incentives. Practically no American intellectual need worry about satisfying his or his family's basic needs, but as he is classed in accordance with his income, his susceptibility to material inducements remains very great.

The pressures which restrict intellectual freedom can be divided into three main kinds: (1) pressures exerted by public opinion; (2) economic pressures; (3) penal actions. Naturally, these categories overlap considerably. For example, the possibility of public disfavour constitutes a very palpable economic threat to a physician or playwright. Lynching is sometimes a genuine expression of public opinion. Wealth may enable its owner to organize a private police force, while political authority occasions the dispensation of patronage.

It is important to note that whereas economic and opinion pressures bear directly upon the production of ideas, penal action mainly affects their dissemination.

The aforementioned pressures are more effective in restricting the freedom of thought (or another area of choice) if they are focused; that is to say, if the limitations which they impose coincide. Many examples show that this need not be the case. The restraints imposed by the Tzars in their part of Poland on the freedom of culture were obeyed only in so far as the police were feared. Cultural creativity went on in spite of hindrances to the dissemination of ideas. There even existed secret 'universities', with professors maintained by donations. The situation was very different in German Poland, where penal repression was rather less severe, but where the bulk of the wealth passed into the hands of the Germans. A similar lack of correspondence between penal repression on the one hand and the economic and opinion pressures on the other, manifested itself in India towards the end of the British rule, in France before 1830, and in many other cases.

As Gaetano Mosca predicted in 1902, a thorough application of the socialist doctrines of state ownership of the means of production was bound to constrict the freedom of thought because, by concentrating economic and political authority, it ensured that the pressures emanating from them are focused. Yet circumstances might arise under which adherence to this formula would cover the control of industries by self-perpetuating directorates, able to defy the central organs of government. Obversely, the existence of private property ensures neither the separation of economic from political power, nor any discrepancy in the pressures emanating from them. There is not much justification for talking about political power as distinct from economic in an 'oil sheik-dom' or a 'banana republic', or in Venice in the 18th century.

Public opinion creates our language, forms our tastes, shapes our consciences. I shall leave aside, however, the problem of internalization, as it involves the question of partial pre-deter-mination of the will, and therefore, would have to be framed in terms of variety rather than freedom. I shall consider public opinion as limiting intellectual freedom only in so far as the desire for applause and the fear of ostracism dissuade intellectuals from doing what they would otherwise do.

Two factors affect the efficacity of public opinion in restricting the freedom of thought: (1) its unanimity; (2) the possibility of escaping its pressure by anonymity, by withdrawing from social intercourse, or by forming segregated coteries. The operation of these factors depends principally on the heterogeneity and size of the social aggregate. It is well known that public opinion is most irresistible in closed peasant communities, and most easily cir-cumvented or defied in large cosmopolitan cities. Ethnic and religious diversification enlarges the scope for dissent without ostracism. So does stratification, because it supports a plurality of standards. Tocqueville attributed – rightly, I think – the remarkable conformity of opinion which he found in America to the absence of social inequalities. And it is a certain fact that all levelling movements exhibit a strong hatred of individualistic intellectuals.[1]

The influence of heterogeneity in promoting intellectual freedom depends on the extent to which: (1) The dividing lines intersect, which means that the compartments into which the population is divided are not always mutually exclusive – that there is no necessary coincidence between, say, occupation and religion, club membership and employment and so on; (2) The demarcation lines are gradual and blurred, and not clear cut; (3) There is social mobility ie movement of people from one social compartment to another. A division of the population of a city into Christian Greeks, Moslem Turks and Jews, each speaking a different language, inhabiting a separate quarter, not inter-marrying, keeping apart except for business, in no way enhances intellectual freedom. The same can be said about a division of a society into hereditary, endogamous and strictly endo-convivial strata (by endo-conviviality I mean a customary or legal prohibition of entering into convivial relations with outsiders). Social mobility enhances intellectual freedom only in so far as it is accompanied by cultural heterogeneity, because only then is there a possibility of choosing a way of life. This explains why very high social mobility in the USA is compatible with remarkable conformity.[2]

[1] This was admitted, and even illustrated, by the famous Marxist Karl Kautsky in his *History of Communism in Antiquity and Middle Ages.*

[2] This statement does not contradict the thesis of Bendix and Lipset presented in their well-known book *Social Mobility in Industrial Society.* They maintain that the rate of entry into non-manual occupations of sons of fathers in manual occupations has been roughly the same during the recent decades in all highly industrialized societies although they have no data for the Communist countries. Even excluding the latter, it does not follow that social mobility is the same, unless we choose to define it as inter-generational transfer between manual and non-manual occupations. As originally formulated, the concept of social mobility included horizontal mobility (that is to say, movements of individuals from group to group without changes of status) and there is no reason why we should narrow it to vertical movement only. Even in the latter case it can be shown that the rate of entry into the *élites* fluctuates much more widely than the rate of transfer between manual and non-manual occupations which is determined chiefly by changes in occupational structure, and to a large extent involves no changes in status in highly industrialized societies. Moreover, as Lipset and Bendix say themselves, 'The length of the step up or down the

A person's susceptibility to the pressure of public opinion depends also on his prestige. It has often been observed that aristocrats are usually much less concerned about the impression they make than those whose status falls with their reputation. People view more benignly the eccentricities of those whom they regard with awe. Moreover, the prestige enjoyed is internalized: a person becomes (to use David Riesman's terminology) more inner-directed. Other-directedness, that is to say, the tendency to modify one's attitudes so as to fit in with other people, is tied up with lack of self-assurance. It has been suggested that the anxious avoidance of controversial issues, so common among American and British sociologists, is less due to the fear of reprisals than to 'other-directedness' induced by their low status within the academic community, and the low status of the intellectuals in their countries. It is significant, incidentally, that in Britain as well as in America the dignity of a titular head of a university is considered to be too high to be bestowed on a famous scientist or scholar; it is reserved for people from higher walks of life.

Public opinion may crystallize spontaneously or may be engineered, that is to say, moulded by some deliberate and concerted action. We must not mistake, however, contents of printed materials or performances of prescribed incantations for genuine expressions of public opinion. The latter is not easy to engineer – not even for a totalitarian government. The most successful effort in this sphere was that of Hitler in Germany. The Russian Communists were only partly successful, the Czech even less so, their Polish and Hungarian colleagues not at all. The Chinese Communists, it seems, succeeded in this respect better than the Russians, but less completely than the Nazis. Two factors account principally for these differences. In the first place, it is easier to engineer public opinion in harmony with the current of nationalism than against it. Secondly, it is easier to do so when the standard of living is rising than when it is falling. Hitler abolished unemployment, and arranged holidays for the workers. In China the majority of the people were starving at the time of the Communist victory which brought some improvement. The Russian Revolution

---

ladder of occupations might be substantially greater in one country than in another, although in each the same proportion of the population could obtain better positions than their fathers when we compare them solely in terms of movement across the manual–non-manual line' (op. cit., p. 26).

diminished the aggregate wealth, while enabling some hitherto handicapped people to better their lot: this produced a division into a converted minority and a hostile majority. In Czechoslovakia the application of the Communist economic doctrines was felt as a dubious blessing and in Poland and Hungary it brought about a collapse of the economy, only slightly remedied by the recent partial retreat from doctrinairism. Nationalism helped the Nazis and the Chinese Communists; was a hindrance to the Bolsheviks before the Second World War, and a help since 1942. In Czechoslovakia the position was ambiguous, and in Poland and Hungary there was a head-on clash.

What happens when the official ideology and public opinion clash depends on a number of circumstances, such as the cohesion of the ruling body, the means of coercion at their disposal (including aid from abroad) and the urgency of the need to elicit active cooperation from the ruled. It will be remembered, for instance, that when the Germans approached Moscow, Stalin became more tolerant towards the Orthodox Church. When a government can neither mould public opinion, nor completely suppress its manifestations, it cannot elude being influenced by it. In consequence some interstitial areas of freedom of thought may survive even under a totalitarian régime. The strength of the influence of the general public opinion over the ruling section depends on the extent to which the ruling and the ruled are united by the bonds of connubiality and conviviality. This influence is weak where the ruling personnel constitutes a caste; it is least where endogamy and endo-conviviality are coupled with racial or ethnic differences. In contrast, the unsegregated position of the Polish Communist party seems to account for the relative freedom of thought in Poland, which, though severely limited, is nevertheless surprising in view of the structure of the state. Nearly all party men have relatives and friends among non-members and seem to care about how they are judged by them. The party is not – not yet, at least – a caste, nor even a class, if by class we mean an aggregate which is not strictly hereditary, but biased towards endogamy and endo-conviviality. Under these circumstances, the faith and courage of the party men is weakened by the unanimous condemnation by public opinion of most aspects of the official ideology. The independence of the public opinion in Communist Poland is probably due to four factors: (1) the collective sufferings endured under the German occupation; (2) the near disappearance of class privileges at the same time; (3) the strengthening of the influence of the Church; (4) the disappearance of ethnic minorities with which a game of divide and rule could be played.

The first proposition concerning economic restraints on intellectual freedom is that it diminishes as the required equipment becomes more costly. An experimental atomic physicist cannot undertake any research which the authorities do not deem worthwhile. Unlike Galileo and Einstein, he cannot radically diverge from the opinion of his senior colleagues. For the same reason, large scale social research is condemned to triviality: it will be financed only if it is sufficiently uninspired to be appreciated by the officials in charge of the funds. Secondly, the dissemination of ideas becomes less free as its costs rise, for thereby the control over it passes from the producers of ideas to owners and administrators of wealth.

An intellectual who has a private unearned income, on which he can maintain himself at a customary standard, and defer expenses connected with his work, is completely immune from economic restraints on his freedom. A holder of a sinecure, or of a post with secure tenure and no supervision, is somewhat less free, though his freedom is still substantial. Below them on the scale of independence come those who work under supervision, or whose tenure is insecure, or both. The position of freelance intellectuals is unclear, for it depends on the state of the market: if there is only one buyer, or only a few, the independence of a freelance writer is illusory, and may in fact be less than that of an employee working under supervision. This is the position of script writers for films and broadcasts. The emergence of powerful book clubs, the concentration of control over book publishing, the growth in size and the diminution in number of newspapers and periodicals, the linking of the publishing business to other financial interests, governmental ownership and censorship, all diminish the areas of choice open to the intellectuals.

The intellectuals' economic freedom could be roughly measured by the proportion of them belonging to the following categories: (1) owners of wealth; (2) holders of sinecures and posts with secure tenure, and no supervision; (3) part-timers; (4) the freelance (excluding those whose dependent position puts them into the category of *de facto* employees); (5) supervised employees.

To obtain a fuller picture, these ratios would have to be interpreted in the light of information on the nature of the supervision, and on the way in which the posts of the second category are assigned, or to be more precise, on the extent to which upholders of a single doctrine control the appointments. Here again we must beware of taking nominal appearances for reality. For instance, in many countries on the Continent a minister of education appoints university professors, whereas in England this is done by co-optation. Nevertheless, academic life is no freer from control by petty orthodoxies in England than elsewhere. The truth is that the cohesion of informal cliques can be just as effective in imposing an orthodoxy as an administrative centralization.

In a general way, we can say that, other things being equal, freedom of thought is inversely related to *de facto* concentration of control over the economic bases of intellectual activity. The changes in the economic position of intellectuals which took place within the last hundred years can be summarily described as the widening of opportunities for entering the ranks of intellectuals, accompanied by the narrowing of their freedom.

Another tendency strengthens the influence of the factor mentioned above. Allegorically, it could be described as the law of lighter weights rising to the top. More precisely – and with due regard to many individual exceptions – it can be stated as follows: in any organization devoted to some kind of intellectual activity those who rise to the top of the hierarchy are, on the whole, not likely to be the best intellectually; and the larger the organization, the more pronounced is this tendency. This is partly due to the psychological incompatibility between intellectual vision and the skill and taste for administration and practical politics, partly to divergent specialization, and partly to the simple fact that somebody who single-mindedly seeks power is more likely to get it than a person who is distracted by his desire for knowledge or artistic fulfilment for its own sake. This is particularly so in branches of intellectual activity such as literature, art, philosophy and the study of society, where there are no immanently meliorative orthodoxies[1] and where the criteria of achievement are

[1] By an immanently meliorative orthodoxy I mean a system of principles which enable those who accept them to extend and improve their understanding without questioning the basic assumptions, by applying the accepted principles, permutating them and drawing further deductions from them. Mathematics,

vague: because, other things being equal, in the competition for awards the prevalence of intrigue varies inversely with the clarity of the criteria of achievement. This important sociological law is almost self-evident: it is obvious that runners, for instance, can gain less by slandering and sycophancy than literary critics or novelists, and physicists less than sociologists.

The foregoing statements can be verified by a comparison of names appearing in histories of science, literature and art with lists of principals of educational and cultural bodies: there is an overlap, but it is not large. Lest it be objected that it was large-scale research teams that produced such marvels as nuclear bombs and artificial satellites, I hasten to say that the construction of these things by no means constituted a revolution in thought: it was merely a matter of filling in the details within the basic framework erected earlier by unorganized investigators. Generally speaking, we can say that large scale organization of intellectual activity tends to stultify originality. It does not follow, however, that it can never be advantageous or indispensable.

It may be worth noting that, under certain circumstances, administrative inefficiency may promote intellectual freedom by creating accidental sinecures.

Every government tries to justify its right to rule: this is both prudent and satisfying. The nature of an official ideology, and the thoroughness with which a government is determined and able to impose it, circumscribe intellectual freedom. Ideologies differ in the ratio of the judgements of fact to the judgements of the

physics or chemistry are such immanently meliorative orthodoxies. In contrast, strictly Freudian psychoanalysis provides an example of immanently degenerative orthodoxy. Guided by intuition, Freud has arrived at valuable insights through vague reasoning on mostly wrong assumptions, often falling into grave errors; and those who adhere blindly to his principles, and draw additional conclusions from them, get further and further away from the truth. It follows from what was said in Chapter One that the orthodoxies which dominate many fields of sociology are mostly of an intermediate and stationary type: consisting of nebulous and circular statements they do not lead either to truth or error.

Marxism is an orthodoxy which is degenerative but not immanently so. When reasoning within its framework, one neither discovers anything that Marx did not know nor adds to its stock of internal logical contradictions; but as the system remains static and nevertheless claims to be applicable to the reality of today (which is, of course, very different from what it was when the system was created), the views of its exponents become more erroneous with every successive change in social circumstances.

values which they instil. Confucianism, for instance, contained almost solely apodictic injunctions, not tied to any particular cosmology or other factual beliefs. This explains its tolerance of foreign religions, and the absence of a struggle between science and religion. It was not persecution that stultified Chinese science.

Every ideology rests upon a selection of values, and therefore, cannot be indifferent to all brands of exhortation, but the restraint it places upon freedom of enquiry depends on the number and reach of the judgements of fact which it contains. These judgements can be concentrated in different fields. For example, various branches of Christianity prescribed beliefs about cosmology and the supernatural. Later they withdrew gradually from the former field. Never, however, did they concern themselves with interpretations of the parts of history which did not bear upon religious or ecclesiastical matters. Marxism, on the other hand, leaves questions about the material world more or less open whilst inculcating sociological theories.[1] In contrast to Marxism, the ideology which buttresses British institutions comprises few judgements of fact. In harmony with the ritualistic conception of life which pervades British culture, it consists of apodictic, emotionally conservative assertions about what is 'done' or 'not done'. A certain amount of ritualism permits a combination of freedom of thought with a rigid conformity of behaviour.

The pressure exercised in order to inculcate an ideology depends on the relation of the resistance it meets to the determination of its promulgators, and the means of coercion at their disposal. Resistance to an ideology is inversely related to: (1) its credibility; (2) the emotional satisfactions it provides; (3) the docility of prospective adherents.

The credibility of an ideology depends on: (1) the extent to which it harmonizes with workaday mental habits; (2) its newness: (3) its falsifiability. The first factor is a very complicated phenomenon, and I cannot say anything sensible about it within the space available here. The influence of the second is quite clear: habits of thought are not easy to change. The third factor calls for

[1] The Lysenko affair was an excrescence of despotism with the attendant sycophancy and delation, rather than of doctrinairism. The few other similar cases were of very minor significance.

closer examination; particularly as it accounts for an important feature of contemporary Communist régimes.

Religious persecutions are nothing new. The Holy Inquisition was quite efficient, and so was the police of Japanese Tokugawa Shoguns, but the apparatus of thought control in Stalin's Russia was something unprecedented. This was connected with the ease with which the essential parts of the official ideology can be found to be untrue. The tenets of traditional religions may seem incredible to non-believers, but hardly ever can they be directed tested; there is no way of disproving transmigration or immortality of the soul. The gods are high in the sky, the devil appears at midnight in dark forest and caves; miracles happen far away or long ago; nor is there any need to cope with revendications from those whose after-life is not what they were led to believe. Communist ideology may fascinate those who wait for the day of the delivery, and dream of revenge and a reshuffle of the cards, but once salvation has arrived, its orthodox version makes greater demands on credulity than any religion of the past. Surely it is easier to believe even nowadays in magic spells and witches' sabbaths, than to believe that social equality has arrived when one sees others living very much better than oneself; or that the state is withering, when its agents never leave one in peace. The semantic contortions of propagandists are a way out of the quandary of having to make palpably untrue assertions. It is not, moreover, a matter of abstruse arguments, like the controversies about heliocentric cosmology or evolution of the species, but of ocular evidence accessible to everybody who is not a mental defective. Under these circumstances, an enormous army of police spies is needed in order to stamp out all expressions of disbelief. In contrast, commandments such as to be ready to die for the king, or to respect our betters, or to keep to our stations in life, containing judgements of value and not of fact, cannot be disproved by adducing evidence, but only eroded by changes in mental climate. This is why philosophical and sociological enquiry could flourish under Kaiser Wilhelm but not under Stalin.

The traditional religions provided many emotional satisfactions; they gave the hope of a better life in the hereafter, the certainty that justice will be done and sufferings compensated, the comfort of feeling under the protection of mighty beings. The conviction of the efficacity of prayer alleviated the feeling of helplessness which everybody must sometimes experience. Once it is established, Communism offers no solace to the lowly and the lame: it demands self-sacrifice in the name of materialism. This is another reason why it could not survive in its unadulterated form without coercion.

So far we have looked at Communist ideology from the point of view of passive recipients; now we must examine the motives of its exponents. In the first place, we must consider the nature of the vested interests which they may have in it.

We shall say that somebody has a vested interest in an ideology if his power or wealth or status depend on its widespread acceptance. However, an interest can prompt to appropriate action only in so far as it is correctly perceived; every day we see people acting against their interests. So we must pose the question of whether the vested interest in Marxism of the rulers of Communist states is real or imaginary. For it is wrong to assume that an ideology used to justify a structure of power must be indispensable to it – that no other ideology could serve the same purpose. In some cases this seems to be so. We can hardly imagine, for instance, Hindu society without the Hindu religion. Customs of stringent avoidance could not be enforced without ritual sanctions stemming from the notions of uncleanliness and pollution. Nor can a better doctrinal prop for a caste structure be imagined than believing that pious clinging to one's inherited position will be rewarded with rebirth into a higher caste. In Russia we see the opposite: a despotic government justifies its rule with the aid of an egalitarian, nay anarchist ideology, which makes the task of the rulers harder than need be. In all probability a technocratic and paternalistic ideology à la Auguste Comte, frankly offering to the masses prosperity under tutelage, would improve the efficiency of the Soviet state without necessitating anyradical changes in the distribution of privileges and power. It might be difficult to justify state ownership of barber shops in non-Marxist terms, but arguments could be found for maintaining control over large-scale industries. It does not seem rational for a powerful boss, keen on discipline and morale, to preach class struggle and the withering of the state, praise equality and glorify revolutions. Such practices are largely, no doubt, the result of inertia: the ideology under the banner of which the power was won appears indispensable to its perpetuation; but it may be disavowed when the supreme authority passes to those whose careers were not changed by the revolution.

There is, however, one rational ground (rational from the point of maximizing power) for upholding the orthodox doctrine: it is its utility for subjugating lands which have not yet received the dispensation, and where there is a revolutionary situation. So, there is a dilemma between the awkwardness of the ideology for the purpose of internal administration, and its extreme usefulness for external expansion.

The most severe restrictions on the freedom of enquiry into matters other than technology, physics and chemistry, do not stem from the totalitarian structure of the Soviet state but from the fact that the official ideology not only does not justify this structure, but implicitly condemns it. It follows from this, in conjunction with the preceding remarks, that the scope of freedom of thought in the Soviet Union will be greatly affected by how promising the opportunities of conquest by subversion will be.

Even if it is admitted that the orthodox ideology does not constitute an indispensable prop of the régime – that ingrained habits of command and obedience, economic dependence on centralized co-ordination, and lack of immediately applicable alternatives would ensure the continued functioning of the administrative machine – it may still be objected that the party as such would lose its position if orthodoxy were abandoned. This could very easily happen if the doctrine were rejected suddenly and totally, to the accompaniment of an acute struggle for power: but if a gradual, even though radical, reinterpretation took place under cohesive leadership, the party might well maintain its power and privileges. Such a possibility should be viewed in the light of the proposition that, other things being equal, the extent of the vested interest which the upholders of a doctrine have in it depends on the degree to which propagating it is the sole function related to their privileges. The Christian clergy, like many other priesthoods, were occupied mainly with officiating and preaching, and their power rested on the real faith among their flock, which might be weakened by radical alterations of the dogmas. In contrast, the full-time theologians and preachers of Marxism constitute only a small and subordinate appendage of the party executives. Therefore, in spite of many resemblances, Communist parties differ basically from traditional priesthoods, and do not need the same degree of fixity of doctrine in order to maintain their positions.

Given the nature of the official ideology, and the importance which the rulers attach to its widespread acceptance, the dissemination of dissenting views may be tolerated either if the régime is so strong and its ideology so deeply rooted that there is no danger that the heresy will spread, or if the government realizes that it is powerless to stamp it out. The latter possibility may materialize either because there are independent centres of power which can curb governmental policy, or because its administrative machine is inadequate for the task. It must be noted, however, that the perception of danger depends on the sense of security, which need not correspond to reality. On the whole, long established governments underestimate the danger (for instance Louis XVI and his ministers) whereas revolutionary rulers are over-suspicious.

It is, alas, not true that ideas cannot be eradicated by persecution. There is no need, however, to dwell upon this error as it was refuted long ago by De Tocqueville, Mosca and others. But there is another point which, although first made by Hume in a letter to Diderot, has not attracted the attention it deserves. Hume suggested that the freedom of thought prevailing in England had a lulling effect on the minds, whereas the persecution of writers in France was not ruthless enough to strangle thought, whilst sufficiently exasperating to stimulate it. Something similar could be said about Poland today as compared with the West. The censorship there is much more harmful than it was in pre-revolutionary France, and the economic conditions not very propitious in fields other than the exact sciences, nevertheless as far as the valuation of cultural creativity goes, the effect is comparable: thought acquires the flavour of a forbidden fruit.

Influence

The unfettered play of the intellect continuously brings out new combinations, and therefore fixity of beliefs can be obtained only if some curb is put on intellectual activity. There are three factors which can bring this about: (1) restrictive pressures (discussed previously); (2) circumstances which lull the mind (say, a way of life which fosters listlessness or boorish sybaritism);

(3) social isolation of the intellectuals, which blunts the impact of their views on public opinion. The last named possibility requires that (1) the masses are satisfied with their way of life; (2) that the prestige of the intellectual is low. On the whole, ordinary people are satisfied with their way of life if: (1) their bodily needs are satisfied; (2) they are not lonely; (3) they are neither humiliated nor bullied; (4) entertainment is available. Recent improvements in these respects have diminished the influence of intellectuals in the countries of north-western Europe. The marginal role of intellectuals in American society is largely due to the fact that these needs were always better provided for there than elsewhere. We are talking here about direct persuasive influence over public opinion – not about the way in which the intellectuals' activities may affect society by paving the way for technical inventions.

Pauperized intellectuals played an important part in various revolutionary movements. It is not true, however, that intellectuals are always hostile to the régime under which they live. The question, then, is under which circumstances do they turn to subversion. To a very large extent this can be explained in terms of supply and demand.

The supply of intellectuals depends primarily on educational opportunities; often, by widening them, governments prepared rods for their own backs. In Tzarist Russia poverty was no bar to higher education. Many students (if not the majority) supported themselves by giving private lessons or some other work. The word 'student' evoked the idea of poverty. Many died of tuberculosis, owing to malnutrition. To the police every student was *a priori* suspect. England was exactly the opposite. University students were few and with negligible exceptions came from opulent families. The residential requirements of Oxford and Cambridge did not permit working one's way through the university. Moreover, a degree from one of these institutions conventionally entitled its holder to a respectable position. There were practically no destitute indigenous intellectuals. The few self-taught outsiders found bearable livelihoods in journalism, teaching evening classes, etc. True, many of them were impecunious, but their situation was not bad if compared with the fate of the majority of their counterparts in eastern Europe. There was some correspondence between the contrast in their economic circumstances and the difference in the violence of their opposition to the social orders under which they lived. No English scholar lived like the Spanish writer Joaquin Costa, son of a peasant, author of many books, who literally starved through most of his life, and ended it in an old barn.

Roughly speaking the situation in Poland and Spain was similar to that in Russia; France and Germany were half-way between Russia and England.

It may be said that the case of America disproves our hypothesis. There, the intellectuals who were violently hostile to the basic institutions were, like in England, in a small minority; and even they, on the whole, confined themselves to the advocacy of gradual reforms or semi-hermitic withdrawal. And yet, nowhere was university education easier to obtain. This contradiction, however, is only apparent. The American universities turn out proportionally fewer intellectuals: in view of the lower scholastic level we could consider only the postgraduate students as potential intellectuals. Furthermore, the proportion of students undergoing training in practical skills is much higher. On the other hand, proliferation of educational and cultural institutions provided numerous niches for the intellectuals; and though their relatively mediocre emoluments and low status foster mild disaffection, there are none who have nothing to lose but their squalor.

It cannot be claimed that it is the existence of representative government which induces docility in intellectuals, for a very large section (perhaps the majority) of them violently attacked the parliamentary régime in Italy before Mussolini. The same was true of the Weimar republic, and is true of Italy, India and Japan today.

Pauperization of the intellectuals may result not only from their all-round superabundance, but also from a wrong assortment. Often the educational institutions turn out too few scientists and technologists, and too many people qualified in the humanistic disciplines. In pre-war eastern Europe – and the same can be said about Spain and Latin American countries – this led to a pullulation of lawyers, candidates for posts in public administration, men of letters and ideologues, who were all engaged in cut-throat competition. These circumstances largely account for the spread of subversive movements, anti-semitism and other ethnic frictions.

In pre-industrial societies there was not much scope for work requiring intelligence, and many people who had it were pushed into occupations where it was entirely wasted; brains were expendable. The expansion of technology, science and what might be called administrative technology, created vast new fields where intellectual abilities might be exercised. Into these fields gravitate people who might otherwise become 'pure' intellectuals, but feel no overpowering calling. In the overgrown apparatus of public administration there are not a few niches where intellectuals can quietly cultivate their own gardens. So highly industrialized societies found a remedy against the intellectuals' subversive inclinations: less freedom and more comfort. In this respect Soviet Russia differs profoundly from the empire of the Tzars: there are no pauper intellectuals. There are, of course, still many intellectuals in prison camps, though the habit of jailing them wholesale had to be abandoned owing to the increasing need for 'brains'. But the obligation to have a job leaves no room for living like the heroes of Dostoievsky. It is therefore highly unlikely that, even if the police relaxed their surveillance, there would be a large supply of prophets of a new revolution.

Prestige

In the light of an inductive survey of the data, it appears that the prestige of intellectuals in a society is determined by the interplay of several factors, the nature of which can be briefly described in the following propositions:

1 Other things being equal, the prestige of intellectuals is higher in nations which command little power. Many observers remarked that in Europe it was higher in small than in large states. Its level in Imperial Germany, although very high in comparison with Britain or America, was rather lower than in Holland or Denmark. It was, moreover, a legacy of pre-Imperial days. The intellectuals' prestige was very high for a very long time in China, which was no mean power, but this was due to the factors discussed under 3 and 4.

2 Other things being equal, the prestige of intellectuals is higher in poorer countries. In the same way as women and men often find a compensation for their physical disabilities in intellectual achievements, it is possible that lack of success in the quest

for power and wealth induces nations to value their cultures more highly, and therefore, also those who add to them.

3 The disdain for manual labour lends a certain distinction to intellectual occupations (genuine and spurious), but only if they are valued on other grounds as well. In many societies dominated by a military nobility or the hereditary rich, both intellectual and manual work were held in disdain.

4 The prestige of intellectuals is high if educational qualifications are indispensable for attaining a high rank in society. We have here a process of extrapolation: if, in order to obtain a post in the civil service, it is necessary to demonstrate a certain amount of bookish knowledge, then the standing of the repositories of such knowledge is enhanced; particularly if the civil service alone constitutes the upper layer of society. This explains the low status of intellectuals in commercial, as well as militaristic, societies. It also accounts for the high status of intellectuals in China, which has the longest tradition of bureaucracy, and where entrance examinations for the civil service were invented a thousand years ago. These were introduced, incidentally, not so much out of a regard for knowledge as to forestall the hereditary appropriation of administrative posts; as can be seen from the fact that, apart from graft and wire-pulling, castration was an alternative road to high office. We can explain along similar lines why the status of intellectuals was higher in Germany and France than in England, and in England higher than in America; and why in spite of all persecutions it has risen rather than declined in the Communist countries of eastern Europe. There, a massive elevation of un-educated men occurred only when the régimes were founded. Now the acquisition of diplomas and normal bureaucratic promotion are gradually becoming the only channels of ascent. In the future this trend may be reversed by the infiltration of hereditary privilege.

5 The prestige of intellectuals, like that of any other social category, is greatly affected by their wealth. Except for those who inherit property, 'wealth' means current remuneration, and this depends on the relation of supply to demand. There is, however, an element of circular causality here, for demand depends on the perception of need for the services of intellectuals, and this is affected by their prestige, which in turn directly influences remuneration.

6 In view of the fact that true intellectual quality, as distinct from hierarchic positions or the possession of a diploma, can never become the basis on which a whole population can be graded, being an intellectual can confer high status only if it is not determined by any single criterion, such as wealth, descent or hierarchic rank. In other words, intellectuals can enjoy high status only in a society where grading is synthetic (to use Ossowski's terminology); that is to say, where status is assigned on the basis of an intuitive synthesis of assessments in respect of several distinct criteria.

7 Past association with successful popular movements enhances the prestige of intellectuals. This is true of individuals as well as of the intellectuals as a social category. The intellectuals were the standard bearers of the *bourgeoisie* in their struggle against the aristocracy in France and Germany. This explains why their status in these countries became very high after the victory (or partial victory) of the *bourgeoisie*; as well as why it remained lower in England where this was not the case. Likewise, the prominent part played by intellectuals in the Polish and Czech liberation movements ensured their extremely high standing in the resuscitated states. The new ex-colonial states present interesting similarities in this respect.

Intellectuals cannot avoid being marginal. In so far as they are really preoccupied with intellectual matters, and are by implication unusually intelligent, they are deviants whose specialization keeps them away from the levers of power, and who are therefore, like other powerless minorities, always exposed to persecution. Their greatest difficulties, however, stem from the inherently subversive nature of cerebration: thinking is always dangerous to the established order, whatever that order may be. An intelligent person who thinks hard about something, be it washing dishes or foreign policy, is likely to discover a way of doing these things which is better than the current methods; and if he tries to persuade people to put his suggestions into practice, he disturbs their habits, threatens vested interests and brings upon himself the wrath of the lovers of routine. As Bertrand Russell once said 'people would rather die than think'. The subversiveness of intellectuals differs from that of vandals and other disturbers of peace in not being purely negative: no matter how misguided, an intellectual usually tries to create something to put in the place of what he attacks.

As the history of so-called revisionism shows, an intellectual is likely to be subversive even in relation to a subversive movement which he supports, by being undisciplined and critical of the dogmas which ensure the unity of the movement. It is a sad fact that powerful pressure groups or movements cannot be organized on the basis of an open mind but require dogmas.

Even purely intellectual institutions quickly develop orthodoxies and bureaucratic rigidities, not to speak of corruption and clique politics, with the result that the normal fate of the creative faculties of the human mind is to be squashed (except in recent times in technical fields). Only under exceptional circumstances – when the domineering bureaucracies and pressure groups are entwined in a stalemate – can the fragile tree of the higher intellect strike roots in little enclaves of no-man's-land, and push its branches to the open air through the cracks between the power blocks. This gentle plant has, however, the peculiarity that its effusions may eventually erode the foundations of these monolithic structures.

PART FOUR

CLASS STRUCTURE AND ECONOMIC PROGRESS

CHAPTER FIFTEEN

PARASITISM AND TECHNICAL STAGNATION

PARASITISM IS a polymorphous and ubiquitous phenomenon in the social life of human beings as well as in nature. Social parasitism can be defined as a mode of existence based on extraction of wealth from producers without assisting them in any way to produce it. Classification of concrete situations with reference to this category presents no difficulty so long as we deal with clearcut cases: it is perfectly clear, for instance, that a band of nomads, which swoops periodically upon an agricultural village to levy tribute, stands in a relation of parasitism to that village; and that, on the other hand, the relationship between an engine driver and a signalman is that of indispensable collaboration, not parasitism. It is very difficult, however, to analyse more complex cases from this point of view. An absentee landowner who does nothing except collect the rent is clearly a parasite, but with a landowner who administers his estate the matter is by no means simple, because he obviously does contribute something to the process of production, even though his contribution may be defective and his share of the proceeds unjustly large. In passing a judgement of this sort upon the worth of a contribution and the justice of a division of proceeds we imply a number of hypothetical judgements: we assume, in this case, that the said landowner would be able to continue to administer his estate in return for a much smaller share of the proceeds, or that somebody else could do it much better or for a smaller reward. Or take the relationship of an army to a civilian population. The army only consumes commodities, but may it not make production possible by ensuring order and by preventing potential invaders from destroying the means of production? Obviously Batista's army in Cuba, which was useless for defence, could not maintain order (of which it was in fact the chief disturber) and was fleecing the civilians mercilessly and disorganizing production, must be regarded as a parasitical body; but it is not equally obvious that the French army at the time of the Dreyfus affair was purely parasitical: it is not certain that French producers would have been able to produce more had that army been dissolved, as an invasion or a civil war might have ensued which would have caused more severe impoverishment than that produced by the burden of military expenditure.

In cases of complex symbiosis, a diagnosis of parasitism implies a large number of judgements about alternative possibilities of ordering not only production but social life in general. The matter is further complicated by the fact that economic parasitism may provide the ground for cultural creativity which may eventually benefit the toiling masses. For example: modern technology could not have arisen without creations of Archimedes, Euclid, Descartes and many others, who from a short-run economic point of view were parasites because they in no way helped to produce the goods which they consumed. Thus a reasonably adequate analysis of intermediary and complex forms of parasitism (including those described by 'Parkinson's laws') would require a comprehensive treatise on sociology written from this point of view, and for this reason I shall deal now only with the fairly pure forms of parasitism, uncomplicated by intricate interlacement of activities, which I propose to call simple parasitism. Simple parasitism is an important social phenomenon: many societies were clearly divided into consuming and producing classes, with the former giving no assistance to the latter. Indeed, this was the rule since the state and stratification came into existence. Defence hardly constituted assistance to producers because usually it merely meant a change of masters and had little effect upon the condition of the producing classes, which usually remained abject. In some countries priests and officials supervised irrigation but those so employed constituted a negligible part of the governing classes. The landowners seldom took part in directing production. Notwithstanding the extreme exploitation of the slaves, the *latifundia* of the Hellenistic and Roman world were exceptional in being administered as fairly cohesive units of production, as in most seignorial societies the peasants were left to produce as best they could, and the owners or holders of estates, as well as the state, were interested solely in wringing out of them the largest part of the produce. This phenomenon, which I propose to call simple parasitic extraction of surplus (surplus being defined as commodities produced in excess of minimal subsistence and reproduction requirements of the producers), accounts for the stagnation of the techniques of production in oriental civilizations. The causal link here is extremely simple because it is quite obvious that such a state of affairs destroys all incentives to technical ingenuity.

'Before urban revolution' – says Gordon Childe (in *Man Makes Himself*, London 1935, pp. 257 ff) – 'comparatively poor and illiterate communities made an impressive series of contributions to man's progress. The two millennia immediately preceding 3000 BC had witnessed discoveries in applied science that directly or indirectly affected prosperity of millions of men and demonstrably furthered welfare of our species by facilitating its multiplication. We have mentioned the following applications of science: artificial irrigation using canals and ditches; the plough; the harnessing of animal motive power; the sailing boat; wheeled vehicles; orchard husbandry; fermentation; the production and use of copper; bricks; the arch; glazing; the seal; and – in the earliest stage of the revolution – a solar calendar, writing, numeral notation and bronze. . . . The two thousand years after the revolution – say from 2600 to 600 BC – produced few contributions of anything like comparable importance to human progress . . . the crucial discovery (of iron smelting) was due not to the rich and long civilized communities of Babylonia and Egypt, but to a hitherto unknown community, dependent upon the Hittite Empire. . . . The alphabet brought reading and writing within the reach of all. . . . Yet again this revolutionary simplification of writing was not carried through in the old centres of learning, but in the relatively young cities of Phoenicia.'

The Near East, the cradle of civilized arts and crafts, has remained singularly uninventive ever since. Egyptian, Syrian and Mesopotamian peasants and craftsmen employ to this day essentially the same methods as their ancestors of the fourth millennium. Nor is the situation different in Persia and India.

This lack of technical innovation must have been due to inhibitions inherent in the social circumstances, because technology is intrinsically cumulative. The material culture of small illiterate tribes may remain static because its simplicity does not permit many new combinations, or because all the possibilities of the environment have been exhausted (as is notably the case with the material culture of the Eskimoes, which cannot be improved except with the aid of gadgets produced elsewhere), or because isolation restricts opportunities of imitation and stimulation. But the same could not be said about the material culture of the large societies of Asia, within which innumerable improvements were theoretically possible. Moreover, until the end of the first millennium of our era these populations were not blighted with absolutely universal mental sterility, since they continued to produce religions, philosophies and artistic styles.

Ever since considerable states arose through the conquest of one city by another, or of agricultural regions by nomads, Near Eastern peasants have lived under the sway of masters – warriors, scribes and priests – who took away from them everything beyond what was absolutely necessary for them to live and continue to work. A vivid picture of grinding extortion is given in this description of tax-levying, translated from a papyrus in A. Moret's *Le Nil et la Civilisation Egyptienne* (Paris 1926, p. 311): 'the scribe of the treasury arrives to tax the harvest . . . and with him Negroes with canes . . . They say: give us the grain! There is none. It was destroyed . . . Then they beat him stretched on the ground; he is tied up and thrown in the ditch, he falls in the water and crawls with the head bent down. His wife is tied in front of him, his children chained, his neighbours abandon him and run away . . .' Empires rose and fell but the lot of the peasant remained essentially the same. More than three thousand years later the great Arab social philosopher thus explains the general disdain in which the cultivators of the soil were held: 'This degradation is due, in my opinion, to the fact that cultivation of a field entails the obligation of paying dues, thus placing the cultivator under the sway of arbitrary power and violence. Abasement of the payer results, and he falls into misery under the burden of oppression and tyranny.' (*Les Prolègomnes d'Ibn Khaldun*, Paris 1936, vol. 2, p. 346.)

The following extract from an uncompleted manuscript by the late Z. Rajkowski throws a lurid light on conditions in Iraq under the Abbassids: 'Slow tax-payers were subjected to beating and imprisonment irrespectively of whether it was their fault or not. Often collective punishment was inflicted upon whole villages: the inhabitants kept in the sun without drinking, or herded into caves and held there for days in conditions of indescribable filth and degradation. In order to procure cash for tax collectors villagers had to borrow from usurers without a hope of ever getting out of their clutches. Out of the fear of tax gatherers many villagers fled from their abodes and roamed in the country as thieves, beggars or bandits. Although there was no law in virtue of which the peasants were tied to the soil, they were savagely punished for leaving their villages. When the newly converted peasants began to migrate to towns an order was issued that they be sent back with names of their villages branded on their foreheads.'

The fate of the Indian peasants was no better. The successive waves of conquests imposed numerous masters on them – landlords, usurers, feudatories, kings and their officials, priests – whose only concern was to exploit the cultivators of the soil. Speaking of Moghul India, W. H. Moreland says in his *From Akbar to Aurangzeb* (London 1923, p. 300–1): 'The demands made by the various governments on producers were so large that there is no exaggeration in the statement that the administrative activities were the most important factors in the distribution of the national income. Speaking generally, their effect was to leave to the producers very little, if anything, above the minimum required for their subsistence, and to offer the surplus in rewards to energy and ingenuity exerted in unproductive ways . . . Almost throughout India the tendency was to reduce the reward of production to a point where it ceased to offer an adequate incentive, and to attract brains and energy to the struggle for a share in what had been produced by others.'

In *India at the Death of Akbar* by the same author (London 1920, pp. 187–9, 299) we read: 'Bernier, writing to Colbert, said: "No artist can be expected to give his mind to his calling in the midst of a people who are either wretchedly poor, or who, if rich, assume an appearance of poverty, and who regard not the beauty of the excellence but the cheapness of an article: a people whose grandees pay for a work of art considerably under its value and according to their own caprice." He goes on to point out that the degradation of artistic handicrafts was retarded by the influence of imperial workshops, and by the protection of a few powerful patrons, which resulted in the payment of rather higher wages, and adds: "I say rather higher wages, for it should not be inferred that the workman is held in esteem, or arrives at a state of independence. Nothing but sheer necessity or blows from a cudgel keeps him employed: he can never become rich, and he feels it no trifling matter to have the means of satisfying the cravings of hunger and of covering his body with the coarsest garment . . ." Producers as a whole were at the mercy of an administration conducted by men who were accustomed to extremes of luxury and display, and who were discouraged by the conditions of their tenure from taking measures to foster the development of their charge, and who were impelled by the strongest motives to grasp for themselves the largest possible share of each producer's income.'

Speaking of Siam in the 17th century, a French traveller, La Loubère, remarked that no one dared to distinguish himself in any art for fear of being forced to work, not only for the six months legally owed to the government, but all his time and without pay. 'And because that they are indifferently employed in these works, every one applies himself to know how to do a little of all, to avoid bastinados; but none would do too well, because that servitude is the reward of ingenuity. They neither know, nor desire to know, how to do otherwise, than what they have always done. . . . It is no matter to them to have 500 workmen, for several months, upon what a few Europeans would finish in a few days.' (Quoted from H. G. Qauritch Wales, *Ancient Siamese Government and Administration*, London 1934.)

In the Roman Empire the cessation of conquests reduced the supply of slaves who then had to be given conditions which would permit reproduction, but the decline of slavery did not bring a radical improvement in the condition of the toiling masses, who continued to be the victims of parasitic rapacity. The big landowners and the tax gatherers ruined the producers with their extortions, disregarding their own long-term interest. The tax gatherer, 'who had obtained his office by intrigue, came down with a powerful retinue demanding old receipts, presenting a mass of cooked accounts, which no one could check, least of all the simple farmer. What followed resembled the worst scenes in Turkish provincial government, outrage, torture, imprisonment, murder; and all these enormities were countenanced, and actively supported, by officers of the palace and the praetorium, with the aid of the soldiers of the neighbouring garrison.' (S. Dill, *Roman Society in the last century of the Western Empire*, 2nd ed., London 1933, p. 276.) In the chronicles there are cases mentioned of people who fled from exploitation to live among the Huns.

To these examples many more could be added: whether we look at the Byzantine Empire, or Togukawa Japan or the Turkish Empire, or Persia under any of its dynasties we find a picture of grinding oppression of the working by the parasitic classes. Thus in societies which differed from one another profoundly in many respects, parasitic appropriation of surplus was accompanied by stagnation of technology. In China this was also the rule, but it was not quite as steady as in other states of Asia: on several occasions colossal rebellions tore down the fabric of the state, and reinstatement of order after these upheavals was normally accompanied by some abatement of parasitism. The Chinese have made during the last two millennia more inventions than any other nation in Asia, and it is arguable that this was due to the relative respites from parasitism which they occasionally enjoyed.

The undisputed pre-eminence of western Europe in the field of technology dates only from the 17th or perhaps even the 18th century, but its roots lie as far back as the 12th; and it was a partial elimination or weakening of parasitism which made this development possible, as is shown in the following passages from P. Boissonnade, *Life and Work in Medieval Europe* (London 1937, pp. 193–251):

'The movement began in the eleventh century in those Western countries in which the renaissance of commerce allowed the merchant classes to realize their power and gave them the will to break their bonds. The merchant patriciate, upheld by the mass of small artisans and traders, leaning now upon the Papacy and clergy, now upon the smaller nobility, profited by the divisions of the feudal classes and played off each against the other. . . . In the twelfth and thirteenth centuries merchants and workers joined in vast federations, sometimes public and sometimes secret . . . In vain the Church tried by the voice of her canonists and saints, Yves of Chartres and Bernard of Clairvaux, to bar the way to these confederations of workers "of new and execrable name", as the historian Guibert de Nogent describes them. In vain the feudal baronage, and sometimes even the monarchy, tried to stay the revolution by a policy of rigorous and often atrocious repression. Everywhere the movement of emancipation triumphed more or less completely, sometimes by peaceful, sometimes by violent means . . . The more intelligent among those in authority made spontaneous concessions of authority to their subjects, in the hope of increasing their productive power by emancipating them.'

'The general result of the communal movement, which may perhaps be called the first syndicalist revolution, was favourable to the masses who gained a livelihood in the towns by their labour and by the pursuit of commerce and industry. For the first time thousands of men, forming perhaps a tenth of the whole population of the West, won equality and civil liberty, benefits which throughout antiquity and the Dark Ages had been enjoyed only by infinitesimal minorities . . . In economic affairs these urban communities, boroughs, centres of colonization, and communes possessed . . . powers, the extent of which astonishes the historian. Everything was done to endow the mercantile and industrial *bourgeoisie*, in all its elements from the humblest to the greatest, with a body of privileges, monopolies and regulations destined to stimulate the power for work, the expansion of trade, and the growth of wealth. . . . This dominant preoccupation of urban policy . . . had magnificent results. It made the medieval towns living and progressive centres of activity. To most of them it brought wealth, due to the productive capacity of a labour which was emancipated, honoured and protected.

'The emancipation of millions of men belonging to the commercial and industrial classes . . . is one of the capital events of history. The urban commune, which was the work of the merchant and the artisan, took its place in the political and social hierarchy side by side with the feudal lordship. Henceforth it was, for the West and for the whole world, one of the most active instruments of progress and liberty. At the same time it gave the commercial and industrial classes a framework in which they could group themselves and give themselves a powerful organization, and thanks to which they were able to improve the conditions of their existence and for the first time enforce a recognition of the value and the power of work.

'The rural masses profited by the movement of reclamation and emancipation to win in their turn the ownership or quasi-ownership of that landed capital which up till then it had been their part merely to make fruitful by their work for the profit of others. . . . The peasants, resolved to be free, stopped at no sacrifice, no ruse, no means of coercion. Sometimes they offered their needy lords large sums of money, the fruit of long economies, for the purchase of a charter of enfranchisement. Sometimes they usurped clerical privileges to escape from jurisdiction of lay lords. Sometimes they stole or burned the seignorial charters, or else by innumerable quibbles contested the validity of feudal rights. More often still they evoked their customary privileges; they disavowed the lord; they threatened to abandon his land and fly to a neighbouring town or a royal domain, upon which peasants were free. Finally, like the *bourgeois* and the artisans, they had recourse to the invincible weapon of association. They formed rural unions, fraternities and conjurations; they bound themselves together by oaths. . . . The movement began in the eleventh century by a series of agreements, often individual, which fixed the obligations and lightened the duties of villeins; it proceeded more widely by dint of collective agreements in which large rural groups were concerned. This became general in the twelfth and thirteenth centuries.

'Extending to a much larger mass of people than did the emancipation of the towns, this emancipation of the peasantry was one of the greatest events in history. It endowed the rural multitudes, who never in the past had known such a régime, with the most precious prerogatives. For the first time liberty of person and of contract was proclaimed and put into practice among the country people. . . . The rural masses ceased to be passive herds and became groups of men, proud of their liberty and determined to have their rights respected. A new era began in the history of the peasant, and the conditions of life of the rural classes were improved to an extent hitherto unknown.'

The rise and development of machine industry, which required the creation of large units of production, was a complex process, which to be interpreted in terms of the incidence of parasitism would require more space than is available here, and for this reason must be reserved for a later publication, together with the problem of factors determining the incidence of parasitism, some of which have been discussed in my *Military Organization and Society*. However, as far as pre-industrial civilizations are concerned, the evidence adduced here suffices to show that parasitism constituted the most powerful brake upon the progress of the methods of production, and was chiefly responsible for the age-long technical stagnation of ancient and oriental civilizations.

CHAPTER SIXTEEN

VERTICAL MOBILITY AND INDUSTRIAL INNOVATION

THE NOTION that high vertical social mobility is a monopoly of Western civilization is as erroneous as it is widespread; and as technical progress constitutes the most distinctive characteristic of this civilization, the idea came to prevail that vertical mobility and technical progress are inseparable. This view calls for some qualification, because although there can be no rapid technical progress without intensive vertical as well as horizontal social mobility, it does not follow that vertical mobility cannot attain a high level without such progress. Indeed, several oriental societies whose technology was stagnant were characterized by extraordinary vertical mobility. In view of the economic structure, short range inter-occupational movements must have been less massive and regular in oriental societies, but in some of them the recruitment of the *élite* was based on the principle of a meteoric career to a greater extent than has ever been the case in the Occident, apart from the times of revolutions. The most striking example is that of the Ottoman Empire.

'Perhaps no more daring experiment has been tried on a large scale upon the face of the earth than that embodied in the Ottoman Ruling Institution. . . . The Ottoman System deliberately took slaves and made them into the ministers of the state; it took boys from the sheep-run and from the plow-tail and made them courtiers and husbands of princesses . . . [It] . . . took children for ever from parents, discouraged family cares among its members through their most active years, allowed them no certain hold on property, gave them no definite promise that their sons and daughters would profit by their success and sacrifice, raised and

lowered them with no regard for ancestry or previous distinction
. . . and ever kept them conscious of a sword raised above their
heads which might put an end at any moment to a brilliant career.
. . . With hardly an exception, the men who guided Suleiman's
empire to the height of unexampled glory were sons of peasants
and herdsmen, of downtrodden and miserable subjects, of un-
lettered and half-civilized men and women. . . .'[1]

Between 1453 and 1623 only five out of forty-eight Grand
Vezirs were of Turkish blood. Apart from ten whose ethnic origins
are unknown, there were six Greeks, eleven Albanians, eleven
Slavs, one Circassian, one Italian, one Armenian, two Arabs and
one Georgian, which means that 88 per cent of the chief executives
of the state came from the subject races.

The Mamluk régime in medieval Egypt was equally remarkable
although, not having attained such power as the Ottoman Empire,
it did not amaze Western observers to the same degree. The
Mamluks were a military oligarchy of slaves, slaves of varied
origins, ruling an alien land. Originally, they constituted a slave
army of the Ayubid sultans of Egypt, until one of their leaders
usurped the throne. He did not, however, succeed in founding a
stable dynasty. In many instances slaves rather than sons of the
sultan succeeded him. Many sultans met with violent death and
the throne was captured by men risen from the ranks, who
managed to obtain the support of the troops who, it must be
stressed, continued to be recruited by purchase in slave markets,
principally in Southern Russia and the Caucasus. It seems that
owing to their predilection for marrying imported women of their
race who were unadapted to the Egyptian climate, their reproduction rate was below the level of replacement.

It is quite erroneous to believe that social strata in all oriental
societies were closed. Naturally, these societies greatly differed
from one another and were constantly changing in the course of
their long histories. But on the whole they seem to have been
more, not less, vertically mobile than Europe until the 20th
century. The French and Russian revolutions stand out in
European history as examples of the ruling group's almost complete displacement. But many revolutions of this kind occurred
elsewhere. The first unifier of China replaced feudal nobility by

[1] A. H. Lybyer, *The Government of the Ottoman Empire in the Time of Suleiman the Magnificent* (Harvard 1913, pp. 45–6, 196).

his officials recruited from lower classes. Then, in consequence of the revolution which brought about the fall of the Ch'in dynasty, a leader of rebellious peasants, Liu-Pang, rose to the throne, founding a dynasty bearing the name of Han. The highest posts and honours were naturally bestowed upon his lieutenants. During the times of disorder which followed the fall of the Han dynasty, potentates rose and fell with astonishing rapidity. Many of them were barbarian mercenaries. All subsequent revolutions, all of which except the last ended with the foundation of a new dynasty, caused extensive replacements of in the ruling personnel. Similar examples could be given from the history of Japan and Islamic states, although there it was usually soldiers, not peasants, who rebelled. It is significant that in European history from the Dark Ages onwards one cannot find an example of a founder of a dynasty who rose from being a peasant, like Liu-Pang, or a stable boy, like Reza Shah, or a slave, like Iltumish, the Sultan of Delhi.

Revolutions are cases of group vertical mobility whereby an organized group displaces another at the top of the social pyramid. Peaceful vertical mobility is usually individual, though not always. Apart from revolutions there was plenty of individual, peaceful, vertical mobility in oriental societies. We find already in the Old Kingdom of Egypt an example of a commander-in-chief who had risen from the rank of a simple soldier. On one inscription an anonymous father admonishes his son to study hard so that he may become a revered scribe instead of being a peasant who 'always sweats' or a miner who 'stinks like a fish'. Such advice can only be given in a society where there is considerable opportunity for social ascent. The Chinese examination system also afforded opportunities for climbing, by making official appointments dependent in principle on academic qualifications. Naturally in reality these opportunities were not equal for everybody, and sons of officials enjoyed various advantages which were legally entrenched in varying measure. Nevertheless, there were always some individuals who managed to climb from the bottom to the top of the social ladder. According to the estimates of Wittfogel (*Oriental Despotism*, pp. 351 ff) during the period of the T'ang dynasty about 10 per cent of the high officials were commoners, under the Sung dynasty about 15 per cent and under the Ming (whose founder was of humble origin himself) about 23 per cent.

'Chu Yuan-chang, who became the founder of the Ming dynasty, was born in 1328, the son of poor peasants in the Hual Valley, the country between the Huai and Yangtze Rivers. When still a boy his parents and almost all his relations died in a famine, and the orphan became in turn a shepherd boy, and then a Buddhist monk. The cloister, however, did not satisfy his ambitions; he abandoned his monastery and became a beggar, turning, by natural transition, into a bandit. In the ranks of the insurgents who were then multiplying on all sides, Chu Yuan-chang found his true vocation. He rose rapidly until he became commander of a large band, and then breaking with his normal superior, set himself as a partisan chief with independent ambitions.' (C. P. Fitzgerald, *China*, p. 453.)

A striking example of how autocracy favours vertical mobility is the case of Harun al-Rashid, the Caliph of Baghdad, who during one of his wanderings incognito met a beggar and made him a governor of a province. In order to appreciate the importance of this example one must realize that in most of Europe until the French Revolution, only nobles could hold high military and administrative posts, and that an appointment of this sort would be unthinkable.

Speaking of the Mogul Empire in his *India at the Death of Akbar* (pp. 63, 66, 71), W. H. Moreland says:

'Men came to court in search of a career, or at the least a livelihood; if the search was unsuccessful, they withdrew, while success meant the attainment of military rank, administrative functions, and a remuneration, sometimes in the form of a cash salary, and sometimes by the grant of the whole or a portion of the revenue yielded by a particular area. There was no independent aristocracy, for independence was synonymous with rebellion, and a noble was either a servant or an enemy of the ruling power . . . certainly there was at that time no other career in India which could offer the prospect of such prizes, and we need not wonder that the service should have attracted to the court the ablest and most enterprising men from a large portion of Western Asia.

'There was nothing approaching to the orderly promotion which is now so familiar; there were huge prizes to be won, but there were also many blanks in the lottery. It must have been very difficult to make a start, and from a subordinate position attract the favourable notice of the Emperor, but the start once made promotion might be rapid . . . Hakim Ali, for instance, came from Persia to India poor and destitute, but won Akbar's favour, and from being his personal servant rose to the rank of 2,000 (a commander of 2,000 horsemen). Peshrau Khan again was a slave who was given to Humayun as a present; he rendered service in many different capacities and died a commander of 2,000, leaving a fortune. . . .

'The Emperor was heir to his officers, and neither rank nor fortune could be passed on; the most that could be hoped for was that enough would be left for the maintenance of the family, and that the sons would be given a start in consideration of the father's services. Some officers may have accumulated secret hoards to meet this and other emergencies, but at any rate it was impossible to establish a family in a position of open independence, and each generation had practically to start afresh.'

In the early days of the Roman Empire the emperors were descendants of Julius Caesar who was, it must be remembered, an aristocrat. Generals and high officers were drawn from the senatorial nobility. It is true that very few of them descended patrilineally from ancient senatorial families of the republic, but the social ladder could only be ascended in the course of several generations. The 3rd century may be considered to be a turning-point in this respect. From then onwards the senatorial nobility was precluded from serving in the army. All officers were drawn from the ranks, and we see simple soldiers of peasant origin, like Diocletian and Constantine, mounting the throne. On the other hand, it became impossible to ascend through any channels other than the army since after Diocletian's reforms everybody was compelled to follow his father's profession. The accumulation of wealth in commerce or industry, which had been an important channel of climbing up till now, became impossible because of disorders and fiscal extortion. It is difficult to say whether vertical mobility in general increased or decreased. All that is certain is that its form had changed. Military service, and not finance or commerce, was now the sole means of ascent, as these were the times, of technical stagnation and definite economic decline, we can see that vertical mobility will not stimulate economic and technical progress, if it is canalised into non-productive activities.

A comparison between Byzantium and western Europe is very instructive from this point of view. As far as political positions are concerned, there can be no doubt that vertical mobility was far greater in the former. In principle it was only scholastic attainments, mainly juristic, that carried the right to official appointments. Naturally, nepotism and unequal opportunities of acquiring these scholastic qualifications led, as in China, to the formation of a semi-hereditary stratum of officials. Nevertheless, there are numerous records of poor provincials who came to the capital as beggar-students and rose to the ranks of highest dignitaries. Such careers could not be made in medieval western Europe. There all governmental functions were reserved for the nobility. As for military service, the contrast between the two civilizations was even more striking. In western Europe only nobles could be fully fledged warriors, and only barons could be leaders. In Byzantium soldiers were recruited from among the peasantry and the surrounding barbarians. Generals rose from the ranks and, a thing unheard of in the West, some of them, in spite of their humble origins, mounted the throne.

The magnificence of Constantinople was a source of constant wonder to Western travellers, and Byzantine crafts had no match in Europe till the Ottoman conquest. Nevertheless it is true that while new forms of economic organization and new methods of production were developing in western Europe, Byzantine craftsmen and merchants stuck to their traditional ways. In the West new forms of economic activity were being created by 'new men', men who gained wealth and rose in status in virtue of their pioneering efforts. In the rigidly controlled economy of Byzantium, on the other hand, there was no place for innovators and pioneers. The ascent was slow in medieval western Europe, far slower than the corresponding movement in military and bureaucratic channels in Byzantium. It took many generations before descendants of vagabond hawkers became respectable merchants. In spite of its slowness, however, it was this kind of vertical mobility, and not the more rapid kind which existed in Byzantium, that was accompanied by technical and economic progress.

Although, as we have seen, great vertical mobility is not sufficient for technical progress, certain forms of it seem to be a necessary accompaniment. Technical progress involves not only the invention but also the organization of new units of production able to apply new methods. The motives of inventors are complex: it is quite probable that disinterested curiosity is more important than any thought of material reward. But in the case of businessmen, it is fairly obvious that they are motivated by the quest for wealth and power. The attainment of these involves climbing the social ladder. New methods of production will therefore be introduced only if innovating activity is rewarded by a rise in status.

Men whose status and wealth were assured and independent of their efforts seldom become industrial and commercial pioneers. New forms of economic activity were as a rule created by 'new', 'self-made' men. Already in the 7th century BC in Greece there was a conflict between the aristocracy and the newly rich, who made their fortunes by developing commerce and industry. It was the freedmen who were the bearers of capitalistic development in Rome. Vagabond hawkers, not the nobles, created urban industry and commerce in medieval Europe.

'As early as the first half of the 15th century . . . a new class of capitalists began to make its appearance . . . almost everywhere in Flanders, France and England, and in those cities of southern Germany which maintained commercial relations with Venice. It consisted of new men; it was not in any sense the continuation of the old patriciate. It was a group of adventurers of "parvenus", like all those groups that made their appearance during each economic transformation. They did not work with old, accumulated capital. This they acquired only at a later stage. Like the "mercatores" of the 12th century, and inventors and industrialists of the late 18th and 19th centuries, these pioneers brought as their sole investment, their energy and their intelligence and cunning. . . .'[1]

Many more examples could be added in support of this thesis. Conversely, there seems to be no case of a society in which economic and technical progress would not be accompanied by considerable vertical mobility. In 17th and 18th century Europe, France, England and Holland – countries which were the bearers of industrial progress – were characterized by much greater

---

[1] Henri Pirenne, *A History of Europe* (London 1939), p. 516. This theme is further elaborated in the same writer's '*Périodes de l'histoire sociale du capitalisme*' (*Bulletin de l'Académie Royale Belge*, 1914).

vertical mobility than Poland, Hungary, and Spain – countries whose economies were stagnant. In Italy and Spain there are good grounds to believe that in the 15th and 16th centuries, the epoch of their economic efflorescence, vertical mobility was much greater than during the next two centuries, when the number of inventions made by their nationals dropped, not only relatively to other countries, but absolutely.[1] The pronounced decline of Polish science and economy, which occurred in the same period, coincided with the stoppage of the ascending movement.

The importance of the canalization of vertical mobility is brought out by comparing western Europe (excluding Spain) during the modern period with vertically mobile but technically and economically stagnant societies. In the Ottoman Empire, as we saw, vertical mobility was extraordinary, particularly until the 17th century. It was certainly far higher than anywhere in Europe, and probably in the world, except during revolutions. The important difference between western Europe and the Ottoman Empire was that in the former at least some of the men who climbed the social ladder did so by trying new methods of production and exchange, whereas in the latter, as in China, they were drawn upwards by a rigidly organized bureaucratic machine.[2] Their ascension did not depend on successful innovation but on successful conformity. In western Europe a political career was difficult for a commoner; a military career was altogether impossible. It is possible that the small capillarity of these channels, instead of inhibiting, definitely stimulated economic and technical progress by diverting the energies of those who aspired to wealth and power into the fields of industry. The Catholic Church was the most effective elevator during the Middle Ages. The Protestant ecclesiastical bodies ceased to perform this function because the abolition of the celibacy introduced an element of inheritance into the recruitment of the clergy; and it was the Protestant countries which were most successful in the fields of industry and technology. Admittedly, the connection here is very complex but it is reasonable to suppose that the redirection of energies of climbers had some bearing on this superiority.

[1] P. A. Sorokin, *Social and Cultural Dynamics*, vol. 2, p. 150.

[2] China, however, was a less extreme case as there the acquisition of wealth through trade or usury was not entirely without significance as a channel of social ascent.

The conclusion of this discussion is that it is not vertical mobility in general but its specific form, canalized into industrial innovation, which is correlated with technical progress. Industrial innovation, that is to say, must be the way to wealth, power, and high status, if there is to be the progress of discoveries and inventions.

CHAPTER SEVENTEEN

POVERTY AS A STIMULANT OF PARASITISM

THE IDEA that parasitism is inimical to economic progress is not new: Adam Smith broached it, and in 1826 Charles Comte – one of the great founders of sociology, unjustly overshadowed by his namesake Auguste – published four volumes devoted entirely to elaborating and verifying this principle, under the title *Traité de Législation, ou Éxposition des Lois Générales Suivant Lesquelles Les Peuples Prospèrent, Dépèrissent ou Restent Stationnaires*. This great work still remains the most exhaustive survey of parasitism and class oppression. Karl Marx and Charles Comte complement each other: Comte deals with pre-industrial forms of exploitation, whereas Marx concentrates on the fate of the factory workers. As a result of looking at different forms of exploitation, they differed in their assessment of its consequences: Comte regarded it as an insurmountable obstacle to the growth of wealth, whereas Marx viewed it as essential to the accumulation of capital and, therefore, to the progress of capitalism. These views, however, are not really contradictory because reducing the workers' share in the fruits of their labours has different effects according to whether the resulting surplus is consumed by the parasitic classes or used for developing production.

Marx has exaggerated the role of accumulation of funds and of exploitation as the causes of the rise of machine industry. Naturally, capitalism could not have developed without the accumulation of capital. But with slow population growth, the simplicity of early machines and the relatively slow progress of inventions, the amount of capital necessary to assure a moderate rate of development was not large, and sufficient funds were in existence in most large societies. The factors which were crucial in producing industrial capitalism were those which canalized an important fraction of available wealth into improving productive equipment. The influx of capital into a country where the social structure fosters wasteful and parasitic use thereof, far from stimulating economic progress, can ruin it, as the case of the decline of Spain shows.

The causal relationship between parasitism and poverty is not unilateral but circular. The principle of circular causation between parasitism and poverty arises from a combination of Charles Comte's principle that parasitism causes poverty with the principle that in a fairly complex society poverty fosters parasitism. The qualification of complexity is necessary because poverty has no such effect in simple unstratified tribes: parasitism can flourish only in societies in which there are differentiated groups, some of which can exploit others. Instead of 'causes' the word 'fosters' is used in the second component because the effects of poverty upon parasitism are less immediate than the effects of parasitism upon poverty, and can be temporarily counterbalanced by such factors as ideological fervour or the power of an austere despot: in Russia under Lenin there was more poverty than under the Tzars but less parasitism.

The assertion that poverty produces parasitism does not imply that parasitism cannot grow in its absence. Actually, bureaucratic parasitism is growing in the wealthiest countries and, although it is probable that eventually it may arrest technical progress, at present it is even stimulating it by preventing crises of over-production, such as the one which nearly destroyed capitalism in the thirties. In order to clarify the issue we must make a distinction between a relatively benign parasitism in opulent societies, where a fairly large number of people may be parasites without severely depriving the rest, and more malign forms which occur in poor societies where unproductive and comfortable existence of a minority can be secured only by ruthlessly exploiting the majority. Putting it into medical parlance, we can say that tolerance of parasitism (that is to say, immunity to its deleterious effects) depends on wealth. The medical analogy is exact: a dose of bacteria which may be fatal to a debilitated body may scarcely affect a strong one, but nearly every illness increases vulnerability to other diseases.

Granted that poverty in complex societies is in the long run invariably accompanied by parasitic exploitation, it may be argued that this correspondence is accounted for by the principle that parasitism breeds poverty. However, there are reasons to believe that the reverse is also true. Firstly, there are examples of how impoverishment caused by extrinsic factors stimulated parasitism, which then produced further impoverishment. This was notably the case with Italy at the close of the Renaissance, when a shift in the trade routes reduced commercial opportunities and stimulated the conversion of entrepreneurs into landlords and rentiers. Secondly, if the relationship between poverty and parasitism were in the nature of one-way causation, then it would be much easier to abolish them both: it is because they are enclosed in a vicious circle, entangled with other vicious circles, that this is so difficult. We can deduce from general principles of cybernetics that in a system of interdependent variables, containing stochastic elements, only those variables can be consistently maintained at a maximum which are included in positive feedbacks (ie vicious or virtuous circles). Thirdly we can trace the social mechanisms through which poverty produces parasitism.

The said mechanisms exemplify the principle of the least effort: men seek the wealth necessary for the satisfaction of their basic needs, and everywhere where wealth can be conserved there are men who amass it in order to gain more power and glory. If the easiest or quickest road to minimal prosperity as well as to riches leads through participation in activities which add to the collective wealth, then men will put their energies into socially useful occupations. If, owing to circumstances among which general poverty usually occupies a prominent place, productive activities are unrewarding, then men will concentrate on devising ways of wresting from the others such wealth as already exists. In other words, the energies which in an expanding economy will be applied to production, in a stagnant or contracting economy will be canalized into open or veiled predation. Naturally, everywhere there are people who will always opt for parasitism and predation, and others who will never do so; but the great majority can be swayed by the relative advantages of these alternatives.

The social mechanism in question offers an analogy to the mental mechanism brought to light by Freud (although we need not agree with his detailed interpretation of it): when the basic propensities of human nature find no outlet, mental energy turns inwards to consume itself in internal conflicts. In the same way, when social energy finds no outlet in constructive activities, it is used up in social conflicts.[1]

Another mechanism of conversion operates between internal and external conflicts. It has been analysed at considerable length in my *Military Organization and Society*, and it can be succinctly described as follows: external and internal conflicts represent alternative manners of predation; they constitute alternative and mutually compensatory releases of population pressure, as they are alternative methods of organizing emigration to hereafter; finally, by displacing resentments and aggressiveness towards the outsider, an external conflict helps to smooth internal quarrels, and vice versa. Thus, social energies can be regarded as having three main outlets: construction, internal strife and external conflict. The relationship between them is such that a blockage in any of them produces an increased flow through the others, whereas a widening of one tends to drain off the flow through the other channels.

[1] An interpretation of the history and the present situation of Latin America from this point of view is given in my forthcoming book *Parasitism and Subversion in Latin America*.

CHAPTER EIGHTEEN

PARASITIC INVOLUTION OF CAPITALISM

THE CHIEF CONCERN of businessmen is to make money, and their choice of the means to that end depends upon the relative difficulty of various types of activity. So there is no reason to assume that they will choose to behave in ways that are socially useful if socially harmful methods of conducting business bring larger rewards. Many critics of capitalism, most notably Ruskin and J. A. Hobson, long ago pointed out that neither the happiness nor even the bodily welfare of a nation depends only on the amount of goods produced, and it is quite clear that many increases in 'real income' as calculated by economic statisticians are in fact purely fictititious because they make no allowance for such negative positions as the diminution of space to move about, pollution of the air, discomfort engendered by compulsory 'consumption' of transport and so on. But these disutilities constitute a phenomenon distinct from that which is the subject of the present chapter.

Even before Adam Smith it was generally known that merchants and producers tend to conspire to raise prices. However, what I mean by parasitic involution of capitalism is something wider than monopolistic pricing policies – something that does not come within the purview of the economic theory at all – namely, the tendency to seek profits and to alter the conditions of the market by political means in the widest sense of that word. This tendency is absolutely ubiquitous but its intensity marks off the indigent from the affluent societies.

The least laborious of all possible ways of acquiring wealth is to seize what has been produced by somebody else, and for this reason war and politics have a glamour of which productive activities are devoid. Undisguised exaction of tribute is (next to unregularized robbery) the simplest and most transparent form of predation, but in essence this phenomenon is no different from using the machine of coercion of the state for preventing the workers from bargaining effectively or for driving a competitor out of business: in both cases wealth is transferred with the aid of coercion. Capital investment in tax-farming or purchase of offices may be very profitable but socially they are not merely unproductive: their indirect consequences cause a diminution of general wealth.

The gravity of the parasitic involution of capitalism resides not even so much in the waste it causes as in the discouragement of productive activities subjected to parasitic extortion.

As the societies of Asia and Latin America were thoroughly pervaded by parasitism when capitalism began to penetrate into them, it is not surprising that they showed the signs of parasitic involution very early. In a moment we shall look more closely at this process, but in order to understand it better we must consider briefly the situation in the countries where capitalism evolved in a predominantly productive rather than a predominantly parasitic direction.

In Britain, the state, ever since the fall of the Stuarts, was too weak to be an overpowering agent of parasitism, and consequently did not offer a particularly profitable field for parasitic investment. A fairly wealthy man could buy a colonelcy in the army or use his funds for getting himself elected to Parliament, but the gains from such posts were usually negligible and always compared badly with what success in business could bring. Moreover, in Britain wealth could always open the way to political influence and office but not so much the other way round, whereas in Latin America the connection between wealth and political office was and is reciprocal. The relatively limited scope for parasitic investment constituted one of the chief factors bringing about the early development of English industry. The same was true to an even greater extent about the United States. In France, on the other hand, the possibilities of making money through politics have been greater on the whole, and this accounts for the slower speed of French industrialization. In Germany, the state was strong, and could therefore offer a wider scope for investment in politics, but it remained under the control of a military nobility and civil service imbued with traditions of dutifulness which made them fairly immune to graft, and awkward partners for financial manipulations. The case of Japan was analogous in this respect. The Prussian government, moreover, extended some protection over the peasants out of concern for them as the source of recruits for the army. Such considerations never carried any weight with the governments of countries where the supply of manpower was always more plentiful than that of arms.

Taking western Europe and North America as a whole, we can say that where the state was strong it was not in the hands of capitalists, and where it was more or less in their hands it was too weak and restricted in its activities to become their chief tool for making money. When the obstacles to parasitic involution no longer operated new restraints appeared in the shape of democratic government and organized labour which prevented or at least attenuated exploitation. In the United States, where the traditional monarchic and nobiliary constraints never existed, the early establishment of political democracy provided more than a substitute, whilst the abundance of free land greatly enhanced the bargaining power of labour.

The history of imperial Rome provides the best example of how capitalism may strangle itself through parasitic involution. That there was capitalism in ancient Rome cannot be doubted because, notwithstanding the absence of machine industry, all the essential features of a capitalist social structure were present. These were – the legal framework appropriate to commercial and financial transactions, highly developed monetary circulation and banking, gainful employment of capital, production for the market carried on in large establishments. However, the large agricultural and industrial establishments were products of mere concentration of ownership and their methods of production were not more advanced than those employed in very small units. The large industrial establishments consisted of a multiplicity of technically independent small units jointed only because capital could be invested in slave artisans. But the biggest field for the investment of capital consisted of land tilled by slaves, usury and tax farming, the latter amounting to no more than organized robbery. Within such a structure the influx of gold from the conquered provinces could only stimulate parasitic exploitation, which became so extreme that it seriously impoverished the lands of the empire, and stimulated civil wars which finally ruined them, causing the decay of towns and the disintegration of the economy into isolated self-sufficient domains based on serfdom.

An undisputed dominance of capitalists tends to produce a parasitic involution of capitalism, and thus to arrest any progress requiring development of production techniques and accumulation of equipment. On the other hand, the subjection of capitalist entrepreneurs is equally inimical to the growth of capitalism because it exposes them to spoliation and makes orderly pursuit of gain impossible. Extreme subjection also fosters parasitism of an interstitial kind: of usurers thriving in the shadow of potentates and satraps, as was the case in the Orient. Capitalism tends towards a productive orientation when the capitalist entrepreneurs can neither use coercion for the purpose of parasitic exploitation, nor are so devoid of strength as to be exposed to exploitation themselves – in other words, when businessmen are too weak to prey upon the other classes, but too strong to be preyed upon. Such a situation – which I propose to call the situation of equipendency – requires a certain degree of differentiation and segregation between the business *élite* and the political *élite*, or at least an influential part thereof. An important implication of the principle of equipendency is that capitalism can function beneficently only in a society where money cannot buy everything, because if it can, then the power of wealth can have no counterweight and parasitic involution ensues.

Prevalence of graft increases the power of money because it nullifies the force of legal constraints and reduces to impotence even those rulers who might be personally incorruptible; and for this reason governments of countries afflicted by graft seldom oppose socially harmful uses of wealth. Under these circumstances politics becomes a strictly money-making activity, and capitalist groups invest large sums in it – an expenditure equally wasteful but much more pernicious than advertising.

Bribing officials, paying and arming supporters, buying votes, subsidizing the Press, bring rewards in the shape of concessions, permits, appointments, contracts and the leniency of tax-collectors. The nature of such transactions prevents us from discovering the size of the sums involved but we can be fairly certain that they consume a substantial part of the available capital.

Where capitalism has benefited the workers, it has done so by enabling them to obtain higher wages. In the under-developed countries this did not happen, because the population growth kept pace with or outstripped the growth of production, while the arm of the state was continually used to weaken the bargaining position of the workers.

Even when the firms were small, it was clear that only by organizing themselves could the workers win improvements in their treatment and pay or even avoid deterioration. Owners of capital enjoy an enormous advantage in bargaining over those who live from hand to mouth. So long as the employers compete with each other for labour, while the accumulation of capital outstrips the growth of the population, the wages may rise even in the absence of effective unions, but the demand for labour ceases to have much influence upon wages once concentration of economic control deprives the employees of choice – to put it into more technical language, once the demand for labour becomes monopsonic. Now, whereas in western Europe the development of the trade unions more or less kept pace with the process of industrial concentration, whilst there was hardly any movement towards concentration in agriculture at all, in the so-called under-developed parts of the world concentration of economic control was always far in advance of unionization of labour. The large estate anteceded capitalism by a long stretch, and capitalism came from abroad in the form of large companies, backed by the power of foreign governments, which faced a 'pulverized' and degraded indigenous proletariat. These companies acquired the positions of the only buyers of labour over wide areas.

In countries where capitalism was beneficent wages rose as the trade unions grew in size and strength. Their growth was made possible by a number of conditions of which the simplest and most obvious was tolerance on the part of the governments, the consequence of the fairly democratic character of the state. In the violent atmosphere of poor countries there was never much room for such tolerance, and the state has usually functioned as the employers' policeman; and trade unions cannot achieve very much against the police.

In North America the development of the unions was later than in Europe but until almost the end of the last century the workers had the great advantage of being able to acquire land without any outlay of capital. Not all of them 'went west' but enough did so to relieve the pressure on the market for labour and to keep the wages far above those prevailing in the richest countries of Europe. Neither in Latin America nor in Asia did such opportunities of escaping poverty ever exist, partly because tropical lands are less easy to bring under cultivation, but chiefly because the land had been pre-empted by the owners of large estates.[1]

Although unionization has made great strides in those countries during the recent decades, it has strengthened only the position of the privileged sectors of the working class, and failed to improve the lot of the majority whose bargaining power is undermined by the rapid growth of their numbers; and so long as the practice of birth control does not strike root among them there is no way in which the situation can be remedied. As Francis Place observed a hundred years ago, the limitation of births is the most effective form of strike, but like other forms of strike it is difficult to practise in conditions of abject misery.

A thorough involvement of businessmen in political strife and graft not only gives them harmful means to keep wages down but also affects adversely the possibilities of small businessmen who cannot use political influence as effectively as the big capitalists. Particularly important in this context is the stranglehold which small cliques of big capitalists have on credit facilities, which enables them to make enormous profits on usury. The cornering of credit facilities largely accounts for the high degree of concentration of control over industry in the underdeveloped countries.

The purchasing power of the population cannot be suddenly increased because it is limited by the amount of goods produced, which is limited by the existing skills, equipment and resources; whose growth depends on the demand for their products. As is well known, economic expansion consists of a beneficent circle of increasing production creating demand for the goods, which in turn stimulates the growth of production and so on; whereas constriction or stagnation create the opposite – vicious circles. Deprivation of the workers of the benefits of an increase in production is not only unjust, but it prevents the expansion of the economy, by restricting the market. Transfers of the purchasing power from the masses to the privileged few act as a brake upon the growth of production because they reduce the market for goods which can be produced cheaply in large quantities, and swell the

[1] See my *Parasitism and Subversion in Latin America*, Part II.

demand for luxury goods and personal services. Furthermore, they lower the efficiency of labour by debilitating the workers and depriving them of incentives. There would be some advantage in an extremely unequal distribution of income if the rich invested most of their wealth in expanding production, but this is not at all the case in indigent societies.

Karl Marx had good grounds for believing that the misery of the proletariat cannot disappear under the capitalist system. The movement of wages at the time when he wrote the *Communist Manifesto* was in fact downward and many hitherto prosperous artisans were being reduced to the status of miserable wage earners. The so-called law of the Increasing Misery of the Proletariat was no doubt a rhetorical exaggeration because Marx must have known that misery cannot go deeper than the subsistence minimum, but the statement that the proletariat would comprise an increasingly large part of the population of capitalist countries was a perfectly valid and simple inference from the existing trends, which had been made by other economists before Marx. The view that the majority of the wage earners were condemned to misery for ever was expounded by many apologists of the '*laissez-faire*', and found its classic formulation in Ricardo's *Iron Law of Wages*.

Neither Ricardo nor Marx were wrong in their analysis of the situation which existed at the time. Indeed, without factors which entered upon the scene after the appearance of *Das Kapital* the fate of the working class would not have improved notwithstanding the growth of production. The factors which altered the situation, and made Marx's analysis no longer applicable, were three: the decline of the birth rate, the development of trade unionism and the accession of the lower classes to full political rights. The relationship between these trends was that of interdependence, and there was the same relationship between them and the growth of production. The combined effect of all the four factors was to prevent the capitalists from appropriating all the fruits of technical progress (which would arrest it) and to raise the standard of living of the workers. In the poor non-Communist countries the persistence of extremely high birth rates, the late growth and continuous weakness of trade unionism and the undemocratic character of the political institutions ensure that the analysis which Marx made of England a hundred years ago is applicable to the present situation. Functioning under the conditions just described, the system of free capitalist enterprise builds a pyramid of upper-class luxury upon the foundation of the misery of the masses.

Without restraints from institutions rooted in sentiments other than the desire for private gain, capitalism has a bent towards predation – and therefore self-strangulation – whilst the trade unions, which under more propitious circumstances might help to direct it into more productive channels, act as agencies of disruption rather than of orderly and reasonable defence of the interests of the workers, thus stimulating instead of dampening the tendency of the businessmen to seek quick predatory gains to the detriment of long range, socially useful investment.

BOOK THREE

Case Studies

WAYNESBURG COLLEGE LIBRARY
WAYNESBURG, PA.

PART ONE

RACIAL CONFLICT

CHAPTER NINETEEN

ASPECTS OF SOUTH AFRICAN SOCIETY

Rationality of Racial Discrimination

TREATING PERSONS of another race inequitably is commonly dubbed 'racial prejudice', and condemned not merely as ethically wrong but as irrational. This is correct enough as far as the beliefs justifying discriminatory practices are concerned; for there can be no doubt that most notions of racial characteristics belong to the world of fiction. It does not follow, however, that the practices of discrimination themselves must always be irrational. As far as ideologies are concerned, it is quite clear that nearly all the arguments used to justify racial discrimination are invalidated by the mere fact that such discrimination is imposed: because if the Negroes were in fact incapable of learning difficult subjects, there would be no point in laws and riots designed to keep them out of the universities. The anti-semites of eastern Europe were (unlike their German counterparts) more logical when they tried to justify resorting to violence and clamouring for discriminatory laws by the needs of defence against the 'devilish cleverness' of the Jews.

There are good reasons for interpreting racialist ideologies as (to use Pareto's term) derivations – that is to say, as beliefs which are determined by proclivities and interests – which does not mean that such ideologies, once deeply rooted, cannot perpetuate the conditions which brought them into existence. It does follow, however, that attempting to eradicate racialism by pointing out that it is based on intellectual error cannot be much more effective than a cure against fever consisting of cooling the patient.

What, then, is the evidence that intellectual error plays a minor part in producing racial discrimination? The first argument in favour of this thesis comes from psychology: psychiatrists discovered long ago that delusions are impervious to rational argument. A mania of grandeur certainly need not develop from an accumulation of plausible mistakes about one's achievements. Secondly, racial doctrines usually contain such absurdities that only a firm will to believe can account for their acceptance. For instance, in spite of complete absence of racial differences between the nobles and the peasants in Poland, the former used to justify their privileges by claiming that they were descended from Japhet, and the peasants from Ham, which is exactly the same argument as the Boers of South Africa still use. Under the *ancien régime* the French nobles claimed (without any factual justification) that they were descended from the Franks (a supposedly superior race) and the commoners from the Gauls. This argument was later turned against them by the revolutionaries who used it to justify the expulsion and extermination of the nobility. So we see that fictitious racial differences are readily invented in order to justify hostile actions. Such beliefs are rational and irrational at the same time: they are irrational in their content, whilst being rational in the sense of subserving certain interests and desires.

Naturally, a certain kind of behaviour may promote the selfish interests of individuals very well, whilst being harmful to the interests of the community, but it cannot be classified as irrational in so far as the individuals in question do not care about the good of the community. Anyway, it can easily be shown that racial discrimination can be rational in the sense of furthering the satisfaction of two basic and universal cravings: cupidity and conceit. It can also be demonstrated that once hostility strikes root, oppression may be perpetuated out of fear of vengeance.

Racial discrimination enables South African whites to live much more comfortably than they would otherwise be able to do. This applies above all to people who possess neither the wealth nor skill which would enable them to remain in a privileged position if the non-whites were allowed to compete with them for jobs. Barring confiscation, a rich man would not need to fear poverty just because the members of the subject race were permitted to accumulate capital: it would take several generations before an African capitalist could challenge an Oppenheimer. The same is true to a lesser extent about scientists, physicians, managers and other highly skilled professionals who could not be replaced during their lifetime. In contrast, the lower grades of public and private employees would lose at least two-thirds of their income if the markets for their labour ceased to be protected from African competition, because most of them could be replaced by Africans overnight without any loss of productivity. A bricklayer, who must be of European race, earns more in an hour than the African who brings the bricks to him does in a day. Such differences in remuneration could not be maintained if the Africans were not forbidden to lay bricks and form unions. These circumstances explain why the upper classes are less rabidly racialist than the white workers and clerks, let alone the 'poor whites' who are notorious for their inclination to insult the Africans. This impression has been confirmed by a statistical enquiry carried out by psychologists of the University of Witwatersrand, who ascertained a negative correlation between socio-economic status and responses to questionnaires indicating hostility towards the Africans. The greater frequency of vulgar manifestations of this hostility among the lower classes is also due to the more numerous contacts with Africans who are not their servants, and to a lesser concern for manners in general.

The supreme importance of the racial division in South African society proves that the relationship to the means of production by no means determines economic interests: in spite of considerable efforts by liberal, socialist and Communist organizers, white wage-earners remain staunchly racialist, and always side with the employers against the African wage-earners. Whatever we might think about the moral value of this attitude, a simple calculation shows that from the point of view of their own material interests, their behaviour is perfectly rational and cannot be described as prejudice. The whites constitute about one-fifth of the population, and consume about three-quarters of the national product. Should the available wealth be distributed in the way it is in Britain, let alone evenly, the great majority of the whites would be reduced to poverty because the product per head is low. It might be said, of course, that the abolition of the colour bar would stimulate economic progress so much that South Africa would become one of the rich countries, but it cannot be proved conclusively that this would be the outcome, and in any case the general benefit would materialize in a fairly distant future, whereas a redistribution of wealth would cause losses to the privileged almost at once.[1] In spite of its gold, South Africa is not a fabulously rich country and much of its area is unfit for cultivation. With more efficient agricultural methods, it could feed a considerably larger population, but the birthrate of the Africans is so high that the growth of the population might nullify the increment of wealth. Furthermore, to live really comfortably one needs to be served: the easy life of the privileged requires that some people should be poor enough to wish to be domestic servants. Under conditions of equal opportunity for all races, the majority of white South Africans would have to work much harder than they do, even if the income per head were raised to the level of Canada or Australia.

From the point of view of the economic interests of the Africans, the incentives to fight are greater than anywhere else in Africa, because a much larger slice of wealth is at stake. In West Africa only the top positions were reserved for Europeans, and for this reason the attainment of independence benefited only the few who stepped into the shoes of the colonial administrators. In South Africa, on the other hand, abolition of the colour bar would give to large multitudes the prospects of improving their lot.

Next to the desire for wealth, the wish to have opportunities to feel superior is the second most important cause of racial discrimination; and in certain situations may be the most important cause. The fact that open manifestations of hostility and disdain become more frequent as we go down the social ladder of the privileged race can be easily explained in the light of this consideration, because it is only to be expected that those who have no other grounds for feeling superior to others, will cling all the more tenaciously to the only criterion which enables them to look down on somebody. Probably the colour bar in the USA stems almost entirely from many people's desire to have somebody to despise. The economic benefits accruing to the whites as a result of discrimination are much smaller than in South Africa

[1] This fact accounts for the anti-capitalist streak in the ideology of the National Party, many of whose supporters realize that a free play of the market forces, unfettered by legal and customary restrictions on the economic activities of the Africans, would undermine the privileges and lower the standard of living of the common whites. It also stimulates antisemitism, as it is widely believed that Jewish businessmen are especially inclined to be guided solely by economic criteria in selecting their personnel.

because, in the first place, the numerical proportions are very different: even in the Deep South the Negroes are in a minority, and therefore, by keeping the wealth which without discrimination would be possessed by the Negroes in the hands of the whites, the average wealth of the latter cannot be increased so substantially. Secondly, the restrictions on the earning capacity of the Negroes in the southern states are mild in comparison with what goes on in South Africa. For this reason, an interpretation of the colour bar in terms of economic benefits, which fits South Africa, is not very relevant to the case of the southern states, and hardly at all to the USA as a whole. It seems that in the highly competitive American society, with its cruel creed that not getting on amounts to a failure which must be a person's own fault, there are many people who suffer from what American psychologists call 'status anxiety', and they find a consolation in fastening upon a dividing line which places them above a large number of their fellows in virtue of indelible features.

Once a clearcut superposition of races comes into existence, a situation is created in which it is quite rational for its beneficiaries to try to perpetuate it. Even those members of the privileged race who are against racialism as a matter of principle, may find themselves in the position of having to take the side of their own race. The reason is very obvious: the fear of vengeance which will fall indiscriminately on good and cruel masters. There is something incredibly naïve in the faith of many liberals in the power of democratic elections to cure hatreds. As far as South Africa is concerned, I have not the slightest doubt that elections would bring a party of Bantu nationalists to power, possessed by the understandable desire to avenge their past sufferings. There is no reason whatsoever to expect that the blacks would be kinder to the whites than the whites are to the blacks: as among the whites, demagogues, ready to play upon racial hatred for the sake of their careers, would overbid the moderates. Even without the fearsome burden of the accumulated thirst for vengeance, the history of minorities does not encourage optimism as to their fate. It may be, of course, that by persisting in their ways the white South Africans are preparing for themselves a fate even worse than it need be, but their prospects are none too bright in any case, and it is perfectly rational behaviour to delay the day of doom.

Deeply rooted mutual hatred and well-crystallized nationalism make racial fusion utterly impossible. Even in Portuguese Angola and Mozambique this solution to racial conflicts is impracticable. As we are speaking of rationality, I must point out that the desire to preserve national identity is not usually considered as wicked or stupid. If we condemn neither the Jews for not dissolving themselves into the mass of the Gentiles, nor the Poles and the Irish for refusing to become German or English, we have no right to blame the Afrikaners for clinging to their identity as a nation. Another consideration which must also be borne in mind is that racial conflicts are not the only possible conflicts, and that there is no way of proving that a new nation which would emerge from fusion would not resemble those which inhabit the area around the Caribbean which are plagued by violence, corruption and starvation. This might result from a dissolution of customs conducive to regularity in political behaviour.

Analogous arguments cannot be applied to the USA. Being a minority, the American Negroes cannot start oppressing the whites, particularly as they do not form a nation in any sense: nearly all of them are mulattoes, many are difficult to distinguish from people of purely European ancestry, and all they want is to be accepted as Americans with full rights. In contrast, the Bantu of South Africa have their own languages, which are now in the process of concrescence, they have a national anthem and the conviction that the land really belongs to them.

Given the geographical distribution of the population and other circumstances, the white South Africans are faced with the dilemma: to oppress or be oppressed, with rather uncertain prospects of being able to remain the oppressors very much longer. The only measure which could reduce the danger of being massacred one day would be a partition of the country combined with sorting out the population. This would be a true 'apartheid'; for 'apartheid' as practised now is merely another name for colour bar and the policy of 'keeping the native in his place'. Under the present 'apartheid' the line which keeps people of different races apart is horizontal not vertical: it is the barrier between the master and the servant.

Partition would demand enormous sacrifices on the part of the whites: they would have to keep for themselves only the southern part of the country and abandon the gold, diamond and uranium fields. Even if they resorted to the frightfully cruel policy of driving the African population into the peripheral regions or beyond the frontiers into Mozambique and Angola, even then they would lose enormously because, although they would have ample resources, they would have to do all the work themselves. Only on the basis of an unrealistically optimistic view of human nature could we expect a voluntary partition – particularly a partition which would not amount to a *de facto* extermination of the African population. Moreover, from the point of view of the whites the motive which could effectively prompt such a course would be the wish to forestall an even worse fate for their descendants. From the egotistic point of view of those making decisions now, the only rational thing to do is to hang on to their privileges as long as they can.

It cannot be overemphasized that to show that racial discrimination may be rational from the point of view of the selfish interests of the whites, does not amount to arguing in favour of its ethical acceptability. From the point of view of the African it is even more rational to try to loosen the fetters and eventually to break them. Nor do I think that the policy of the National Party promotes its proclaimed aims in all ways. On the contrary: its blatancy, and the needless humiliations of the Africans are partly motivated by the fanaticism of the leaders themselves, but even more, I think, by the desire to win the votes of the most ignorant part of the electorate. Jan Smuts was just as much of a racialist as Malan and Verwoerd, but he knew that hypocrisy is the best policy. One of the most stupid policies of the present government is labelling as a Communist anybody who is sympathetic to the Africans. By doing this they are instilling into the minds of the Africans the idea that the Communists are their only friends.

The absence of lynchings in South Africa can be easily explained: here the apparatus of the state fully backs racial discrimination, and therefore, there is no need for private violence to enforce it.

The Stratification of the White Population

An analysis of the stratification of the white population must take into account a certain degree of separateness of the English and Afrikaner sections, each of which exhibits certain peculiarities in this respect. Nevertheless, there are a number of general features. In comparison with Europe outside Scandinavia, the most salient feature of this stratification is the relative attenuation of what is called social distance, in spite of great differences in wealth. This attenuation is, above all, due to the mere fact that the whites do not constitute a complete society, but only the upper layer of a multi-racial conglomerate: as all whites feel they are standing together against the non-whites, the internal differences lose some of their weight – which is just another exemplification of the principle that hostility towards outsiders strengthens the solidarity of a group. The same principle manifests itself, moreover, in the fact that the National Party, which outbids the United Party in propagating and carrying out measures designed 'to keep the natives in their place', espouses the cause of equality among the whites to a greater extent: it does in fact to some extent protect the interests of the poor whites against the immediate interests of the employers.

The attenuation of social distances within the white sector reveals itself in many ways: personal contacts between whites are marked by easy informality, expressions of deference never assume extreme forms, differences in manners are relatively slight, and even among English-speaking people 'stand-offishness' is incomparably less common than in England.

Very substantial homogeneity of manners is accompanied by extensive vertical mobility. South Africa still remains a country of great opportunities for a man of Europoid race: the great majority of the prominent businessmen of today started from next to nothing, very often as poor immigrants. Only in Cape Town can be found some 'old families', and even there they form only an insignificant portion of the rich. There have been some cases of English 'county families' coming over with their possessions in quest of an easier life than in tax-ridden Britain, but they were very few. On the whole, the South African rich are first or second generation. The immigrants and their offspring show, on the whole, a greater aptitude for making money than those born in South Africa. The poor whites are almost without exception of old Afrikaner stock, whilst only very exceptionally an immigrant or a son of an immigrant falls to that level.

Notwithstanding the absence of appropriate investigations, it can be said with considerable assurance that vertical mobility is decreasing. The downward movement, in many cases amounting to pauperization, was largely the result of the high reproduction rate of the Afrikaner farmers, many of whose descendants migrated to towns in search of a livelihood, some slipping into shiftless existence. Owing to the fall in the birth rate among the farmers, and industrialization which opened wider opportunities of remunerative employment, pauperization of the whites has become rarer than it was three decades ago. A very important role in eliminating pauperization was played by the deliberate policy of the government, which even during the rule of the United Party instituted various measures designed to protect impecunious whites from the free play of the market. In addition a fairly extensive network of social workers was built, whose sole task is the rehabilitation of those whites who have fallen below the level of their birthright.

As far as social ascent is concerned, it also seems that the movement is slackening. The days of the gold diggers have passed long ago, and South Africa is no longer a country where everything needs to be started. Furthermore, commerce and industry are coming more and more under the sway of giant companies, and for this reason it is becoming more difficult to make a fortune quickly. Nevertheless, the opportunities for making money are still greater than in Europe. The disappearance of mass immigration also is bound to reduce social mobility.

It is curious that nearly all people of European race who are poor seem to have low intelligences – they are not just uneducated but plainly dull. The character of the passengers on the trains provides an illustration of this, as travelling by train constitutes in South Africa an indication of a low economic status. The connection between the lack of wealth and lack of intelligence is due in the first place to the universal acceptance of wealth as the most desirable thing in life, connected with the weakness of other ideals and the absence of an intellectual and artistic 'bohème'. The second (and perhaps decisive factor) is the ease with which wealth can be attained. There are good inductive grounds for proposing a generalization that the wider the opportunities for making money, the more evident is the connection between wealth and intelligence. My impression is that gifted individuals are more common among manual workers in Poland, Spain and Chile than in Britain, the explanation being that in the latter country there were some opportunities for able individuals to rise out of this category, whereas in the former countries such opportunities did not exist.

In the case of South Africa, the extent of the opportunities for the whites derives from the denial of them to the rest, and not from general opulence.

The number of jobs requiring any given level of ability and skill depends on the total population and the stage of economic development, so that if recruitment is restricted to one section of the population, the quality of the incumbents is thereby lowered. This effect can be very well observed in many walks of life in South Africa.

The two sections of the white population – the English-speaking and the Afrikaners – are differently placed on the social ladder, and may even be said to possess distinctive social ladders. The lowest class, the 'poor whites', consists almost entirely of Afrikaners. The very rich normally speak English at home, even if they have Afrikaans names. English as the home language has a certain snobbish appeal, or at least had before the Afrikaners became undisputed rulers of the country. The upper class's wider contacts with the world contribute to this effect. The urban middle class used to be composed mainly of English-speaking people, but the proportion of the Afrikaners has been steadily growing, and by now is not far from parity. Outside the province of Natal the farmers – that is to say the owners of sizeable estates cultivated by black or coloured (mixed race) labourers – are almost entirely Afrikaners.

The separation of the political and economic hierarchies is a curious feature of South African society. Industry and commerce are in the hands of English-speaking people, though many of them are sons of eastern European Jews. In contrast, the leading politicians of both parties were Afrikaners even before the victory of the National Party in 1948; with this difference that whilst the United Party leaders were closely associated with the English South African upper class, the National Party politicians are connected with the farmers who (as mentioned above) are mainly Afrikaners. The civil service is staffed exclusively by Afrikaners. The original cause of this state of affairs was the lack of English-speaking people who could comply with the requirement of knowledge of both official languages, and their preference for more remunerative posts in business, but once the Afrikaners came to dominate the civil service, they began to discriminate against English-speaking entrants. The police are entirely Afrikaans. In view of the steady expansion of the sphere of governmental control, these circumstances deprived the English section of the essential levers of power.

The politicians, the richest farmers, the higher civil servants, the ministers of the Dutch Reformed Church and the university professors form the *élite* of Afrikanerdom. In virtue of their power, they are feared by the 'socialites' of Johannesburg and Durban, who nevertheless look down upon them, thus producing resentment.

Money constitutes the only criterion of social status among the English-speaking South Africans. Among the Afrikaners it is slightly different: although money is of prime importance and poverty disqualifies, high status can be achieved with only moderate wealth. Political activity, religious ministry and contributing to Afrikaans culture as a writer do elicit respect. In the English sector the intellectuals enjoy no prestige whatsoever.

The middle class of the Afrikaners is composed of the farmers, the civil servants and intellectuals, and the (as yet not very numerous) businessmen. Below it come the skilled factory workers, clerks, policemen and people of similar occupations. Employment on the railways came to be considered as a stigma because the government provided many white paupers with unskilled jobs there. People doing 'kaffir's work' and paupers are classified as poor whites.

The English-speaking section contains practically no lower class, and can be divided only into the middle and the upper class.

On the whole the consciousness of status is much weaker among the Afrikaners than among the English South Africans: there is less snobbery and more cordiality, their solidarity is strengthened by the brother-in-arms feeling, not only against the Africans but also against the English and the Jews; and is further reinforced by the egalitarian tradition formed during the time, distant only by decades, when there were no class differences among the semi-nomad farmers – the 'trekboers', as they were called.

The position of the Jews is ambiguous. On the one hand they are extremely prosperous, and control business (particularly distributive commerce) to a greater extent than in any European country. On the other hand, they were never able to play an important part in politics, and since the assumption of power by the National Party they have been completely deprived of political influence, because this party does not allow them to enter its ranks. Unlike the Indians, however, the Jews are neither hampered nor humiliated in their activities.

Notwithstanding the greater wealth of the English-speaking section, the Afrikaners by no means recognize it as superior. In fact, each section considers itself to be better than the other, but all these *differends* dwindle into insignificance in relation to the colour bar.

Various Singular Features of South African Society
The Indians

The Indians are predominantly from southern India, and from the lower castes. With the exception of the ideologically minded, they insist on their superiority over the Africans who resent it very much. Many whites dislike the Indians to the point of insane hatred because, as many of them are wealthy and even educated, they upset the coincidence between the colour bar and the line dividing the rich from the poor. The Indians have never been as restricted in their activities as the Africans: they may engage in trade, and they have even succeeded in monopolizing the fruit and vegetable trade. The policy of the National Party of reducing their relative privileges constitutes a height of folly, as it drives them to make a common front with the Africans.

A trait of character which is very common among the Indians is their addiction to large and expensive cars (mostly quite out of keeping with their houses) and to fast driving and overtaking. The explanation is obvious: this is the only field in which they are permitted to surpass whites in a conspicuous manner.

Degrees of Mental Suffering

The poor, of course, suffer most physically, but as far as mental torments are concerned, the most affected are the educated Africans, irrespectively of whether they have received formal education or acquired it unaided. The so-called 'bush natives' in some ways still feel that the whites are something superior. An educated African, on the contrary, feels that he is superior to the majority of whites but is compelled to give them precedence on every occasion. Even worse, he is the favourite victim of white louts.

Acceptance of Immigrants

Immigrants from Europe (unless they come from its southern parts and are swarthy) are received much better than in other countries of immigration. The explanation is twofold: firstly that every European is regarded as a potential ally, and secondly, that the white population is itself divided into two sectors between which there is some hostility, so that a newcomer does not face a unitary wall.

Politics

As far as the colour bar is concerned the differences between the major parties – the National Party and the United Party – are not a matter of principle but solely of tactics: the United Party is in favour of discretion and sugaring the pill, and for this reason it has been disingenuously accused by its opponents of neglecting to defend the interests of the whites. The few whites who advocate attenuating the colour bar are entirely isolated and regarded with suspicion even by the Africans who are developing their own racialism. The real dividing line between the United Party and the National Party is that between people who are pro-English and those who are anti-English. In fact, these parties are essentially, though not entirely, ethnic parties. The National Party is explicitly the party of the Afrikaners: this is the meaning of its name. The United Party has always proclaimed the equality and co-operation of the two sectors, but in view of the connection with Britain, a formally equal partnership was bound to lead to British pre-dominance.

Economically, the United Party represents business, whilst the National Party represents the farmers, civil servants and poor whites, all of whom are predominantly Afrikaans. The Jews have considerable influence in the United Party, whilst being excluded from the National Party. The victory of the National Party was principally due to the higher reproduction rate of the Afrikaners. However, owing to the lack of perfect correspondence between ethnic and economic divisions, the social determinants of party affiliations are not clear cut.

The impotence of the English-speaking South Africans, although they control business and own considerably more than

half of the total wealth of the country, demonstrates the importance of the control of the apparatus of the state. As mentioned
earlier, the civil service, the police and (less completely) the army
are staffed by Afrikaners.

It has been claimed that in the southern states of the USA
racial antagonism has been fostered by the rich planters and
politicians connected with them, in order to keep the lower classes
divided and therefore docile. This thesis may not be altogether
false in view of the fact that in contrast to the states where discrimination against the Negroes is less severe, the southern states
remain under one-party rule, which means that no group rising
from below has been able to challenge the supremacy of the ruling
circles. Furthermore, the struggle against the encroachments of
the Northerners stimulated the solidarity of the Southerners, thus
fortifying the internal position of their rulers, because external
conflict strengthens the internal position of the leaders of any
social aggregate, unless they manifestly fail in the task of directing
the defence.

A similar mechanism operates in South Africa in favour of the
National Party which, having avenged the Boer War and subdued
the British, assumed the leadership of all the whites in their
struggle against the blacks.

The National Party has often been accused of Fascist and
dictatorial tendencies. In many ways it is true, and the sheer lust
for power must never be overlooked in analysing politics. Nevertheless, it appears that most of the measures which undermine
civil liberties were enacted and accepted by the whites without
serious resistance because they were felt to be necessary for their
defence. Even more, these measures are not generally felt to be
infringements upon liberties. The colour bar is regarded as sacred
and infringements of it as indubitably immoral. It is not accidental
that the act prohibiting sexual relations (in or out of wedlock)
between persons of different races is called the Immorality Act.
The rules of racial segregation are regarded by the majority of
white South Africans in the same light as prohibition of cannibal-
ism or of defecation in public. The United Party opposed the
extension of the discretionary power of ministers mainly out of
fear that they might be used not only for ensuring white domination but also for bolstering up the supremacy of the Afrikaners
over the English.

The inner structure of the National Party is remarkably democratic and is marked by the lack of ceremonial distance between the leaders and the ordinary members. In this respect it is not at all Fascist.

The Manners of the Rich

The South African rich exhibit all the traits proverbially attributed to the newly rich: uncouthness, ostentatious display of wealth, lack of appreciation of higher cultural values and so on. Even the second generation rich seem to differ considerably from their equivalents in Europe. The explanation seems to be that in South Africa there was no older upper class whose refinements the new rich could imitate. As far as wealth and hereditary privileges go, the South African upper and middle classes are the equivalents of the defunct nobilities of eastern Europe, but their manners and culture are strikingly less refined.

Racial Purity

Practically all the descendants of the early settlers show traces of non-European, chiefly Hottentot, ancestry. The Afrikaners, who are supposed to descend from the Dutch, differ from them remarkably in physical traits which can hardly be attributed to a different way of life. When people were being classified according to race, attempts to investigate everyone's ancestry were abandoned because some high personages were in danger of losing their status. Actually the mere necessity for identity cards with race marked on them proves that the races cannot be absolutely pure.

There is certainly no lack of sexual attraction between the races: one hears and reads continuously grotesque accounts of the efforts of the police to catch transgressors of the Immorality Act. A private secretary of the Prime Minister as well as a provincial chairman of the National Party have figured among the culprits.

An Explanation of the Distinctiveness of South Africa

In order to disentangle the factors responsible for the chief peculiarities of South African society, we must make clear what these peculiarities are. As suggested earlier, neither the poverty of the masses nor their ill-treatment distinguish South Africa from the majority of the countries of the world. In the present context, it is solely the rigidity of the colour bar that demands an explanation.

It has been suggested that the colour bar is a product of Protestantism because its most extreme manifestations can be found where Protestant Europeans have come into contact with other races. There are some good arguments in favour of this view: the Catholics do not pay much attention to the Old Testament whereas the Protestants study it assiduously, and the Old Testament does contain passages which can easily inspire and justify the ideas of racial exclusiveness and superiority. The existence of the 'coloured' (which in South Africa means of mixed origin) population number over a million, as well as of their equivalents in the former Dutch East Indies and British India, proves that this factor could not by itself prevent a mixture of races; but a comparison of these cases with what went on in Spanish, Portuguese and French territories suggests that it probably did diminish the extent of interbreeding.

The influence of the Old Testament over the Protestants was undoubtedly very important in making the colour bar in South Africa so rigid, but equally important, I think, was the difference in ecclesiastic organization between the Catholic Church and the Protestant congregations. The history of colonization abounds in examples of disagreement between colonizers and metropolitan authorities on how to treat the natives. One of the chief grudges which the Boers had against the British imperial government was the protection it accorded to the natives. This protection did not amount to very much but it did impose some restraints which, together with the population growth, prompted the Great Trek to the north, and the foundation of the independent Boer republics. The recent developments in Rhodesia, Kenya and Algeria also illustrate this type of divergence between metropolitan governments and settlers. The kings of Spain issued a flood of decrees designed to protect the natives of their colonies from the depredations of the conquerors and their heirs. Ever since it was decided that Indians had souls too, the Spanish monarchs were supported by the Church in this endeavour, and particularly by the monastic orders. These efforts did little to alleviate the cruel exploitation but they did attenuate the impermeable barrier between the conquerors and the conquered. Throughout, the initiative in this direction came from the metropolitan authorities and bishops and friars sent out to the colonies, whilst the local clergy yielded more readily to the demands of the colonizers. In the colonies of the Protestant nations, the ecclesiastical bodies adapted their teachings entirely to local circumstances: in virtue of the democratic and decentralized constitutions of the Protestant (particularly Calvinist) congregations there was no outside authority capable of opposing the settlers' pressure. Even today the Catholic Church in South Africa gives less countenance to racial segregation than less centralized religious communities, and for this reason makes converts at their expense.

Protestantism favoured the colour bar in another way too: namely by restraining sexual licence more effectively than did Catholicism. Naturally it is all a matter of degree, and it would be entirely wrong to imagine English and Dutch colonizers as paragons of chastity; nevertheless, it does seem that they never equalled the Spaniards and the Portuguese in the extent of concubinage. It is possible, of course, that the Iberian predilection for harems stemmed from the heritage of Islamic domination, or even from biologically determined tendencies, but the influence of religion could not have been negligible. Among people who take religion seriously, the Protestants usually surpass the Catholics in the gravity of their manners and strictness of adherence to the accepted code of behaviour. These differences are probably due to the Catholic institution of confession, which provides a fairly painless escape from the burden of guilt, and to the paternalistic relationship between a Catholic priest and his flock, which helps them to avoid responsibility for their actions.

Neither polyandry nor monogamy, but only polygyny can produce a very rapid mixture of the conquerors and the conquered; and as polygyny necessitates a low status of women, it follows that a high status of women impedes such a mixing, and thus favours erection of a barrier between the peoples involved. This deduction is supported by inductive evidence: there can be no doubt that the status of women was higher among the English and the Dutch than among the Spaniards and the Portuguese. It does not seem that this difference was in any way determined by religion, the influence of which should have been the other way round, because the Old Testament lends more support to patriarchy than the New. In view of the fact that the Nordic tribes, even before their conversion to Christianity, accorded to women a much higher status than they have enjoyed among peoples farther south, we might assume that some very old and persistent traditions account for this difference. The inequality in muscular strength between men and women seems to be slightly less marked among the Nordics than among the Mediterranean races. We cannot exclude the possibility that smaller differences in bodily strength may have lessened the subjection of women. A more important factor, however, seems to be one noticed by Montesquieu, who attributed the relatively high status of women among northern peoples to the fact that, as they arrive at puberty later, they have more chance of acquiring some knowledge before they are married (and, we should add, to develop some strength of character), and in consequence can better assert their right to have some say in family matters.

These explanations of the differences in the status of women are merely tentative, and their acceptance is not essential for the present argument, because whatever might have been the causes, the fact remains that the status of women among Afrikaners has been and is much higher than among the Iberian peoples, and it could not but impede multiracial concubinage on the scale witnessed in South America.

The coloured (which in South Africa means of mixed race) population resulted from interbreeding between the early settlers – ex-sailors and servants of the Dutch East Indies Company – and Hottentot women. But the Hottentots were few, and disappeared early, except for a few remnants. The Bushmen were even fewer and, as they could not be enslaved with profit, were exterminated. Like the Spanish conquerors of America, the early settlers arrived without women. But, whereas the Spaniards conquered enormous lands before they began bringing women from Spain, the women from Holland arrived and almost eliminated Hottentot wives and concubines when the Boers were still confined to the small area around the Cape of Good Hope with only a sparse Hottentot population; so that the Boers began their wider conquests in family units. They pushed towards the north and the east, and conquered the numerous Bantu tribes, marching as a true nation in arms, families packed on the enormous ox-wagons, women not only loading but also firing guns. This occurred relatively recently: the great Boer expansion commenced at the beginning of the 19th century and the epic Great Trek took place only a century ago.

Finally, it must be remembered that nowhere else in the world did two races so conspicuously different in appearance come into contact in such large numbers. Visible differences between the Spaniards or the Portuguese and the American Indians were small in comparison. The Negroes came into America as slaves torn out of their tribal affiliations, so that they did not form cohesive bodies. The Romans and other early empire builders conquered neighbouring populations which did not differ greatly in physical type. Elsewhere in Africa the European colonizers were few – except for Algeria where the barrier, being religious and ethnic rather than racial, is less impassable but the mutual hatred even greater. By being proportionately more numerous, the white South Africans have a better chance of defending themselves than the settlers in Rhodesia and Kenya, but the same factor exacerbates the conflict.

CHAPTER TWENTY

RACE AND CLASS IN LATIN AMERICA

As FAR AS race is concerned the countries of Latin America fall
into three broad categories: the countries where the majority
is of Amerindian descent (Mexico, Peru, Guatemala, Bolivia,
Paraguay); those where Europoid elements predominate (Argentina,
Uruguay, Chile, Costa Rica); and the predominately negroid and
mulatto nations around the Caribbean. Brazil and Colombia
cannot be classified in this way because they are particularly
varied, and their different regions fall into each of these three
categories. However, as regards the social situation, the distinction
between racially homogeneous and heterogeneous countries is
perhaps more important. Although it is all a matter of degree,
we could say that Mexico, Paraguay, Uruguay, Argentina and
Chile have populations in which it is difficult to distinguish races.
In consequence these are the countries where social characteristics
are least correlated with physical traits.

The proportions of racial admixture are not without significance
because, even if we assume that no mental characteristics are
genetically linked to the physical traits which distinguish the
races, the character of a civilization is affected by the nature of
the initial ingredients (that is to say, traditions); and the impact
of a tradition partly depends on the numbers of its bearers.

The most important differences between the nations consisting
chiefly of European descendants, and those with a large admixture
of Amerindian and African blood, have little to do with genetically
determined mental traits, and reside in the fact that the former are
less burdened by the heritage of slavery and serfdom, because the
immigrants from Europe came as free men and were enslaved only
in exceptional cases.

Sociologically speaking, the most important distinction is that between the populations which regard themselves as forming a nation, and those who do not. The inhabitants of Argentina, Uruguay, Cuba, Chile, Costa Rica and (with more numerous exceptions) of Mexico consider that they form one nation, whereas in Peru, Guatemala, Ecuador and Bolivia important parts of the populations are classified as Indians, and do not have any clear notion of nationality. In Brazil and Venezuela there are also sizeable groups without national consciousness. In all these states there remain Indian tribes which have not yet been subdued, and which are being exterminated or reduced to servitude. Some of them are very fierce and kill any stranger who comes near them.

The barrier between the Peruvians and the Indians of Peru corresponds very little to racial differences, and is chiefly a matter of culture. It is not a question of class because the miserable and mostly illiterate urban proletarians are not counted as Indians. The differentiation rests on language, clothing and the member-ship of a tribe or a village community: an Indian who learns to speak Spanish well, puts on clothes in town style, and leaves his ancestral village ceases to be regarded, or to regard himself, as an Indian. The appellation '*el Indio*' describes a cultural and social condition – not descent or racial features.

There is, thus, a radical difference between the colour bar in North America and the divisions between the Peruvians or the Guatemalans and their Indians. A North American Negro speaks the American brand of English as his native tongue; and if well educated, he speaks and writes it better than most of his Europoid compatriots. He may be wealthy, educated, well-mannered, occupy a high office and be distinguished from his compatriots of similar economic position only by a trace (perhaps very slight) of African ancestry. This suffices to cause him great difficulties and humiliations. If we applied the North American racialist criterion to Latin America, and classified as Indians and Negroes all the individuals who show a trace of Amerindian or African descent, then (outside Argentina and Uruguay) we would find few people who would fall into neither category. Even in Chile most people show traces of Amerindian blood.

The permeability of the frontier between the Indian and 'the national' accounts for the absence of nativistic movements in Latin America. To be sure, there have been many uprisings of Indian tribes, but there has never been any tendency for these tribes to merge into, say, an Indo-Peruvian nation as opposed to Spanish-Peruvian, analogous to the process of merging the South African native tribes into a South African-African nation opposed to the South African-European nation. As soon as the native tribes and village communities lose their identity, they merge into the territorial nation – become Mexicans or Peruvians – and their resistance against the oppressors loses its ethnic colouring and assumes the character of a pure class struggle.

The problem of the Indians has often been, and is being, raised, but all who have raised it proposed only one solution: integration. When the monument to Cortes was demolished in Mexico and the revival of Aztec themes dominated art, the aim was not to eject from the nation the presumed descendants of the Spaniards but to eliminate the vestiges of the division into conquerors and conquered. Thus there has never been any parallel in Latin America to the emergence of new nations in Africa, where the new educated classes are integrating the tribesmen into purely African nations in opposition to the European masters or their shadow. There can be no Indian intelligentsia or middle class in Latin America because any Indian who enters the middle class ceases to be an Indian, and will not be handicapped on the grounds of his racial traits.

One of the important consequences of this situation is that there can be no nativistic nationalism into which social discontent could be diverted. The factor of race neither cuts across the divisions between classes nor complicates their antagonisms; which is also one of the reasons why the Marxist interpretation of society appears so convincing to Latin American intellectuals.

The absence of a colour bar does not mean that there is actual racial equality: in all countries of Latin America the proportion of people with Europoid racial characteristics increases as we go up the social ladder. The adhesion between high status and Europoid features is perhaps least marked in Mexico and Bolivia – the countries which had undergone social revolutions which destroyed the privileges of the old upper classes, and gave to numerous individuals of humble origins the opportunity of far-reaching social ascent. The more frequent occurrence of Europoid features among the rich than among the poor is chiefly the heritage of the conquest, but it has been reinforced by the selective nature of immigration from Europe. Except in Argentina, Uruguay and

Southern Brazil, most immigrants from Europe came as business-men or technicians, and therefore entered directly into the middle class or higher; and even many of those who came poor were able to rise higher in virtue of advantages derived from an upbringing in an environment less conducive to improvidence.

The correlation between Europoid features and high status has a certain self-perpetuating force, because the positive valuation of Europoid features helps their possessors to rise on the social ladder or to maintain themselves on a high level. But it is only a matter of better chance – not of automatic classification into a higher caste, as in South Africa or Rhodesia. In contrast to South Africa, where the chief task of the welfare services is to prevent 'the poor whites' from falling below the minimum prescribed for a white man, nobody in Latin America has ever made any efforts to prevent the social degradation of individuals with Europoid features. The brothels of Rio de Janeiro used to contain blonde girls from Poland; and some of the Polish peasants who emigrated to Brazil fell into debt bondage, or were captured and put into slave compounds with Negroes. This, incidentally, was happening several decades after slavery was declared illegal. So it is evident that the Brazilian planters had no deep feelings about the dignity of the white man.

In Brazil pure afroids (ie people of purely African ancestry) are fairly common in the middle class, but there are none among the land-owning aristocracy, although many Brazilian aristocrats would be classified as Negroes in North America. There are few afroids in the higher reaches of Brazilian society primarily because social capillarity is generally low, with the partial exception of São Paulo. Class barriers are more fluid in the south, which is undergoing rapid industrialization, than in the north where the patterns of social life are still determined by the legacy of the division into masters and slaves; and it is in the north where the majority of the afroids live. There is a Brazilian saying that 'a poor man is a Negro and a rich man white', which roughly summarizes the situation. The majority of the very poor are Negroes, dark mulattoes or mestizoes, the rich are of predominantly European descent and the rest are a mixture of shades.

On the whole the African was more severely handicapped in his rise in status than the Amerindian, which does not mean that the mass of the conquered Indians were treated better than the imported African slaves. Actually, although there was not much to choose between their fates, the latter was perhaps slightly better treated because he had been bought, whereas the Indian serf was (and often still is) 'a free commodity'.

In Indo-America (with the exception of Mexico, Paraguay and Bolivia, which have become more or less homogeneous racially) most people in the upper classes are of predominantly Spanish descent, while the majority of the poor are of predominantly Amerindian blood. The half-way mestizoes predominate in the intermediate strata but are present in the highest and the lowest strata too. Moreover, even in the highest aristocracy there are individuals of purely Amerindian physical type. And even persons commonly considered as Indian by origin (in the social sense) have been known to rise to the highest dignities: the greatest Mexican statesman of the 19th century, Benito Juarez, was an Indian, as is the only living Mexican of comparable stature, Lazaro Cárdenas. Many dictators in Venezuela and elsewhere were Indians, notwithstanding their Spanish names. Though very exclusive socially, the aristocracy of Peru is very far from racial purity. Colombia is probably the country where the descendants of the Spaniards preserved their 'racial purity' most nearly. In some districts of Colombia there are peasants of pure Spanish descent.

The absence of anything resembling the colour bar as known in English-speaking countries calls for some explanation because it was certainly not due to the kindlier treatment of the subject races by the Spaniards and the Portuguese. Like other social phenomena, interbreeding acquires a certain momentum of its own: once it has occurred on such a scale that the individuals of intermediate shades constitute the majority, any barrier based on strictly physical features is bound to cut across social affiliations, and therefore become thereby unenforceable. The mechanism of heredity is such that the siblings of racially mixed ancestry exhibit various dissimilar combinations and traits, thus qualifying for different racial categories. Such cases have caused a great deal of suffering in South Africa but they were never sufficiently numerous to throw the whole principle of the colour bar into confusion. When the overwhelming majority falls into the intermediate grades, the social barriers must be based on criteria other than physical features. This explanation raises the question of why interbreeding took place in Ibero-America on a larger scale than in the English colonies.

The difference in the extent of interbreeding stems primarily from two simple demographic facts. The first is that the colonizers of North America came in family groups, whereas the early Spanish and Portuguese settlers came without wives. Even in the 18th century, when the conditions of life in the chief cities of Ibero-America resembled those of Europe much more than was the case immediately after the conquest, very few women came from Spain and Portugal. As they led a more secluded life, the Iberian women were probably less inclined to travel than their sisters from northern Europe, particularly as the journey to most parts of Spanish America was longer and more dangerous than to the north Atlantic coast. Moreover, it seems that the fertility of the European women in the tropics, and the survival rate of their offspring, were lower than the corresponding rates for the mestizoes. Naturally, there are no statistics on this point, but several physicians reported about it at the time, and it is unlikely that their views on such a simple and un-ideological point should be entirely baseless.

A distinguished Brazilian sociologist and historian Gilberto Freyre attributes the complete lack of revulsion against dark skin to the impact of the Moorish domination of the Iberian peninsula, which implanted in the minds of its inhabitants an association between darkness of the skin and high status. One must also remember that the Iberians do not differ greatly from Amerindians in skin colour, and are somewhat nearer to the African than are the English or the Dutch. These factors, however, could only affect the extent of interbreeding, because, given the fact that the colonizers came as single men, fairly extensive interbreeding could not be avoided. Similarly, although Puritan gravity could, perhaps, have reduced the practice of polygamy (and, therefore, the rate of interbreeding) it could not have prevented it altogether. Even the puritanical colonial officials of Victorian England could not entirely control their concupiscence; and so it would have been very surprising if young adventurers, ready to risk their lives against tremendous odds for the sake of gold, were inclined to self-restraint.

Without polygamy the Spanish conquest of America would have been ephemeral. The men who came from Spain overran only the chief cities of the Aztecs and the Incas, and it is even doubtful whether their legitimate descendants could have maintained themselves there once the Indians ceased to be overawed by the horses and firearms. However, the numbers of the dominating group were rapidly swollen by the products of concubinage. Nearly all the Spaniards had large harems, often running into dozens and sometimes even hundreds, with even more numerous progeny. These children of the Spaniards were baptized and brought up in the Christian faith, given Spanish names, and recognized as heirs by their fathers. The conquest of the interior was their work, and it was they who gave to the empire its firm foundations. Polygamy played just as important a role in the iberization of America as it did in the arabization of the Near East: in both cases the numbers of the conquerors were inadequate to impose a new identity upon the conquered peoples which would outlast the severance of political links. It must be emphasized, however, that massive procreation through non-legalized polygamy would not have buttressed the Spanish rule so much had the Spaniards been inclined to reject their illegitimate offspring. The custom was (and still is in less urbanized areas) that, although illegitimate children rank in precedence below the legitimate, they are regarded as heirs, not only by their fathers but also by society in general. It remains to be added that this mechanism of iberization did not cease to function in the early days of the empire; on the contrary, it works to this day in the more outlying regions, because wealthy Latin American men have never abandoned the habit of concubinage.

The Catholic Church played a paramount role in fostering the fusion of races. It could never force the soldiers and planters to treat their subjects less cruelly – nor did it ever seriously try to do this – but it insisted on gaining converts, and urged the Spaniards to marry their native concubines. The Protestant Church has facilitated the maintenance of racial segregation for two reasons: one organizational, the other doctrinal. The Catholic Church, being a centralized and autocratic institution, could disregard the wishes of its flock: the priests could be ordered to include the Indians and the Africans in the ecclesiastic community whether it suited its European members or not. In any case an inclusion in a strictly hierarchical community does not represent the same challenge to social inequality as does an inclusion into a democratically governed Protestant Church. The Catholic hierarchy, moreover, readily condoned infringements of the Commandments but took its missionary activity seriously, and insisted on equal obedience from all races. The latter feature was a special manifestation of the general tendency of an autocracy to level the rights of its subjects. The crucial feature of Protestantism was the demolition of ecclesiastic autocracy; and in virtue of their democratic constitutions, the Protestant Churches had to bow to the prejudices of their members. Secondly, the essence of Protestantism was direct access to the Bible; and the insistence on its literal interpretation could not fail to stimulate racialism, in view of the abundance of doctrines of racial purity in the Old Testament.

The numerical proportions between the conquerors and their victims play a decisive role in determining the extent of miscegenation. In North America the European settlers lived in greater density and were much more numerous than the nomadic tribes with whom they came in contact. Even if they had killed all the men and taken all the women, they could not have surrounded themselves with harems comparable to those of the Spanish conquerors. On the other hand, the Spaniards were more numerous in proportion to the native population than were the Englishmen who directed the conquest of India. The latter were so few that no amount of polygamy could have enabled them to alter palpably the racial composition of the enormous native population. The British and Dutch travellers to the East were mostly concerned with trade, and for this reason they travelled to and fro more often, and did not lose their contact with their home countries so easily. Moreover, many of them made considerable fortunes, whereupon they left the colonies, whereas among the Spaniards usually only the very high officials and those who found gold went back.

The turmoil which was endemic at the beginning of the empire and after its collapse made the maintenance of social divisions based on race more difficult than was the case under more regular conditions of political life in the southern states of the USA. In the free-for-all fights tough adventurers could rise meteorically regardless of their race, whilst many old-established families were despoiled.

It would be an exaggeration to say that racial discrimination plays no part in generating social antagonisms in Latin America. Nevertheless, its role is relatively minor because racial differences (in the strict sense) correspond only vaguely or not at all to the line which divides the rich from the poor. The conflict between the Indians and 'the whites' rests essentially upon the divisions between the landowners and the labourers and share-croppers, or the townsmen and the peasants. There is plenty of oppression and exploitation in Latin America – no less than in the racialist countries like Southern Rhodesia or South Africa – but people are exploited not on account of their race but because of their social position; and anybody who is defenceless and poor will share their fate regardless of his features.

CHAPTER TWENTY-ONE

AN ECONOMIC INTERPRETATION OF ANTISEMITISM

ONE OF THE chief contributions of Karl Marx to our understanding of society was his insistence on the necessity of explaining political struggles and ideologies in terms of conflicts of economic interest. In the more moderate form suggested by Engels, which admits the possibility of a reflexive influence of an ideology upon the conditions which nurtured it, this idea is very helpful. It does not explain everything, but it does explain a great deal. There is no reason, however, to assume that struggles for economic prizes must always be fought between classes – that is to say, collectivities differentiated principally in virtue of their economic positions.

In a way, the interpretation presented here might be described as a synthesis of Marx's thesis on the economic nature of all conflicts, with Gumplowicz's antithesis, which emphasized the paramount importance of struggles between races. Gumplowicz, who lived in the Habsburg empire, which abounded in ethnic, racial and religious divisions, had ample opportunities for making observations which supported his theory.

On the basis of the following analysis of antisemitism, with some references to analogous phenomena, I propose the following thesis.

The strength of popular movements and currents of animosity directed against a non-dominant minority is stimulated by the following factors:

1 The conspicuousness and indelibility of the distinguishing marks.

2 The coincidence of cultural and religious and racial dividing lines.

3 General poverty and, particularly, processes of impoverishment.

4 The ratio of the minority to the majority, and, particularly, the process of increase of this ratio.

5 The minority's share of the total wealth, and, particularly the process of growth of this share.

6 The extent to which economic complementarity is absent.

7 Absence of common foes.

Among the movements and currents of animosity directed against various racial, religious and ethnic minorities, antisemitism has been without any doubt most thoroughly studied. In the writings on it two kinds of approach predominate: one is psychological, the other is through genealogy of ideas. The latter is wholly inadequate. As shown in Chapter 12, we can throw light on the causes of historical processes by investigating the genealogy of ideas when we deal with ideas which are difficult to conceive, such as in the field of science, technology or the art of organizing, whereas anything so primitive as ideological justifications for the dislike of strangers can occur spontaneously to any untutored mind. Ideas of this kind are always being proclaimed by somebody, and the important question, from the point of view of social causation, is to discover which social circumstances enhance their appeal. It is of little help in understanding the rise of Hitler to be told that he got his notions from Nietzsche or Stewart Houston Chamberlain, because if he did not get them from their writings he could have got them from many others, including the Old Testament. It is ethnocentrism with its ingredients of pride and hatred that has been common throughout history – not its opposites. The real problem is to explain why among the Germans in the thirties of the 20th century these commonplace sentiments turned into an insane passion.

The psychological approach is more fruitful. Unquestionably, sadism and the scapegoat mechanism operate among human beings and play a large part in the persecutions of minorities. These psychological factors must be taken into account but any interpretation solely in terms of them is bound to be inadequate because it cannot explain the variations. There are grounds to believe that sadistic propensities – as distinct from indulgence – are an irradicable feature of the human species. There is probably a little sadism in all men (though perhaps not in all women), and in any population there is a sizeable number of downright sadists who will use every opportunity for venting their lusts. The existence of a non-dominant minority may provide them with such an opportunity, for the obvious reason that its members are handicapped in defending themselves. Naturally, sadism breeds sadism, but there is an apparently irreducible core of it, which it is very difficult to relate to general social conditions even with the aid of the frustration-aggression theory, for it appears even among populations whose material needs are fully satisfied, and where there is no institutionalized brutality. This does not prove that the theory which explains sadism as a form of aggression generated by frustration is wrong: there are many forms of frustration possible even when the material needs are provided for, the most obvious being sexual. It may not have been accidental that the burning of witches began soon after celibacy had been enjoined upon the clergy, and that the most ardent inquisitors were recruited from among the monks, but on the other hand, the wealthy spectators at Roman circuses savoured gruesome sights in spite of indulging in sexual pleasures to the limits of physical capacity. We might still rescue the theory by pointing out that these people had to endure frightful humiliations and insecurity, which might have accounted for their unbridled and perverse sybaritism. There are, however, many cases described by psychiatrists which do not reveal any forms of frustration beyond what is the inescapable lot of all human beings. We must, then, draw the conclusion that in trying to discover the social circumstances which stimulate hostility against minorities, we must consider sadism as a factor which is always present, at least potentially, and which is partially independent of social conditions.

The frustration-aggression theory purports to explain displaced aggression, that is to say aggression directed at objects other than those which cause the frustration. Such aggression obviously is very important in social life and particularly in the persecutions of minorities, but equally important is simple aggression – rational in a way – which assumes the form of attempts to wrest from the minority goods which some or all members of the majority covet, or to prevent the minority from obtaining these goods in the first place.

The scapegoat theory is very enlightening. It can be interpreted as a special application of the frustration-aggression theory, and can be likewise related in some measure to economic fluctuations. It enables us to understand some spectacular events like the massacres of Jews after the epidemics in the Middle Ages, as well as the customs of human sacrifice, but it fails to account for one important feature of animosity directed towards minorities: namely, its connection with the numerical proportions between minorities and majorities.

The stress on the irrational psychopathic elements in antisemitism is due to the concentration on the phenomenon of Nazism, which was essentially a mass psychosis in spite of its economic and military conditioning. For this reason Hitlerism differed profoundly from the more prosaic and less cruel antisemitic currents which prevailed in eastern Europe. Furthermore, Hitlerite antisemitism was ordained by the charismatic leader. Before the rise of Hitler there was antisemitism in Germany, but it was weaker than in Poland and Hungary: its relative strength corresponded more or less to the relation of the proportion of the Jews in the total population of Germany to the equivalent proportions in other countries. The cruelty of the persecution of the Jews in the Third Reich was probably due to the particularly strong streak of sadism, infused into the Germans by disciplinarian social relations, the tradition of unquestioning and dutiful obedience, Hitler's insane hatred and his scheme to bind the German nation inescapably to himself by involving it in complicity in an enormous crime. In the milder antisemitic movements in eastern Europe these features were not present; in Hungary Horthy did try to divert popular discontent into this channel, but in Poland the government tried to contain it within the limits of the law of equality for all citizens.

Persecutions ordered by governments must be clearly distinguished from those which surge spontaneously from the masses. We must remember, however, that all concrete cases present inextricable mixtures of both of these ideal types, though in very varying measures. This distinction is very important for attributions of causal efficacy because a course of action which is decided upon by a small number of persons is less determined by social conditions than an action which is the result of a large number of independent decisions. For this reason acts like the expulsions of the Jews from Spain and quasi-expulsions from Russia are not easily explicable in economic terms: less bigoted monarchs might have left them alone. Ferdinand and Isabella as well as Alexander III ascended their thrones by inheritance, which had nothing to do with their views on this matter, whereas Hitler rose to power in virtue of the appeal of his propaganda, in which antisemitism figured in the first place. So it cannot be said that given the social situation, Hitler's personal inclinations were the cause of the persecutions – they determined only their severity.

Even if we consider only the behaviour of the masses we must take into account a factor which we can hardly call economic: namely, the desire for invidious self-esteem, practically universal among humanity. We assign importance to various criteria of excellence in accordance with what we excel in. One of the most accessible ways of satisfying this desire is to disdain strangers. This tendency, however, though very important in preserving any existing discriminatory institutions and attitudes, and in facilitating their establishment, cannot be regarded as a factor which initiates variations affecting whole societies. There are no reasons to think that this tendency varies greatly from one society to another, although individuals differ greatly in this respect. Among individuals whose desire for invidious self-esteem is of more or less equal strength, and whose economic interests are similar, the ones most prone to espouse the cause of racial or ethnic discrimination are those who have least other grounds for feelings of superiority, given the scale of values prevalent in their environment.

We have thus delimited the field: what is to be explained are the variations in the intensity of spontaneous mass currents of animosity towards ethnic and/or racial and/or religious non-dominant minorities. Antisemitism will be treated as a case which throws light on this general issue.

A comparative survey suggests that (like other minorities) the Jews can live unmolested only where they are few – which does not mean that where they are few they must be unmolested.

The only exception to this rule in New York, but there they are too powerful to be persecuted. Moreover, the enormous wealth of the United States makes economic competition less lethal than it is in the poor countries. For this reason (as suggested earlier in connection with the persecution of the Negroes) psychological factors (other than the simple desire to satisfy elementary needs) play a more important role in the causation of racial and ethnic frictions in the United States than is the case in indigent societies, whilst the opposite is true of the strictly economic factor of the struggle for the division of wealth. Nevertheless, notwithstanding the great wealth available to Americans, there seems to be more hostility and discrimination against the Jews there than in England or France where they are proportionately fewer.

If we take Europe in the 20th century we see that the differences in the intensity of antisemitism roughly correspond to the ratios of the Jews to the total populations. It was most intense in Poland (where more than 10 per cent of the population was Jewish), Hungary and Rumania. It was less intense in Czechoslovakia, where they were fewer and which was more prosperous, and in Germany until Hitler whipped it up. Although the Tzarist government deliberately used the Jews as a scapegoat for the wrath of the populace, antisemitism was less deeply rooted in Russia proper than in Poland, Rumania and Hungary because the Jewish population was proportionately much smaller, and the country offered greater économic opportunities. The Tzarist government pushed most of the Jews into Poland and the Ukraine, thus intensifying antisemitism there. Antisemitism had least effect upon the prosperous countries of western Europe where Jews amounted to less than 1 per cent of the population.

As an approximate rule, there is a critical ratio which is most conducive to popular persecutions, and which seems to lie around 10 per cent. With this ratio the non-dominant minority is very conspicuous, has many points of friction with the majority, but is still small enough to be persecuted with ease. Harassing a minority of 30 or 40 per cent often entails great danger, whereas a minority of 1 or 2 per cent (provided that it is not particularly conspicuous for other reasons) can more easily escape the attention of the majority unless it is put into the limelight by organized hostile propaganda. Naturally even a majority of 99 per cent can be cruelly oppressed but this can be done only with the aid of the entire apparatus of the state – not by unorganized crowds.

The ratio is important. Nevertheless the numerical factor explains neither Hitlerism nor why antisemitism was stronger in eastern Europe in the 20th century than a century earlier, which shows that it is not a simple matter of numbers. One reason why there was less incentive a century ago to violent attacks upon the Jews was that the laws kept them in inferior positions. An exactly analogous consideration explains why there are no lynchings in South Africa as there are in the southern states of the USA.

The story of pogroms and discriminations in eastern Europe is too well known to be repeated here. What might be worth mentioning is the role which antisemitism has played in Stalin's success. When Lenin died there was a mere sprinkling of non-Jews in the highest organ of the party. By the time Stalin died there was only one Jew in the Politburo – Kaganovitch (since removed by Khrushchev). In all Stalin's purges Jews figured more prominently than chance would warrant.

Everywhere there are more aspirants than good places. The struggle for the good things of life goes on all the time. Its intensity depends primarily on how much there is to share out. This struggle is waged with all kinds of weapons, and one can view racial or religious or ethnic discrimination simply as a tool for eliminating some of the rivals. The larger the ratio of the minority to the total population, the more numerous are the points of contact and, therefore, opportunities for friction. It is clear, however, that the intensity of the hostility cannot depend on the frequency of contacts alone. As far as the conflict of economic interests is concerned, the number factor is supremely important because it determines the total amount of wealth held by the minority – for any given level of opulence of its members. A mass movement aiming at spoliation needs a prospect of a booty of some size. Although usually this size is grossly magnified in the imagination of the covetous or necessitous multitudes, there is normally some relation between the reality and the image.

Eastern Europe between the wars was, as it still is today, a poor and over-populated area. The Jews had succeeded in monopolizing certain lucrative trades, and in entering certain attractive professions in very large numbers. For example, about 60 per cent of the doctors and lawyers in Cracow (and more in some smaller towns) were Jews. Something like 95 per cent of the trade in hides and furs in Poland was in the hands of the Jews. This, of course, does not mean that all the Jews were rich (actually most of them were desperately poor) but they did own a sufficient slice of the total wealth to excite the envy of others. Disregarding clearly exaggerated estimates, it seems that it amounted to about 20 per cent. Under these circumstances, it would be surprising if some of the non-Jews did not strike on the idea that they could make a better living if the Jews were eliminated or despoiled, or at least fettered. The rioting students, for instance, demanded that the Jews should not be admitted into universities in numbers larger than corresponding to their proportion in the total population. In a way, eastern European antisemitism was an attempt to counteract the economic superiority of the Jews by the fists of the greater number.

The superior economic prowess of the Jews in eastern Europe was due to a number of causes, of which the first was the increase in importance of the activities traditionally allotted to them: in consequence of urbanization and industrialization commerce was continually gaining in weight as a source of income in comparison with agriculture; and in this field the Jews possessed not only the advantage of acquired positions but also the tradition of necessary skills. Being a closely-knit community, they often combined to try to keep the Gentiles out of their ground, thus defending, in fact, the *status quo* sanctified by tradition. Apart from the very rich families who acquired the habits of the nobility, the Jews were not impeded from attaining business success by the proclivity to conspicuous and ruinous consumption instilled into the Poles and the Hungarians by the example of their nobility, who regarded spendthriftiness as one of the chief virtues.

In intellectual occupations the success of the Jews was connected in the first place with their tradition of reverence for knowledge and the book, and secondly, with the stimulus to excel produced by their inner conviction of superiority combined with their exposure to outward humiliations. Furthermore, the tradition of parental solicitude and family solidarity seem to be particularly strong among the Jews, and, together with the readiness of mutual help within the Jewish community, they provided a counterweight to the hindrances of antisemitic discrimination. As far as intellectuals in the strict sense are concerned, the prominence of the Jews in their ranks was also due to the marginal social position of unorthodox Jews: being suspended at cross-roads of loyalties, beliefs and customs always stimulates curiosity and independence of thought.

In the old Polish kingdom there was an ethnic division of labour: commerce was a Jewish occupation. In the regions which now form part of Poland both the peasants and the nobles were of

Polish ethnic stock. In the eastern territories there was a proper ethnic stratification; the nobility was Polish, the commercial class Jewish and the peasants Ukrainian. As Gumplowicz pointed out eighty years ago, the situation in Java was very similar, the homologous elements being the Dutch, the Chinese and the Javanese. The same can be said about the English, the Indians and the Africans in south-eastern Africa. In the two latter cases, however, the ruling race retained the largest businesses, which just did not exist in old Poland, and where consequently the nobility remained purely rural. The attitude of the Polish or Ukrainian peasant to the Jew was similar to that of the African peasant to the Indian: a mixture of disdain with admiration for the cleverness of the trading race, of resentment at their pretensions to superiority and their economic exploitation. Sometimes this resentment turned into burning hatred, and led to outbreaks of violence.

The pogroms of the Jews in eastern Europe, the recent slaughter of the Chinese in Indonesia, and the anti-Indian riots in Africa, were truly popular movements. Even in such cases as the Durban riots in 1951, or the post-1905 pogroms in Russia, the police provided only a few *agents-provocateurs*, and turned a blind eye on what was going on – they did not hire or command the assailants. The explosive material was there – the *agents-provocateurs* acted as a spark. As mentioned earlier, there is in all such phenomena a constant element: in any human mass, particularly if it consists of uncouth lads, there are many who will jump at the opportunity of beating up somebody with impunity. Being constant, however, this factor explains neither the timing nor the dimensions of the outbreaks. These can be understood only if we take into account the economic processes.

Money flows into the hands of those who manipulate it, and in all cases where peasants coexist with traders and moneylenders, the peasants fall into debt, and the others increase their share of wealth. This is a well-known process already described in the Bible as well as in modern economic studies of India and other countries. On very large estates the conflict between the Jew and the peasant was aggravated by the practice of rent-farming: big landowners, who could not supervise their estates, sometimes gave their Jewish 'factors' the right to collect the rents in exchange for a lump sum. Like the Roman tax-farming, or the sale of offices, this practice produced some of the worst forms of exploitation.

In the Ukraine, where the largest estates were to be found and where the big peasant wars were fought, the slogan of the rebels was: 'Kill the lords and the Jews'. The smaller pogroms, however, which did not form part of peasant uprisings, did not aim at the elimination of the Jews. In so far as they had an aim, it was the cancellation of debts.

The nobles were in a peculiar position: on the one side they had superior force, on the other, many of them were in debt to Jewish moneylenders. This ambiguity led to erratic behaviour in which patronizing friendship and even humble entreaties alternated with insults and assaults. Anyway, the nobles and the Jews lived in a symbiosis: the nobles relied on the commercial services of the Jews, and protected them. Indeed, the decisive fact in the history of Poland was that the nobles succeeded in suppressing the Christian commercial class, and replacing it by the Jews who, being isolated from the rest of the population, were more docile. This explains the downfall of the royal authority: the kings were unable to resist the encroachments of the nobility because – unlike their counterparts in western Europe – they could not use the *bourgeoisie* as the counterweight. The erratic symbiosis between the nobles and the Jews was somewhat undermined after the partitions by the policy of 'divide and rule' pursued by the Tzarist government, but in the main it continued until the appearance of the non-Jewish professional and commercial classes. Antisemitism as a mass movement appeared when economic competition replaced economic complementarity.

If we follow the history of the expulsions of the Jews from various places in western Europe, which took place towards the end of the Middle Ages, we find that whether we take England or the Rhineland these expulsions were preceded by the growth of a non-Jewish commercial class. The princes of eastern Europe welcomed the Jews – and the population did not oppose them – because, owing to the paucity of native traders, they were economically complementary. There was one medieval case which did not fit this rule: the Jews were expelled from Spain in spite of being economically complementary. This expulsion, however, was prompted not so much by mass antipathy as by the kings' bigotry. Moreover, it occurred as aftermath of the victory in a war against the infidel which lasted several centuries. In so far as there was popular hostility to the Jews, it was due to what the psychologists call nowadays 'stimulus generalization', and what they used to call association of ideas: the war against the Moslems made all infidels odious. For nowhere in medieval Europe were the Jews less racially distinguishable, or more assimilated culturally. Whereas eastern European Jews spoke Yiddish (derived from German), some of the Sephardic Jews, whose ancestors lived in the Orient after the expulsion from Spain, spoke Spanish at home until their arrival in the new state of Israel. This example proves that persecutions can occur in spite of economic complementarity, but it does not disprove the thesis that economic complementarity is a necessary condition of the lack of persecutions. This proposition was first advanced by Leon Petrajitski (Petrazycki) forty years ago in a memorable essay which, unfortunately, is available only in Polish. It can be formulated as follows: in any society composed of cohesive, ethnically heterogeneous sections, a relative absence of conflict is possible only if these sections are economically complementary.

The foregoing considerations allow us to view the growth of antisemitism in eastern Europe as a consequence of the erosion of economic complementarity. The abolition of serfdom and the increase in the density of the rural population led to an influx of young peasants to towns. Most of them became servants or journeymen or industrial workers; some took up petty trade (which some of their descendants succeeded in developing) where they came up against the Jewish monopoly. On the other side, the Jews, when liberated from their legal disabilities, began to flock into liberal professions where they entered into competition with impoverished nobles and the 'mobiles' from below. Apart from the argument from co-variance in time, an examination of the class composition of the antisemitic organizations in Poland between the wars also supports this view. This interpretation can be applied to equivalent movements in other countries of eastern Europe.

The Polish Socialist Party, supported in the main by the industrial workers, was not antisemitic. In Russian Poland before the First World War about one third of its members were Jewish; and many remained in it even after the specifically Jewish parties came into existence. Although the peasants rioted against the Jews sporadically, their organizations were certainly not to the fore in demanding that the Jews should be deported to Palestine or locked up in ghettoes. As the peasants sold their produce mostly to the Jews they blamed them for low prices. As far as the industrial workers are concerned, the explanation is not, of course, that their occupation generates superior virtue: there are many examples from all over the world of how xenophobic industrial workers can be when it comes to admitting foreigners into their kind of job. The reason for the relative weakness of antisemitism among the Polish industrial workers was that, although there were Jews in this occupation, they were relatively few, and did not present a serious threat to employment. The political circles connected with the landowning nobility did not propagate antisemitism either: they maintained the tradition of patronizing tolerance. There were two parties devoted to the cause of antisemitism. One was the Radical National Party – a small body of violent men, whose admiration for Hitler's methods and outlook verged on anti-clericalism. (Its ex-leader, incidentally, is now a *persona grata* of the Communist régime, and heads the National Catholics who defy Rome.) It attracted all kinds of desperadoes and delinquents. In so far as its recruitment tended towards any class, it seems to have been what the Germans call '*Lumpenintelligenz*'; failed students with neither jobs nor private means. This party was born at the nadir of the economic crisis. The traditionalist and clerical National Party was far older and bigger.

Owing to the existence of multi-national states, citizenship in central and eastern Europe is clearly distinguished from national-ity, in the sense of belonging to an ethnic collectivity. So, by calling itself 'national', the party proclaimed that it was against the co-citizens who were not co-nationals. The word 'national', incidentally, has the same connotation in the name of the ruling party of South Africa. It must be added that the overwhelming majority of Jews in eastern Europe were not merely distinguished by religion and physical traits, but had a special kind of customary dress, spoke Yiddish and were neither considered, nor considered themselves, as belonging to the Russian, Polish, Hungarian or the Ukrainian nations. With the exception of the Ukrainians, each of these nations had its 'assimilated' Jews. In Poland people whom the antisemites classified as Jews comprised the following cate-gories: (1) Jews resident in Poland who did not know Polish and lived in complete segregation; (2) Polish Jews who spoke Polish (though not always well) and had strong links with the Polish nation without identifying themselves with it; (3) Poles of Jewish faith who did not speak Yiddish, and regarded themselves as belonging to the Polish nation in spite of humiliations; (4) persons of Jewish origin who cut themselves off from the Jewish community and identified themselves wholly with the Gentile Polish nation – they were either converts to Catholicism or free thinkers; (5) persons of partly Jewish origins who had no links with the Jewish community although they would be branded as Jews by the antisemites if their antecedents were known.

Assimilation occurred as a rule only among the educated or the rich. For this reason it was more extensive in Great Russia, where poor Jews were fewer, than in the western provinces of the Russian Empire. In the old kingdom of Poland converts to Christianity came exclusively from among the rich Jews who desired to enter the ranks of the nobility. Notwithstanding the temptation of ennoblement as the usual reward for conversion, very few Jews abandoned their faith. In later times, when the spread of religious scepticism made more of them willing to do so, they were pushed back by the rising tide of antisemitism. The fact that antisemitism assumed extreme forms precisely at the time when increasing numbers of Jews were abandoning their ghettoes and the special dress, and even ceasing to speak Yiddish, proves that its chief roots lay in the growing acerbity of economic competition rather than in sheer heterophobia.

The National Party in Poland drew its strength mainly from the artisans and traders, with a large ingredient of members of the class which used to be, and still is, called the 'intelligentsia', and which has no equivalent in western Europe. The 'intelligentsia' was the section of society which consisted of families who derived their subsistence from employment as civil servants, teachers and army officers, or the liberal professions. In order to qualify as a member of the intelligentsia, a person had to have academic or at least secondary education, do non-commercial work for which such education was at least formally necessary, and have requisite manners. The antisemitism of this group was also economically conditioned: it became acute after the establishment of universities in a number of towns, and the consequent increase in the number of graduates beyond what could be absorbed by the market. It became frantic during the economic crisis of the thirties when redundancy hit even the well-established members of this class. Before independence there were only two Polish universities, both located in Austrian Poland. Even in Warsaw higher education was only intermittently available before the First World War. In German Poland the people who corresponded occupationally to the 'intelligentsia' were mostly Germans, and did not form a class segregated from the business sectors: they belonged to the fairly unified middle class of the western European type, which had no equivalent farther east. In any case, there were very few Jews there, because after the incorporation of these regions into Prussia the Jews who lived there in mass migrated to economically more advanced parts of Germany. In western Poland antisemitism passed from latency to virulence when the Jews from the eastern parts began to arrive after the reunification. To come back to the 'intelligentsia': in Russian Poland there was relatively little antisemitism amongst this class; primarily because of the weakness of economic competition, and secondly because of the existence of a common enemy in the shape of the Tzarist government which oppressed the Poles and the Jews alike. Two factors explain the weakness of the competition on the pasturages of the intelligentsia in Russian Poland: the first was the smallness of the supply, itself the consequence of the virtual non-existence of institutions of higher learning. Secondly, in spite of being oppressed at home, the Poles with professional qualifications of any kind had ample openings in Russia itself, where often they were even given preference over the Russians, owing to their reputation for being more reliable and less addicted to dissipation.

Unlike the persecution of the Jews in Hitler's Germany, the antisemitic outbreaks in independent Poland were entirely unofficial, and the government tried to repress them – with fair success, for they never turned into massacres, and were normally confined to shouting and breaking windows. The police beat the demonstrators as much as these beat the Jews. Pilsudski (the dictator from 1926 to 1935) represented the old traditions of the nobility which regarded the Jews as a natural part of the body of citizens. The chief and the most effective slogan against him was that he sold the country to the Jews. After his death his heirs began reluctantly to make concessions to the mood of the masses: though still maintaining the prohibition of violence, they allowed organized boycott. To understand the situation, one must take into consideration the odd circumstance that in spite of being a dictatorship with a developing taste for totalitarian paraphernalia, the government could not control the masses very well: in fact, in some places it was dangerous to admit that one was pro-government. In the university of Poznan, for instance, the few students who belonged to the pro-government organization were exposed to intimidation and chicanery from their fellows, as well as to victimization from some of the professors. Some professors from various universities, who did not conceal their anticlericalism or disapproval of antisemitism, had to endure whistles and shouts in lecture rooms, and on some occasions were pelted with rotten eggs. Sometimes the students started riots which assumed the proportions of battles against the police.

The curious feature of the National Party was the anti-capitalist streak in its ideology. In this it resembled the National Party of South Africa, and for the same reason: the big industrialists were not of their stock. In Poland they were mostly Germans or Jews, and some of the biggest establishments were owned by foreign companies. Similar circumstances gave an anti-capitalist tinge to nationalist ideologies in a number of Latin American and ex-colonial countries. The Polish National Party fought battles on many fronts, one of them being of the small and middle size business against big business. It remains to be noted that even the wing whose programmes and values could without exaggeration be described as Fascist, and whose members admired Mussolini and Hitler, was violently anti-German. Obviously the creed of sacred egoism of the nation provides no basis for an international.

To understand the whole situation one must bear in mind the extremely hard economic conditions, which did not yet last long enough to induce despondency: aggressive resentment, not fatalistic lethargy, was the prevailing mood of the people. This was combined with the tradition of disobedience and wilfulness, bred by centuries of disorder and foreign rule, and the inclination to violence in everyday life, which was unparalleled in western Europe. These pent-up animosities would probably have discharged themselves in a civil war, were it not for the German invasion.

There is nothing surprising in the connection between antisemitism and economic distress. A similar relationship has been observed in many other cases, and there is no reason to believe that antisemitism is exempt from social causation, or that the sufferings of the Jews are something absolutely unique. Unfortunately, the annals of cruelty are inexhaustible and other minorities have experienced at some time or other all the iniquities inflicted upon the Jews. The extermination of the Christians in Japan was just as thorough as Hitler's genocide. If fewer were killed it was because they were fewer. When massacring the Armenians, the Turks perpetrated all the deeds of which the SS men are guilty. If the history of antisemitism is particularly long it is because the Jews have clung to their separateness with unique tenacity. Most minorities could not be persecuted for so long because they dissolved themselves in the surrounding population.

In so far as there could be no antisemitism without Jews, the economic interpretation is incomplete because it fails to account for the unique continuity of the Jewish cultural tradition and ethnic identity. Nor could the tenacity of the Jews in preserving their identity be the consequence of oppression, because other oppressed minorities did not acquire it.

The most general conclusion which emerges from this analysis of the economic roots of antisemitism, as well as from the preceding examination of other forms of racial discrimination, is that preaching alone will not extirpate them, and that they cannot be attenuated if the economic conflicts do not abate. The lesson for social engineering is plain.

Economic conflict is not a necessary condition of ethnic and racial animosity but it is a sufficient condition thereof. As the position of Negroes in the USA shows, animosity may exist without serious economic conflict, but it is inevitable where such conflict is bitter.

When goods are growing scarce men will fight for the shares, but whether they will divide themselves on class lines, or according to religious or ethnic or racial distinctions, depends on the relative strength of the various kinds of social bonds: a fissure occurs along the line of least cohesion. The difficulty of harmonizing conflicting interests will be greatest if more than one distinguishing mark coincides: if, for instance, class positions correspond to differences in religion, language, culture and physical traits. Obversely, where such differences cut across the stratification they tend to prevent the crystallization of conflict along the class lines.

The part played by the struggle for a share in wealth in exacerbating antagonisms between collectivities in no way ensures that the movements thus generated offer a real solution to economic ills. Normally the contrary is the case: strife aggravates instead of alleviating poverty, and a vicious circle comes into existence.

WAYNESBURG COLLEGE LIBRARY
WAYNESBURG, PA

PART TWO

ANTECEDENTS AND PROSPECTS OF TOTALITARIANISM

CHAPTER TWENTY-TWO

OLD AND NEW ELEMENTS IN
TOTALITARIANISM

What is Totalitarianism?

'TOTALITARIANISM' was invented in order to designate a political régime whereby the government controls the totality of social life. Complications stem from the fact that although some governments have come near the mark in this respect, no government has ever controlled every action of every citizen, and therefore we must decide at which point of extension of governmental control are we prepared to classify a régime as totalitarian. It might be argued, for instance, that the Fascist régime in Italy was not really totalitarian as it never seriously interfered with the activities of the Church. Another difficulty stems from divergencies of directions in which control is extended. Thus, for instance, the control over British economy exercised by the Labour government from 1946 till 1950 was more extensive, and a great deal more effective, than that of Peron over the economic life of Argentina, notwithstanding his suppression of civil liberties. Suppression of political opposition has always been a common phenomenon to be found in many states which accommodated themselves to the independent power of the Church, and even supported the doctrine of *laissez-faire* in economic matters: as was the case of the Second Empire in France, to mention one of many possible examples.

It is clear then that autocracy does not imply totalitarianism, but does totalitarianism imply autocracy and tyranny? Up till now all totalitarian states have been despotic, but we cannot exclude the possibility that the Soviet régime might evolve into a form of totalitarianism which will be oligarchic and fairly law-abiding. To allow for such a possibility it is preferable to define totalitarianism as a régime where a government recognizes no limits to its interference, controls in considerable measure all aspects of the lives of its subjects, and permits no independent organizations. This definition covers Nazi Germany and all present day Communist states excepting Poland. Gomulka's Poland and Mussolini's Italy fall into the category of semi-totalitarianism because of the independent power of the Church within their territories.

Juridical Defence of the Citizen

The least original feature of modern totalitarianism is the lack of restraints upon those who wield supreme authority, which may seem unusual only in the context of European civilization, where a concurrence of peculiar circumstances (above all the split between ecclesiastic and political power) prevented extreme concentration of power, with the result that even so-called absolute monarchs never enjoyed absolute power. In comparison with Suleiman the Magnificent, Louis XIV was almost a constitutional monarch. As Max Beloff puts it in his remarkable synthesis (*The Age of Absolutism*, London 1954): 'That absolutism was limited partly, as De Tocqueville saw, by the existence of intermediary powers in the shape of privileged classes or centres of local autonomy, but also because of the fact that outside those groups through whom power was actually exercised, its reliance had perforce to be upon passive obedience that could not easily, or for long be brought to undergo major sacrifices for public ends. . . . There were recognized rights that were exercised in practice and that were recognized – the right of petition, the right of association for non-political purposes, subject in some cases to official authorization. By the standards of modern totalitarianisms, the France of the 18th century was a veritable sanctuary of liberalism. . . . For if the rights of the individual were an as yet unrecognized abstraction, the rights and powers of social groups were still a formidable force.'

The mere absence of limitations on authority cannot be attributed to the influence of technology, but the increased efficiency of control has been rendered possible by modern means of transport and communication. Tolstoy once said that what he feared most was a Genghis Khan with a telephone, and the fate of his country has proved that his fears were not exaggerated. Nevertheless, the improvements in the techniques of transport and communication contributed to the geographical extension of the areas effectively tyrannized rather than to the intensification of tyranny around the tyrant. Moreover, even this extension has not always added to the sum of misery because the inability of the chief tyrant to sustain his grip on the inhabitants of the out-lying provinces gave a free hand to local tyrants, who most often were no better. Telephone, radio, television, finger-printing, card-indexing have greatly strengthened the hand of the police, but it is surprising how efficient some ancient police systems were, relying mainly on the expedient of collective responsibility.

Thought Control

Persecutions of deviationists are in no way a novelty, for it is ideological tolerance that is something new in human history, and it is the content of the doctrines rather than insistence on their unquestioning acceptance that distinguishes modern totalitarianism. In content the doctrine of Communism is a great deal more original than Nazism or Fascism: the ideal of unquestioning obedience to a ruler whose every word is law is of hoary antiquity, whereas the sanctification of a cruel despotism by a myth of equality and democracy is original.

The imposition of an ideology and the persecution of heretics are relatively easy tasks which could be effectively performed even by very rudimentary administrative machinery: unlike economic planning or mechanized warfare, heretic hunting does not need a complex division of labour and co-ordination. The heterogeneous population of the far-flung Spanish Empire in America was successfully converted to Catholicism, and kept for centuries within the bounds of strict orthodoxy, notwithstanding the state of communications, the relatively small number of clergy and royal officials, and their rudimentary organization. It is possible that the new methods of brain-washing and subliminal persuasion might make the impact of official persuaders irresistible and indelible, but so far they have never been used on a large scale. Lenin and Trotsky combined normal demagogy with terror, Hitler and Goebbels displayed in addition great ingenuity in working out a technique of mass semi-hypnosis, but Stalin relied exclusively on age-long methods of censorship, repetition and the punishment of doubters and critics. Chinese Communists seem to be more inventive in this field because as well as generally known methods they use a technique of persuasion which seems to be derived from psychoanalysis and the practices of revivalist groups in Christianity, as well as from some ancient Taoist traditions, and which resembles collective confession as well as the sessions of psychotherapeutic groups.

Absolute control over belief in no way necessitates governmental control of economy, as can be seen from the example of the régime instituted in Geneva by Calvin. There, and the same was true of Puritan communities in New England, any expression of doubt about the tenets of the official religion was punished by death, which was also inflicted for uttering any remark which could be construed as blasphemy or obscenity. Everybody's private life was continuously scrutinized, and any shortcomings in observance of prayer and church attendance severely punished. There were laws backed by rigorous sanctions about what people could eat, when and how much, what they could wear (all ostentatious ornaments being forbidden), how many guests and how often they could entertain. The Calvinists not only attempted to stamp out adultery and fornication, but even issued regulations on the subject of frequency and times of marital intercourse. Even more: expressions of affection came within the purview of criminal law, and there have been cases of married couples burned at the stake for having kissed on a Sunday.

It is probable that the Puritan obsession with the sinfulness of sex was a product of the mental shock to the populations of Europe caused by the spread of venereal diseases brought from America. Be that as it may, the fact remains that in Puritan communities the agents of the government, guided by the religious leaders, pried into details of people's lives which even Stalin's police informers left out. Nevertheless, we cannot describe Calvin's Geneva as a totalitarian polity because its government never interfered with the freedom to produce, buy and sell. In fact, they even widened the area of economic freedom by abolishing the prohibition of taking interest. Calvin, of course, was not a Cobdenite and he neither abolished the old municipal regulations concerning economic activities nor dissolved the guilds – as a matter of fact he even sponsored municipal aid to spinners and weavers in order to help the refugees of his faith to establish themselves in Geneva – but on the whole he left production and exchange alone, whilst concerning himself with consumption in so far as it affected morals. Moreover, Calvin's régime in Geneva was not a despotic autocracy. Calvin never claimed the right of arbitrary rule, and acted in accordance with the laws promulgated by the Council, under his guidance. Nevertheless the relationship between the elders of his religious community on one side and the organs of the municipal government on the other, resembled more the relationship between the party and the government in the Communist states of today than the relationship between the Church and the Crown in Catholic Europe. The Puritan communities of New England were thoroughly democratic, and this proves that democracy, in the sense of government by the consent of the majority, is not at all inseparable from liberty, in the sense of tolerance of dissent; and may be accompanied by intransigent doctrinairism and persecutions of nonconformism.

It has been said that one of the most significant differences between old autocracies and modern totalitarian régimes is that, whereas the former were satisfied with passive obedience, the latter demand manifestations of active enthusiasm. This is broadly true if we compare Stalin's or Hitler's régimes with European monarchies or military dictatorships like that of Primo de Rivera in Spain; but if we go further back or out of Christendom, we find cults of rulers no less obligatory than the famed 'cult of personality': the Christians were thrown to the lions for refusing to worship the emperor. As far as ordinary sycophancy was concerned, neither Hitler nor Stalin pushed their demands for obeisances to the limits which were usual at oriental courts or at the court of Louis XIV, where courtiers had to enthuse whilst witnessing an opening of the royal bowels. Stalin's sycophants merely resorted to ancient tricks, for in this sphere the possibilities are limited, and all possible methods of flattery and self-abasement had already been tried. Here, the employment of mass media amounts to a difference in quantity rather than in kind.

Stalin's reliance on terror proves that his propaganda machine was only moderately successful. Defections of soldiers provide a fairly good index of loyalty, and these were much more numerous during the Second World War than during the First, which means that Stalin never inspired so much devotion among the Russian people as Tzar Nicolas II. Indeed the German invaders were welcomed in many regions, and it is extremely probable that they would have won if they had not committed so many atrocities, which convinced the Russian people that this was a war of extermination against them as a nation.

Whereas Stalin's rise was due to his skill at organizing and intrigue, not at propaganda, Hitler's career would have been impossible without loud-speakers and radio, because without them the impact of his uncanny gift of hypnotic demagogy would have been circumscribed by the reach of his voice. There have been great demagogues before, able to send crowds into a trance, but they could only directly influence relatively small numbers. So the modern media of communication made possible on a large scale what had previously been possible only on a much smaller scale.

On the whole it seems that the media of mass communication have a greater impact on democratic than on authoritarian régimes: that they undermine democracy more than they fortify authoritarianism. Government by consent requires multiplicity and real independence of the agencies diffusing information, and therefore, concentration of this function in the hands of a few gigantic concerns makes democracy largely illusory. In authoritarian régimes, on the other hand, diffusion of information is anyway controlled by the government, and so the mass media merely add to the amount of repetition, without altering the essential feature of the situation which is the monopoly of propaganda. The greater frequency of repetition is probably unimportant in view of the well-proven efficacity of such old-fashioned means as the pulpit and the stake. Moreover, so long as there is rivalry between states, radio has weakened rather than strengthened authoritarian régimes, by providing their subjects with access to outside sources of information: in spite of jamming, the inhabitants of the Soviet Empire have more contact with heresies than the subjects of Philip II of Spain. As far as the techniques of indoctrination are concerned, it seems that modern technology has bolstered totalitarianism less than is generally believed, although it is quite possible that the latest methods invented by American advertisers may prove more efficacious. Dogmatism, intolerance and persecution flourished in the past, and indoctrination was as effective as it is now. However, radio, film and television have greatly accelerated the processes of mass conversion.

Mobilization

Hitler's régime was frankly dedicated to conquest, and therefore, it is not surprising that its structure was largely determined by military considerations; but even the Soviet state, notwithstanding its very different ideology, owed its structure to the requirements of mass warfare. Its basic features can be regarded as a reaction to the old régime's defeat in war, and as counter-measures against its three most notable weaknesses: first, the rulers' executive incapacity, principally due to the entrenchment of hereditary privilege; second, insufficient industrialization; and third, the inability of the government to control the mass of armed peasants.

An increased need for a certain kind of service does not always redound to the advantage of those who render them, because those who need them may resort to more systematic coercion or even enslavement. Thus, slavery and serfdom flourished principally in sparsely populated regions, like those of America, where it was worth the employer's while (at least in the short run) to restrict workers' freedom to leave. In densely populated countries like India and China, the abundance of supply made legal ownership of labour unprofitable; and this was the factor, incidentally, which led to the abolition of slavery in the West Indies once they became densely populated. Enslavement, however, is possible only if the balance of power between the prospective parties permits it, and if it does not, then the people whose services have become more necessary may have to be more amply rewarded. Thus, democracy and the welfare state on the one side, and totalitarian control and the apparatus of coercion on the other, may be regarded as alternative responses by governments to the increase in the need for participation by the masses in the war effort. These responses are alternative only in so far as their general direction is concerned, for in reality there is a great deal of overlap: the instruments of indoctrination and control possessed by the democratic welfare state are a good deal more powerful than those that absolute monarchs had at their disposal, whilst on the other hand, totalitarian governments by no means rely on the stick to the exclusion of the carrot. Freedom from the need to think for oneself, satisfactions of gregariousness, canalization of frustration into xenophobic passions, opportunity to imagine oneself in a child-father relationship with the ruler, combined with vicarious enjoyment of his power and glory constitute important sources of satisfaction. To these must be added the doctrine of mystic democracy and an abolition, or at least substantial diminution, of hereditary privileges.

The armies of Hitler and Stalin endured greater exertions and defeats than the armies of the Kaiser and the Tzar, but unlike the latter they never revolted because their masters had taken due notice of the events of 1917 and 1918, and organized machines of indoctrination and terror which made any repetition impossible.

Production

Governmental regulation of the economy has been more usual than *laissez-faire* throughout history. Above all, the state's claims on available manpower have often been great. The building of the Chinese wall was a tremendous undertaking, requiring hundreds of billions of man-hours. The irrigational works on the Yangtse or the Nile, the Pyramids, the Roman and Inca roads were undertakings on a comparable scale. Most governments before the 19th century attempted to control prices, albeit with slight success. Greek 'tyrants', Roman emperors, municipal councils of medieval cities, Ottoman sultans and many other rulers issued edicts on this matter. It remains nevertheless true that owing to the rudimentary state of accountancy and administrative techniques in general, these efforts were on the whole futile, and never even remotely approached the efficiency of Nazi economic controls.

Restrictions on the freedom of movement were a regular feature of many empires. In Byzantium, for instance, nobody was allowed to travel except officials on mission and licensed merchants following approved routes; and the same was true of Egypt towards the end of the Caliphate. In Rome from Diocletian onwards all professions were made hereditary, and to leave one's father's occupation constituted a crime. Many forcible transplantations of populations have also been recorded. The difference between these arrangements and the practices of modern totalitarianism, lay chiefly in the fact that neither the technology nor administrative techniques of traditional despotism permitted detailed and continuous marshalling of human resources.

Apart from various forms of community of property among kinship groups, the sphere of private property has more often than not been restricted by the rights of the state. To recapitulate what has been said in the chapters on feudalism and oriental despotism: in despotic states the kings claimed to own everything that existed within the boundaries of their realms, and regarded all private possessions as temporary concessions. The legal basis of feudal land tenure was the notion that all land belongs to the king, who grants the use thereof as a reward for service. In Europe the nobles succeeded in converting feudal land tenure into allodial (ie full property), but in thoroughly despotic states this conversion never took place. In the Ottoman Empire, for instance, the greater part of the land was distributed to soldiers on a tenure which was strictly dependent upon satisfactory performance of duties, whilst the rest was held by religious corporations in perpetual trusteeship known as 'wakf'. Some of the examples quoted (in the chapters on Mobility and on Parasitism) also show how precarious the rights of property in despotic states were.

The empire of the Incas provides a sociologist with much food for thought because although it was the most totalitarian state of the past it rested upon technological foundations which were more primitive than those of any state of Asia or Europe. The Incas had neither the wheel nor animals of traction; neither iron nor bronze. They knew how to smelt copper and gold but as these metals are soft, all their tools and weapons were made of stone. They knew neither the plough nor the scythe, nor the potter's wheel. They administered their totalitarian state without being able to write, and solely with the aid of a system of symbols in the shape of knots on a cord. The structure of society consisted of two parts of unequal age: the ancestral village communities and the superimposed machine of the state, constructed by the conquerors, principally by the ruler regarded as the founder of the empire, whose name was Pachakutek, which means in Kechua reformer of the world. The Incas did not destroy the village communities which they subjugated, but standardized their size, customs and habits of work, and supervised them closely. Their inspectors saw to it that the land was assigned and re-assigned to families for cultivation in such a way as to maximize production, that dues in labour and in kind were promptly paid, that there were no idlers, and that everybody dressed and ate in accordance with the regulations. As marriage was obligatory, royal inspectors paired off and married those who were shirking this duty.

Conscription for war and construction was universal in principle, and in practice limited only by technical possibilities. The emperor was the son of the sun, and therefore a god; the religious rites were incorporated into the state religion and practised under official supervision. The entire structure was, of course, very much simpler than anything in an industrial civilization, but as there was no sphere of social life which was not rigorously controlled by the government, we are justified in classifying the Inca state as totalitarian. Its élitarian ideology, as well as the fact that it was constructed by extending control over existing economic units rather than by shattering the whole framework and then reconstructing it, bring it nearer to the Nazi than to the Communist pattern.

The systems of control over economic life instituted by the Fascists and the Nazis neither contained radically new devices nor were entirely unprecedented in the extent of their supervision. They were, of course, more complicated than the administration of Ptolemaic Egypt, but they can be regarded as the application to modern technology and economy of some very ancient methods of organization. This link with the past was, in a sense, recognized by the ideologues of these régimes, who depicted them as a reversion from degenerate individualism to the sounder principles of pre-capitalist society. The Soviet economic system, on the other hand, represents something much more novel.

The theories of Karl Marx incited the Bolsheviks to destroy the embryonic capitalism of Russia, but provided them with no guidance as to what to put in its place. Marx was a great interpreter of the capitalist society, and he made unforgettable though one-sided contributions to its understanding, but as a planner of socialism he was not even second-rate because, unlike Saint-Simon, Proudhon and a number of other early socialists, he never produced even the slightest blue-print of what was to be done after the revolution. His views on the importance of class struggles, and their economic motivation, are perfectly applicable in analysing Soviet society, but his economic writings throw about as much light on the organization of the Soviet economy as the Sermon on the Mount does on the working of the papal administration.

The construction of the Soviet state was the most original piece of social engineering ever attempted, and it was the work of Lenin, Stalin, and their assistants who had to improvise in order to put something in the place of what they had destroyed. The orthodox Marxists, on the other hand, wanted to allow capitalism to develop until it reaches the level of industrialization and concentration of ownership which, in accordance with Marx's postulates, would make a socialist revolution possible as well as inevitable. The startling originality of Lenin's conception consisted in regarding governmental control over the economy as a tool of industrialization and technical progress, instead of viewing it (as Marx did) solely as an instrument of redistribution of wealth. The chief source of Lenin's inspiration on this point was the spectacle of the German war economy, with its planned allocation of resources, mobilization and direction of labour, rationing, price control and so on. Seeing the extraordinary efficiency of economic mobilization, Lenin came to the conclusion that the same must be done in order to do away with Russia's backwardness. Now Russia's technical progress provides a standing, even if in many ways a misleading, example to countries where capitalism brought no opulence.

The most essential feature of the Communist variant of totalitarianism, which distinguishes it from its forerunners, as well as from its Nazi-Fascist opposite numbers, is not its egalitarian ideology, respected more in word than in deed, but its dynamic nature: the old totalitarian régimes were oriented entirely – and the modern Fascist brands mainly – towards maintaining the economic structure, whereas Communist governments make gigantic efforts to transform their economic basis. A Marxist interpretation would suggest that by doing so they make a transformation of their political institutions inevitable.

The Party

There is nothing new in one party rule: we can find many examples of it in ancient Greece and Rome. What is new in modern totalitarian parties is their elaborate organization, their numbers, and their ideological functions. In these respects they resemble much more an army or a priesthood than the old fashioned political parties. The Nazi party resembled the Janissaries much more than the Whigs or even the Jacobins; whilst the nearest analogy to the ruling Communist parties are the ruling priesthoods of the past. There are not many examples of such priesthoods, because although the priests had great influence and equally great privileges in most societies, they rarely held undisputed sway. Among such cases were Egypt at the time of Herihor, Tibet under the Dalai Lamas and the Papal State in Italy. The Pope was a prince as well as the head of the Church, and many of his assistants were officers of the state as well as dignitaries of the Church. In none of these cases, however, did the priests alone constitute the upper class, as there were also lay nobilities. In the state founded by the Teutonic Order in what later became East Prussia the warrior monks were the only rulers, but they were primarily a military and only vestigially an ecclesiastic community. The colony which the Jesuits established in the 17th century in Paraguay offers the closest parallel to the modern Communist states (Poland excepted) in respect of the undisputed dominance of a theocratic (or ideocratic) body and the pervasiveness of its sway. Naturally, the methods and the machinery of control were on a completely different scale. The Indian collective farms were very primitive and their joint population never surpassed 150,000; but the control exercised over them by the Jesuits was absolute and total: the Jesuits planned and supervised production and distribution of goods, organized and led the army, administered justice, and regulated morals and everyday habits. Neither native chiefs nor a privileged nobility nor wealthy merchants existed in their state: the Indian subjects were indeed socially equal.

Further parallels between ecclesiastic bodies and the Communist party can be found in the realm of techniques of social engineering. Thus the practice of criticism and self-criticism obviously derives from the Catholic institution of confession and from the customs of some monastic orders. In their techniques of infiltration the Communists have learned much from the Jesuits.

Modern totalitarianism had many antecedents but although many of the ingredients are old, their combination with a progressive technology constitutes a new phenomenon in the history of mankind.

CHAPTER TWENTY-THREE

FACTORS OF LIBERALIZATION

LIBERAL RÉGIMES have been products of very special circumstances connected first with the division between Church and state, and later with some measure of division between political and economic power. The countries where liberalism has flourished have never lived under the harsher and more thorough varieties of despotism: even the absolutism of Louis XIV was very mild in comparison with the traditional despotisms of the East. The process of cumulation of power is not easily reversible. Helvetius, writing in the 18th century, thought that the natural trend of human evolution was towards despotism, and that if the régimes of the countries of Europe were milder than those of the East it was only because they had lasted a shorter time. Without being so pessimistic, we can doubt whether in this age of enormous organizations a liberal tradition can strike roots where it had none before. Perhaps the liberal political régimes are something that has been formed by circumstances no longer existing, and that persists by the sheer force of tradition.

On the other side of the balance we must take into account that with modern technology (including the techniques of birth control) it is feasible to eliminate the poverty which was an underlying condition of the despotisms of old. There is then a further argument that in these days when scientific knowledge is indispensable for the very existence of a state, we might hope for a somewhat more rational solution to the problem of how to live in society than could be expected in magic-ridden ages.

Undoubtedly, there are factors which might deflect the evolution of the Soviet régime in the direction of liberalization. The USSR is not only the strongest but also the oldest of the totalitarian states in existence. Revolutionary idealism, which may still pervade

China, has ceased to play an important role in its life. Its administrative machine is propelled by the will to power, and the nature of its action is determined mainly by its structural properties.

A number of arguments have been advanced against the possibility of the Soviet régime ever evolving in the direction of liberalization. The first is that masterfulness and submissiveness – the two complementary psychological correlates of despotism – have struck such deep roots in the Russian national character that no other form of government is at all possible in Russia. This argument can be rejected on two grounds: firstly, because it assumes a permanence of national character for which there is no evidence (in the case of the Russians we can see that they have become much more circumspect than they used to be in the olden days); secondly, because there are proofs that the dislike of tyranny is fairly widespread in Russia even among people who do not reject the Communist doctrine.

The second argument is based on the character of this doctrine. It is perfectly true, as Mosca predicted sixty years ago, that a sincere attempt to put Marxist doctrines into practice must produce a totalitarian despotism by eliminating all social forces which can oppose the government. On the other hand, however, the Communist practice of twisting any tenet of the doctrine to suit their ends of aggrandizement demonstrates that the Marxist view of ideologies as mere cloaks for pursuit of interests applies to Marxism itself with greater force than it does to traditional religions. In contrast to believers in traditional religions, the Marxists are not discouraged from altering their doctrine by any belief that the tenets of their faith have been enjoined upon them by a Being mightier than themselves. Marxism, moreover, has neither enchanting rituals nor does it provide much consolation to the unfortunate: indeed, it ceases to function as 'the opium of the masses' once the revolution is over and the 'workers' paradise' has arrived. We may surmise therefore, that changes in the structure of power might bring about appropriate modifications in the official ideology.

The third argument stems from Helvetius' idea, mentioned above: it is claimed that accumulation of power is irreversible. Now, although it is true that so far no case of radical liberalization of a perfectly totalitarian régime has been noted (for the obvious reason that apart from the present Communist states there has been only one other case: that of Hitler's Germany), there are many old and recent examples which prove the possibility of decumulation of power, resulting in liberalization through internal transformations. Prussia under Wilhelm II was a great deal more liberal than under his great-grandfather. Argentina under Peron was well on the way to totalitarianism and nevertheless the trend has been reversed. These examples of the decumulation of power, to which others could be added, do not prove that a thorough liberalization of the Soviet régime is probable, but they do indicate that such a possibility cannot be *a priori* excluded.

All serious students of Soviet affairs agree that since the death of Stalin there has occurred in the USSR a process which might be described as liberalization. In some respects it may have been halted recently, or even reversed, but in other respects it seems to go on. The extent and the pace of this process are continuously debated among specialists on Soviet affairs, and not being one of them I have nothing new to say on this matter: as far as the facts of the case are concerned, I take the prevalent opinions of sovietologists as my premise. What I shall try to do here is to analyse the causes of this phenomenon in the light of comparative sociology. A causal analysis is of great importance not only from the purely intellectual but also from the practical point of view: for practical action can be effective only in so far as it is based on correct predictions; and correctness of predictions depends on our knowledge of causation. In what concerns the case in hand, it makes all the difference whether the relaxation of the Stalinist tyranny took place because his successor lacked the taste for blood, or whether it resulted from some structural changes at least partially independent of the ruler's will. If the latter is the case, the question arises: are these changes reversible or not?

The necessity of ascertaining causes will, no doubt, be readily admitted but it may be objected that this is a task for specialists on the area. The answer is that reliability of prediction depends not only on correctness of the factual information but also on the knowledge of regularities, which enables us to make inferences from this information about future events. My task here is to examine the major premises underlying various hypotheses about the evolution of the Soviet system. The reason why historians and area specialists are nearly always wrong in their predictions is that their sole inductive method consists of simple extrapolation: they simply assume the permanence of characteristics or existing trends. Alternatively they tacitly adopt premises which do not bear scrutiny. For example, Isaac Deutscher asserts that the Soviet régime must become democratic because the country has been industrialized. The assumption here is that the condition of being industrialized produces a democratic system. Unfortunately, it is contradicted by the evidence of the rise of Nazism in Germany, which was proportionately more industrialized in 1933 than Russia will be within this decade.

In view of its etymology 'liberalization' should have something to do with increasing freedom, but 'freedom' is a tricky word. Nimble wits have spun enormous webs of casuistry around this word, although few have outdone Hegel in his definition of freedom as the opportunity to obey the state. It might be better to follow the common-sense meaning of this word – but only when it is used in the adjectival form, for common sense makes sense only when it deals with concrete everyday actions. When we ask somebody: 'Are you free this afternoon?' we want to know whether he can choose what he is going to do. By liberalization, therefore, we might mean a process of giving the population more opportunities of choice. However, a widening of the area of choice in one respect might be accompanied by a restriction in other respects. Even if we found some ways of assessing the equivalence of being free in various respects, the difficulty of estimating differences in total freedom would remain enormous. We can be sure that Byron was freer than a galley slave, but it is by no means obvious that on the whole people were less free in the England of his days than they are today. We must, therefore, further delimit the object of the present study: firstly, I shall consider only the limitations on freedom imposed by the apparatus of the state, and secondly, only certain aspects of these limitations.

To approach the problem from the other end, I shall interpret the process of liberalization as consisting of the following elements: (1) elimination of terror; (2) attenuation of severity and frequency of punishments; (3) growth of tolerance of non-regimented activities; (4) diminution of doctrinairism.

One of the most important differences between the Communist régimes and the old-fashioned despotisms is that the latter demanded obedience and an occasional show of deference, whereas the former give a religious twist to their systems by insisting on active manifestations of enthusiasm: the Communists do not like ideological indifference and generally do not allow their subjects to keep aside from politics. Recognition of a right to merely passive obedience would constitute the first step towards liberalization, already partly taken. As the second step in this direction we could consider the toleration of unorganised grumbling, which within the Communist orbit is permitted only in Poland up till now. Intolerance in this respect was not, of course, invented by the Communists, but has been the rule rather than an exception throughout history. Permission to enter into contacts with foreigners would constitute another step towards liberalization. Restrictions of this sort were not invented by the Bolsheviks either: they were common in Russia before Peter I, and in Japan any contact with foreigners was punishable with death for over two centuries. A rather common form of freedom of which the Communist subjects are deprived, is the freedom to form politically neutral associations; and there can be no liberalization without a restoration of this right. A much higher grade of tolerance would consist of permitting criticism of high officials in public, and criticism of the official doctrine. The freedom to do so is quite exceptional, and constitutes one of the most precious and fragile achievements of the Western civilization. The most extreme form of tolerance, is the tolerance of associations which advocate an overthrow of the government by force. There is, of course, no question of such tolerance within the Soviet orbit even in the remote future.

There is a difference between tolerating what one does not approve of and being indifferent to an issue. Expression of some opinions may become permissible because the ideology ceased to take cognizance of them as its sphere of influence. The Catholic Church, for instance, used to prescribe opinions on astronomy and biology but now is indifferent upon these matters. At one time Soviet exegeticists condemned Einstein's theory as an excrescence of *bourgeois* perversity, but later they let the matter drop. Stalin pontificated on biology and linguistics, but his heir keeps out of these fields. We can say then that there has occurred some contraction of the sphere of ideological regulation. Such a contraction need not involve a weakening of belief in the remaining tenets of the doctrine, although it may be accompanied by such a weakening.

How far can an ideology contract without losing its influence upon society? The answer seems to be that it can shed items which are unnecessary for justifying the existing structure of power. Gaetano Mosca proposed the term 'political formula' for the body of beliefs which justify the existing political order. A process of shedding those parts of the ideology which do not constitute a political formula might amount to liberalization.

States differ very much in the severity and frequency of punishments which they mete out to their subjects, but so far nobody has succeeded in formulating a theory which would account for these variations. According to Durkheim, punishments are more severe in societies which are not troubled by doubt and dissent. Sorokin, on the other hand, maintains that they are most severe and frequent where the rulers are trying to impose upon their subjects a code of behaviour which commands no assent, or at least no support, from the moral sentiments of their subjects. It seems that these theories can be reconciled, but that other factors must be brought into consideration as well.

There would be no crimes if nothing were forbidden, whereas everybody would be committing crimes all the time if breathing and eating were illegal. Reflecting upon these obvious truths, we see that punitivity – that is to say, severity and frequency of punishments – must depend on the extent to which the laws prevent satisfaction of basic needs, and on the determination of the wielders of power to enforce such laws. No poor nation has yet been discovered where thefts and robberies were not common. Only when nobody is driven to steal by lack of food, clothing or shelter, is a fair degree of law-abidingness at all possible, though by no means inevitable. There are also many examples which show that an attempt to impose on an unselected population a puritanical sexual code produces an outcrop of crimes and punishments. The well-known example of the Prohibition in the USA illustrates the same point. The same is true of piety and ideological fervour: it is fairly easy to make people perform occasional rituals but there are strict limits to what can be exacted from ordinary people. After much trial and error the churches have discovered that one hour once a week is about the maximum that can be obtained from the majority without resorting to frequent and severe punishments. Only a small minority wish to enter into ideological debates, but nearly everybody wants to have some opportunity to decide on the use of his time, to be left in peace occasionally and to be able to grumble. Any régime which tries to stamp out all manifestations of these propensities is bound to be extremely punitive. The same is true about demands for excessive effort which can be enforced only by severe punishments: overworked horses or galley slaves can be driven only with a whip. Furthermore, everybody likes to make little decisions about the matters of his own everyday life, and particularly about the use of leisure, and will be tempted to break the rules which deprive him of opportunities to do so: in other words, regimentation necessitates punitivity.

It makes a great deal of difference whether punishments are administered according to known rules prescribing what is punishable and how, or whether they are meted out at the whim of the wielders of power. Severity of punishments does not depend entirely on the absence of the rule of law. In the early days of the Roman republic punishments were extraordinarily severe but were inflicted strictly in accordance with the laws. In the oriental sultanates they were severe and unpredictable. There are no cases of punishments being mild and at the same time administered without regularity, the explanation being that irregularity in this sphere amounts to a lack of restraints on the wielders of authority, and under such circumstances at least some of them will punish savagely, either out of sadism or in order to enlarge their sway.

If we apply the foregoing considerations to Soviet Russia, it follows that economic progress is a necessary (though not sufficient) condition of liberalization. We must not forget, however, that liberalization is not the same thing as democratization: the subjects may come to be treated much better without acquiring more say in the conduct of government.

There are reasons for thinking that gross poverty may soon be eliminated in Russia. True, its economy is in many ways extremely wasteful, but the rate of building up of productive equipment is extremely high, the resources enormous and the birthrate not inordinately high and declining. The vicious circle of poverty maintaining a high birthrate, which in turn prevents elimination of poverty, is being broken, and a virtuous circle of an increase of wealth leading to a reduction of the birthrate, which in turn permits the attainment and maintenance of opulence, is being established.

The economic prospects are much brighter in Russia than they are in Poland, where scarcity of resources and a high birthrate aggravate the situation. The latter feature is connected with the influence of the Church, which is greater now than it was before the war because the people feel that the Church is their sole protector. Moreover, a system which involves complete regimentation and suppression of unsolicited initiative is more congenial to the Russians, inured to fatalistic obedience by centuries of despotism, than to the Poles with their traditional rebelliousness which is further stimulated by the knowledge that the régime has been imposed upon them by the Russians. How complete is the disloyalty of the Poles towards the régime can be seen from such facts as that (according to an official party newspaper) during 1958 over one million persons were caught travelling on the railways without tickets; this was out of a population of less than thirty million which includes many people who never travel. As normal people do not try to commit an offence unless they have some chance of impunity, this means that practically everybody who uses the railways in Poland tries to travel without a ticket. Even more revealing is the fact that during the same year nearly one thousand ticket collectors and railway policemen were beaten up while carrying out their functions. A confidential estimate of one of the chief planners is that about one third of the total industrial production is stolen. As the Russians are much more secretive, little is known about the corresponding figures in Russia but, although thefts are a regular feature of life there as well, it seems that on the whole the attitude of the Russians to the system is considerably less negative, and this facilitates the operation of the system. For this reason, in addition to the fact that there are superior resources in relation to population, we cannot base our assessment of the economic prospects of the Soviet Union on the parlous situation in Poland.

Growth of wealth ought to bring about some liberalization in several ways. Not only does it lessen the need for draconian punishments, designed to keep starvelings in order and working hard, but it makes slave labour wasteful even from the employer's strictly economic point of view. This is very important because Soviet forced labour camps, which at their peak probably contained about ten million inmates, were designed (unlike the Nazi concentration camps) not just for punishment and extermination but also as a measure of economic exploitation. With machines in plentiful supply, it becomes very wasteful to make a crowd of slaves dig with spades when one man with a bulldozer could do it much quicker, and when even starvation rations for a couple of hundred slaves cost more than petrol and wear and tear of a bulldozer. So, the most brutal features of Soviet life – mass deportations and slave labour – will probably disappear entirely. But there is more to it. Contrary to what many romantically inclined critics of contemporary civilization say about the dehumanizing effects of machines, I believe that contact with machines (particularly with complicated machines) exercises a profoundly humanizing influence in the sense of making people less brutal. The reason for that is very simple: machines do not respond to shouting and beating – to make them work one has to think and be patient. In contrast, the use of animals offers a standing lesson on the advantages of brutality. One only has to reflect upon the fact that in an industrialized country people do not carry whips.

Industrial progress increases the need for the workers not only to be skilled but also to be responsible. As the processes of production become more complicated, bosses become more dependent on the good will of their subordinates because they are less able to supervise everything directly. For this reason it does not pay to ill treat the employees. Indeed the machine deserves our gratitude: it has made the crudest forms of exploitation of labour unprofitable.

Terror on the scale practised by Stalin constitutes an enormous waste of human material which can be maintained only in a country with a very high birthrate. In so far, therefore, as economic progress is conducive to a lowering of the birthrate it makes such practices more ruinous. In the same way as Roman slavery declined when the supply of slaves dried up at the end of the conquests, so must terror as a permanent institution disappear when the birthrate goes down. (An important deduction from this statement is that any tyrant who wants to indulge in terror on the scale of Stalin's exploits must stimulate the birthrate.) This argument applies with particular force to highly skilled personnel because industrialization (particularly in the age of automation) continuously inflates the demand for them, whilst the supply is limited by the scarcity of individuals with the requisite ability to learn. When Stalin 'liquidated' large numbers of officers, managers, officials and technicians, he had at his disposal a plentiful supply of people who, though not so experienced, had the necessary ability to learn on the job. Even so, his purges gravely injured the economic and military strength of the state. With the present size of the Soviet industry – let alone its size in the near future – such hecatombs would cause catastrophic dislocation.

The eagerness to detect and punish every expression of discontent, no matter how trifling, may stem from a sheer love of bullying, but it may also be stimulated by the fear that every flicker of sedition which is not stamped out at once might kindle a fire which will devour the whole edifice. Such fears may be paranoiac but quite often they are not altogether unrealistic. Unlike Lenin and Hitler, Stalin did not command the loyalty of his subordinates, and was in continuous danger of being overthrown: there are good grounds for believing that he was in fact killed. From the point of view of maintaining himself in power, terror was not an irrational procedure, and its extension to the whole population was his response to the discontent of the masses produced by illtreatment and misery. Elimination of these makes terror less useful as a ruling instrument. Even the need for disciplining wayward intellectuals and political rivals diminishes with the growth of wealth because the masses become less susceptible to inflammatory propaganda: as the experience of the countries bordering the North Atlantic shows, prosperity favours the powers that be. Most men limit their preoccupation to what touches them immediately, and begin to take interest in high politics only when they are thoroughly disgruntled. When the population is not suffering severe privations, the rulers need not concern themselves with ordinary grumbling.

There is, as is well known, far greater freedom to grumble in Poland than in Russia. The explanation of this difference seems to be twofold: firstly the party is less able to control the people; and secondly, it has less need to do so. With the example of Hungary before their eyes, the Poles know that there can be no revolution in Poland so long as Soviet power remains intact; therefore, the party is safe and can let the people grumble.

Continuous preoccupation with instilling enthusiasm into the masses, which is so characteristic of the Communist as well as Fascist régimes, is aimed not so much at preventing revolts and sabotage as at mobilizing energies. Since the time of the pyramid builders, the mobilization of labour always had two main aims: construction and war. With abundant provision of machinery work becomes less unpleasant and shorter, and there is less need to spur on the crowds to frantic efforts. At this stage, moreover, further development of production depends primarily on the few technicians and managers whose output will not be best stimulated by the methods applied to starved labourers just emerging from illiteracy. It is not without significance that Soviet scientists and technicians are exempt from the more onerous ritual obligations, and are not much persecuted for ideological tepidity. This incidentally, is one of the chief attractions of the profession, and explains its plentiful supply of brains. More urbane forms of indoctrination might still be useful for stimulating production, but excessively inquisitorial thought control is economically disadvantageous. In the days of computer civilization, terror for the sake of production is just as out of date as the hammer and the sickle.

With economic improvement the chief reasons for penalizing contacts with foreigners should disappear. Up till now the contrast between Western opulence and Soviet poverty was such that it was dangerous from the point of view of the régime to expose its subjects to evidence which might sow dismay and heresy in their souls. This cloistering had another advantage: it isolated Soviet citizens from sights and notions which might whet their appetite for consumer goods and strengthen resistance against collective investment. From now on the accumulation of productive equipment should be less painful. The danger would still remain that the intellectuals might become dissatisfied on seeing the much greater freedom of their Western colleagues, but if the masses were more or less satisfied the feelings of the intellectuals would matter less. Many restrictions, however, will probably remain in order to safeguard the secrets of military technology.

The rule of law – that is to say, security from arbitrary and unpredictable punishments – need not be a product of a struggle for freedom. In England it came into existence when the parliament succeeded in curbing the authority of the kings, but in Prussia it was instituted by the absolute monarchs in the interests of efficiency. Hohenzollerns, unlike other absolute rulers, normally observed the rules which they laid down, and inculcated this principle into their officials. Likewise, the rulers of the Soviet Empire may promote what they call 'socialist legality' in the interests of efficiency, particularly as the increasingly complex structure of their state more than ever demands elimination of arbitrary excesses. It must be noted, however, that legality does not imply tolerance: the laws which are observed may provide for severe punishments of nonconformists. Stalin's excesses were made possible by the fluid state of the Soviet society, and their elimination might be viewed as an aspect of its consolidation.

When Christianity was imposed upon the peoples of northern Europe by their princes, frightful punishments were meted out for non-observance of its commands and for practising pagan rites. When these peoples finally became Christian by conviction, these harsh punishments for religious shortcomings fell into disuse. In the same way, it is not surprising that as the Soviet régime comes to be regarded by its subjects as part of the natural order of things, the savage hunts for deviationists diminish in intensity. Moreover, in the early days of the régime its *élite* was largely composed of fiery revolutionaries and unruly ideologues, whereas now it consists of well-disciplined bureaucrats. The consolidation of the régime strengthens the efficacity of regular and unspectacular disciplinary pressures, and thus makes resorting to terror superfluous. Economic progress acts in the same direction by permitting a wider use of 'the carrot', and thus lessening the need for 'the stick'. It may be questioned, of course, whether all this amounts to liberalization in any acceptable sense of the word; perhaps we should rather describe it as a process of civilization, consisting of an elimination of barbarian practices.

Given the poverty and cultural backwardness of the Russian nation, the chaos produced by the war and the revolution, and the aims which its rulers were determined to pursue, the extremes of tyranny could not be avoided. Now the circumstances which made terror inevitable no longer exist, but it does not follow that it cannot recur. Although harmful economically and militarily, a recrudescence of terror may result from a flaring up of the struggle for power. Its non-recurrence may be insured only by: (1) general acceptance of a rule of orderly succession to the supreme authority and (2) establishment of some limitations on the authority of the chief of the state. Prediction in this matter is much more difficult than when dealing with economic factors. On the whole it does seem that the development of orderly bureaucratic procedures and the routinization of the party, militate against personal despotism but do not rule it out. One can make, however, a conditional prediction: consolidation of the ruling class constitutes a necessary condition of a definitive elimination of autocracy. In all historical cases, the curbing of despotism was the result of collective action by the most privileged class. Such an action is possible only if the privileged class has developed a strong spirit of solidarity and a fairly rigid code of behaviour. The presence of these characteristics among the nobilities of Europe struck Montesquieu and Hume as one of the most important differences between Europe and Asia, causally connected with the prevalence of despotism in the latter part of the world. Indeed, it is difficult to imagine how a despotism, particularly a totalitarian despotism, could be curbed in any other way, because the essence of such a system is pulverization of the masses by suppressing all independent organized bodies; and in such a situation only those inside the governmental machine, and close to the levers of power, can possibly oppose an incipient, let alone an actual, autocrat. As Klyutchevsky – the author of the great work on the history of Russia – put it, 'the light of freedom is like that of the sun: it shines on the tops of the mountains before it reaches the low valleys'. As we saw in the earlier chapters, ancient as well as modern despots understood this mechanism very well, and tried to prevent a solidification of a ruling class by reshuffling it continuously, decimating it and replenishing it with men elevated from the lower reaches of the social pyramid. Stalin's purges can be viewed as an example of this technique. So, paradoxically from the point of view of democratic preconceptions, the progress of liberalization of the Soviet régime depends on the consolidation of its ruling class.

In contrast to what George Orwell believed, the progress of technology has not tilted the balance between autocratic and oligarchic tendencies in favour of the former. Perfection of weapons, improvements in police techniques, and development of the means of propaganda weakened the independence of the masses and made them more malleable, without, however, strengthening the hand of a ruler in dealing with his immediate subordinates.

Stalin's methods of keeping down his assistants did not differ from those of Ivan the Terrible. The growing complexity of the business of governing favours in fact the oligarchic tendency because it compels the ruler to rely to an ever-growing extent on the judgements of his subordinates.

As far as the process of formation of a ruling class is concerned the signs are equivocal. The complaints about idle and pampered sons and daughters of influential officials which one reads in the Soviet Press, the information which we have about the positions occupied by the children of the potentates, and about their tendency to marry within their own social circle, point to the existence of hereditary privileges. On the other hand, there is a spate of decrees aimed at combating the tendency to shun manual labour. Although he makes an exception for his descendants and his son-in-law, Khrushchev is evidently trying to counteract tendencies towards class exclusiveness by his school reforms, but it is difficult to estimate the success of these measures. Their weak point is that every official tries to make an exception as far as his own children are concerned; so that even in a totalitarian state decrees and Press campaigns may remain powerless on such an issue. On the whole, it seems unlikely that the consolidation of a ruling class can be entirely prevented without wholesale purges. We should remember, however, that social mobility is a matter of degree, and that a certain amount of hereditary privilege is quite compatible with fairly wide opportunities of social ascent for selected recruits from the lower classes, particularly if the economy is expanding.

The early Communist prophets regarded the abolition of the family as a condition of social equality. This view may appear objectionable or impracticable but it cannot be said that it is wrong: as all societies are dominated by men, only promiscuity, which would make paternity impossible to ascertain, could ensure the equal chances in the next generation. The present policy of the Soviet government of strengthening family bonds makes it certain that the trend towards hereditary privileges will continue. It must be taken into account, however, that the family has ceased to be the sole purveyor of knowledge, and that the schools and employing organizations perform the function of sifting the entrants. There are no reasons, therefore, for imagining that a society of castes is the only alternative to equality. It is probable, indeed, that as far as social mobility is concerned, Soviet society will not differ radically from what we know in the West.

Many rulers of the past knew very well that hereditary privileges undermine the instrumental efficacity of an administrative machine, and this explains such practices as the employment of eunuchs in official positions. The Catholic Church, which is unique in having preserved its vitality over so many centuries within an essentially unchanging organizational framework, succeeded in preventing hereditary appropriation of offices by enjoining celibacy upon the clergy.

As shown in Chapter Eleven, large accumulations of property, secure from seizure by the government, were in the past a necessary condition of existence of régimes which could be called liberal. If we follow the history of liberalism as a political movement, we see that it flourished only in the countries where there was a numerous class of economically independent and prosperous city dwellers. As mentioned earlier, Gaetano Mosca – who in contrast to other early critics of socialism did not deny the feasibility of a collectivist economy – predicted as early as 1902 that any attempt to put into practice the Communist doctrines would inevitably produce despotism by concentrating control over all the economic resources in the hands of the government. For this reason we must consider briefly the question of the possible re-emergence of capitalism. How we answer this question depends, of course, on what we mean by capitalism. If we mean existence of private property in any form, then we already have capitalism in Russia, as there are people there who own houses, bank accounts, cars and so on. It is very likely that the area of private ownership will be extended. This, however, does not mean that large scale private enterprise will come into existence. This is unlikely because the trend in the capitalist world itself is towards concentrating control over economic life in the hands of giant corporations. The French word for them, 'société anonyme', describes their social character well. Ford, Rockefeller, Carnegie and other great captains of capitalism built their empires when the field was still free. When the market is controlled by state-owned giant firms, it will not be easy to build new business empires even if it were permitted by law.

If there is not much chance of private property emerging as a rampart against autocracy, how, then, could a dispersion of power come about? It seems that the only possibility is a gradual fortification of some forms of autonomy of various parts of the bureaucratic machine – not purely legal autonomy, of course, but some entrenchment connected with solidification and segregation of the controlling cliques. This would require a replacement of the present fluid structure of the Soviet society by a structure which could be described as cystic, which would involve a fair degree of consolidation of the ruling class. Only in this way, it seems, could something resembling a balance of power come into being in the Soviet society. Such a development would not amount to democratization but merely to a liberalization in the sense of eliminating despotism and regularizing the behaviour of the wielders of authority. In this context it is very important to bear in mind that general despotism is just as uncomfortable to the privileged as it is to the burdened layers of society: privileges have much more value if they can be enjoyed in security. A very serious aggravating circumstance is that under a régime of this kind nobody can contract out of the 'rat race': one either treads on others or is trodden upon; or rather, everybody except the dictator and those at the very bottom both treads and is trodden upon. Such a situation inevitably creates an all-pervading atmosphere of bullying and sycophancy. It lies in the interest of those who hold privileges to introduce some measure of regularity which would give them security.

An injection of some hereditary privilege could attenuate the harshness of the Soviet régime in other ways too: it could reduce somewhat the intensity of the struggle for power. Apart from obvious direct benefits, such an attenuation could bring the benefit of occasionally putting into positions of authority men who have not been embittered by the gruelling long climb uphill, who do not crave for power to the point of being ready to sacrifice everything for its sake, and who have other pleasures in life than the exercise of power. Naturally, an evolution in this direction would not be an unambiguous blessing because it would advance men who might be incompetent to discharge their functions, and it might bring back the old vices of a useless and selfish aristocracy. Nevertheless, it must never be forgotten that under many circumstances the sloth of the bosses is the salvation of the underlings.

It has been suggested that the spread of scientific education must in the long run undermine the faith in Marxism. This is quite possible, but alone such a process would lead only to an elimination of doctrinarian absurdities, and not necessarily to a radical change in the character of the Soviet state. In view of the human capacity for wearing blinkers, and the political obscurantism of many scientists and technologists, it is not at all certain that technical progress must contribute to general enlightenment. The level of social and humanistic studies in the country of sputniks is well below what it was in the France of Louis XVI; and it could be argued that even in the West these disciplines are in a state of decline. Science fiction, too, shows us a world of individuals ethnically well below the better (let alone the best) existing standards – nay, true Neanderthal men – manipulating wonderful gadgets. There is no evidence to show that science fiction writers are entirely unrealistic in this respect.

The essential structure of the Soviet state could withstand a very substantial modification of the ideology and an abandonment of doctrinairism, but there is one part of the administrative machine which would lose its position by any lessening of insistence on doctrinal purity: that of the professional propagandists – the people, that is to say, who have a direct vested interest in the doctrine. Changes in the number of such people provide a good pointer to the prospects of intellectual liberalization.

An elimination of terror and of doctrinarian excesses, a slight relaxation of control over every act of every citizen, can be described as a liberalization but not, of course, as an establishment of a liberal polity. In fact, such a liberalization amounts merely to a rationalization of the régime which strengthens it – using 'rationalization' in the sense in which it is employed by management consultants. However, we must not underestimate the importance of this process for alleviation of human suffering.

The apparatus of the party, with its insatiable thirst for power over everything, still exists and there is no outside force in sight which could restrain it. For this reason, a true liberalization – in the sense of a radical widening of the area of tolerance – could come about only through internal dispersion of power, entrenchment of semi-independent groups and attenuation of the intensity of the struggle for power, which would mollify the rulers. Naturally, such a process takes time.

Unlike Stalin, Mao Tse Tung has never resorted much to terror against members of his party. Having organized it and led it to victory, he enjoys personal ascendancy of the kind that Lenin had among the Bolsheviks. With very few exceptions the original team of leaders still remains at the helm. Even the terror against class enemies was less spectacular than what went on in Russia. The victims of vengeance in the aftermath of victory are estimated at three million, and, owing to the weak resistance offered by the forces of Kuo-min-tang, many of whose generals even sold newly arrived American arms to the Communists, the losses on both sides in the civil war which followed the surrender of the Japanese probably did not amount to a million. Even absolutely, let alone in proportion to the population, the corresponding numbers in Russia were greater, and to these must be added the victims of Stalin's purges and the '*kulaks*' (prosperous peasants) deported to forced labour camps on the collectivization of the agriculture.

The lesser brutality of the Chinese régime, as compared with Russia before the death of Stalin, must not be imputed to a greater measure of freedom enjoyed by its subjects. Indeed the contrary is the case, because in China the party controls the lives of its subjects even more thoroughly than in Russia, and the less frequent use of terror demonstrates the superior efficiency of the Chinese party machine and the greater docility of its subjects. The latter can be understood when we take into account that Russia in 1914 was a wealthy country in comparison with China in 1945, and that the régime of Chiang Kai-Shek was a great deal more oppressive, brutal and corrupt than that of Tzar Nicolas II.

The prospects of liberalization of the Chinese régime – in the sense of the growth of tolerance and relaxation of control over the details of the daily lives of the inhabitants – seem considerably bleaker; partly because being newer the Chinese régime commands a larger fund of fanatical doctrinairism, but principally because it lives in an environment of misery which it has much less chance of eliminating. The poverty of Tzarist Russia was entirely due to inefficiency and was not, as is the case in China, a consequence of overpopulation. For some time the Chinese government conducted propaganda in favour of birth control. It seems that whether for doctrinarian or imperialistic motives, this policy has recently been reversed, and there can be no doubt that without an energetic and successful policy in favour of birth control the régime will grow more and more savage, unless it collapses through internal disorder (which is not very probable). Even if in consequence of a policy of birth control the population does not grow exorbitantly, the elimination of poverty will present an enormous task for a long time, and the population will have to be goaded to gigantic exertions by violent stimuli. Under such circumstances, moreover, it might be unsafe for the rulers to loosen the reins: as a Chinese proverb says, 'he who rides a tiger cannot dismount'.[1]

The problem of liberalizing the régimes of the Soviet satellites in eastern Europe requires no extensive treatment because the conditions there are narrowly circumscribed by the situation in Russia. There is a margin within which the conditions in the satellites may vary in response to internal factors, but it is not very wide. Even in the case of Poland, which since 1956 deviated furthest from the Soviet norm, the divergence is by no means enormous and tends to become narrower because Russia is moving slowly in the direction of liberalization while Poland retrocedes or stands still.

Speaking of Russia and China, I have so far analysed only the internal forces, and so before concluding I should like to say something about the possible effects of a hypothetical reversal of alliances, which cannot be ruled out as impossible: the longest land frontier in the world separates overpopulated China from the scarcely populated expanses of Soviet Asia; and as community of faith has never been able to prevent strife in the past, there is no reason to imagine that it must do so in the future, particularly

---

[1] Since this was written the Chinese government has once again changed its attitude towards birth control, which it now favours. The new course has greatly improved the chances of China attaining power and freedom from misery. The enlightened population policy completes the raising of the position of women brought about by the Communist victory.

In assessing the merits of the present régime in comparison with those of the past, we must remember that in pre-Communist China women and children were chattels except in very small highly Westernized circles. For the great majority of the women the curtailment of private power by the totalitarian régime signified a liberation from domestic or commercial slavery which was a great deal worse than governmental regimentation. A number of travellers have remarked that young women seem particularly enthusiastic about the present régime, and it appears that many of them help the police to ferret out the opponents.

The same applies in a smaller measure to young men who were also liberated by the Communists from paternal tyranny, which often assumed atrocious dimensions. The Chinese Communists were able to enmesh and indoctrinate the population much more thoroughly than their Russian comrades ever could (not to speak of eastern European satellites) because the family relations in traditional China rested upon coercion to a much greater extent than was the case in Eastern Europe, and the party had much less difficulty in finding daughters, sons and wives willing to spy on now powerless patriarchs.

as genuine partnership does not come easily to governments which have no internal experience of tolerance and rule by compromise.[1]

Just as community of faith cannot ensure friendship, so an alliance need not bring about a common outlook. When Churchill drank toasts to 'Stalin the Great' the beneficiary of this eulogy was ruling 'the gallant Russian ally' with a ferocity rivalled only by their common enemy Adolf Hitler. In spite of hurling insults at the statesmen of the West in a way that 'Uncle Joe' never did, his successor appears as an embodiment of benevolence in comparison. The régime of Franco has survived the change-over from an alliance with Hitler to an alliance with the USA without any substantial reforms. It is also to the point that there is a great deal more freedom of speech in Poland, which is a Russian satellite, than in Yugoslavia, which has been expelled from the Communist International.

There are many other examples which show that external alignments may have little effect on internal politics – which does not mean, however, that they have none. Possibly if Russia were forced to seek support from the West against a menace from China, its ideology might become less impervious to the enchantments of 'bourgeois decadence'. On the other hand, notwithstanding that old-fashioned totalitarianism is militarily out of date, strenuous preparations for war remain an almost insuperable obstacle to liberalization.

[1] This was written before the breach between Moscow and Peking became open. On this point I can claim to have made a correct forecast which was rejected by specialists on Communist affairs as 'purely theoretical'. In 1950 I wrote that 'China will undoubtedly emerge as a great power and, driven by the land hunger of its swarming masses, may yet become the most dangerous enemy of Russia. . . . The community of faith is no guarantee of friendship; innumerable historical examples prove that amply. The Catholic kings of France, who persecuted Protestants in their domains, allied themselves with the German and Swedish Protestants against the Catholic Habsburgs, who in their turn found allies in the Persians, co-religionists of the Turks. In order to envisage a rift between the Russian and the Chinese governments, it is not necessary to imagine that either of them must abandon its creed. Despotic states are much less able to co-operate on equal terms than states whose rulers are accustomed to compromise.

'If the two continue to stick together, the danger is that western Europe will be overwhelmed and the American continent besieged. In India, parliamentarianism has feet of clay; elsewhere in Asia it has no feet at all. Therefore, should the cleavage in a future war run on purely ideological lines, the Atlantic Union has a rather small chance of victory. But the discord among the dictators saved western Europe and America in the last war; it may do so again' (*Military Organization and Society*, p. 180–1).

CHAPTER TWENTY-FOUR

COMMUNISM AND CAPITALISM:
ARE THEY CONVERGING?

IN STRICT LOGIC the question constituting the title of this chapter is absurd, for if we define Communism and capitalism as different social systems, then they cannot become one. Leaving apart Communism as a designation of movements in non-Communist states, we can say that as a social system its fundamental features are totalitarian rule by the party and complete state-ownership of the means of production, whereas capitalism implies private ownership of the means of production, and requires limitations on the authority of the government. What can then be legitimately asked is whether the polities which at present can be classified as Communist or capitalist are evolving towards some common type. The basic ideas of Marx, incidentally, suggest that this should be so, because if technology determines 'relations of production' and constitutes together with them the infrastructure which determines the superstructure (ie social structure and culture), then we should expect that societies employing the same technology should become similar in their essential features. Secondly, if we adopt the point of view of Hegelian dialectics, we can regard capitalism as a thesis, Communism as its antithesis, and await the arrival of their synthesis.

Similarity could conceivably come about through transformation of the polities in question into something entirely unlike either of the existing types; in which case we could speak or developmental convergence but not of synthesis, because the latter term implies retention of some of the elements constituting the initial entities. However, all the processes of social transformation which we know about lead to fusion of the old elements with the new, and we have no reason to believe that it will not be so

343

with the changes which capitalism and Communism are undergoing. In addition, we have to take into account the ubiquitous
tendency to imitate which operates even between embattled
nations, and which the improvements in transport and communications cannot fail to foster. Indeed, conflict is one of the
most important stimulants to imitation because the urge to maintain parity is much stronger in military techniques than in the
field of consumer goods.

There is no reason to assume that either totalitarian control
or private enterprise must produce similar results everywhere.
It could be argued that although the Communist system achieved
strength in Russia, it will collapse in China; and that whereas
no internal threat to capitalism is foreseeable in Switzerland, in
Peru capitalism is doomed. One can imagine that under the
pressure of overpopulation certain areas of the globe may remain
prey to warfare and chaos, and alternate between semi-capitalist
and semi-Communist régimes. However, the fate of the poorest
part of humanity is a separate question, and I mention it only in
order to delimit the field: in examining the possibility of convergent
evolution, I shall consider only the states which are growing in
economic and military strength, and whose régimes are in no
danger of collapsing – in other words, the countries where capitalism and Communism have attained success as measured by
stability and strength, and which happen to be situated in the
northernmost belt around the globe, divided by the so-called
Iron Curtain.

If we compare the Soviet system as it is now with its earliest
forms, we may reach a conclusion that during the last forty years
it has moved towards capitalism, in the sense of having re-adopted
some of the institutional arrangements which the Bolsheviks had
abolished when they seized power. Equality of remuneration,
workers' control of factories, the principle of 'from each according
to his ability and to each according to his needs', have been
completely abandoned and relegated to a mythical future. Wage-
differentials reappeared almost as soon as they were abolished,
and eventually became steeper than in the capitalist countries.
The badges of rank and deferential behaviour became very
prominent during the Stalin era. But on the other hand, the
concessions to private enterprise made by Lenin (and known as
the New Economic Policy) were always regarded by the Bolshevik

leaders as merely tactical withdrawals, forced upon them by the lack of cadres needed for organizing a collectivist economy. A few years later Stalin mounted a full-scale counter-attack against all vestiges of private enterprise. Thus, the abandonment of equality, far from constituting a reversion towards capitalism, amounted merely to a re-introduction of social patterns which greatly ante-date capitalism, and invariably accompany large-scale coercive organization. Notwithstanding the adoption of the technology which had evolved under capitalism, the bureaucratic despotism of the oriental monarchies affords the nearest analogy to the social system erected by Stalin. In order to assess the direction of its evolution we must take as the starting-point the year in which it became fully formed that is to say, 1938.

The Standards of Living

The abundance or scarcity of goods colours every aspect of social life: every custom functions differently in an opulent society than in one stricken by poverty. At the moment, in respect of standards of life, the difference between the chief capitalist countries and the Soviet Empire remains enormous: only the most privileged small minority in Communist lands enjoys the amount of material goods which an average British (let alone American) worker has at his disposal. Even a single separate room for a family is regarded as good average housing in Russia and Poland, and only big bosses have flats similar to those which the middle classes have in the West. How to obtain a bearable minimum of food and clothing remains a great problem for most families. Clearly, the social systems cannot converge so long as the discrepancy in economic levels remains so large. A narrowing of this gap could take place through an economic collapse in the West which, like the crisis of the thirties, could cause a downfall of democratic governments and a rise of totalitarian dictatorships, thus producing a con-vergence in the political sphere as well. Let us, however, leave this possibility aside. In any case, owing to the improved understanding of the functioning of monetary circulation, a simple bogging down of the economic mechanism would nowadays be prevented, and (barring some extraordinary collective folly) only overpopulation or the drying up of the sources of raw materials, or war, could bring back general poverty to the chief capitalist countries.

If we take as the starting-points the years in which the Communist economic system was firmly implanted – which is 1937 in Russia and 1952 in the satellites, there can be little doubt that the standard of living has risen since then; although it has not risen as much as the figures of growth calculated by the economists indicate, because the populations have grown too, and also because very high rates of growth can be found only in industries concerned directly or indirectly with armaments, and in the statistics of total production they cover up the relative stagnation in agriculture and house-building, which are the basic determinants of the standard of living. It must also be remembered that estimates of real income are made on the basis of various rather arbitrary assumptions, so that a rise in the index may cover a very dubious improvement consisting, for example, of an increase in the number of television sets accompanied by a deterioration in nutrition. Notwithstanding these qualifications, we can accept the view widely held among students of Soviet economy that the standard of living has risen during the past decade and in all probability will continue to rise. It does not follow, however, that the Russians must catch up in this respect with the chief capitalist countries, because there the standard of living has also been rising during the last decade. Indeed, if we take 1946 as the starting-point and compare Western Germany with Russia, we find divergence rather than convergence because whereas in 1946 the Germans lived as miserably as the Russians, now they live much better. Nevertheless, Western Germany was a case of recovery rather than development, and therefore no conclusions about long-term trends can be drawn from it.

The profound difference between the Russia of today and the Russia of 1937 is that, even though the standard of living has risen only a little, the Russians now have the technical means of raising it, which they did not have in 1937. With extremely rapid expansion of heavy industry and phenomenal increase in the number of personnel qualified in all branches of technology, a very substantial improvement in the standard of living could be achieved very rapidly. This has not happened so far for two reasons: the priority given to armaments, and the top-heavy, red-tape ridden organization of production. The first factor was decisive in the past but the second will be more important in the future because with the present rate of growth of industry and the advent of automation, the Russians, like the Americans, should be able to produce arms as well as a sufficient quantity of consumer goods. Whether they will be able to do that seems to depend on their willingness to be rational rather than dogmatic in devising a more efficient organization of production and distribution. It remains to be added that absolute parity is not necessary for producing some similarity in social situation. Adequate provision of food, clothing and shelter constitutes the turning-point, and the most important dividing line runs between economies which can do that and those which cannot. The difference between a family which has to live in a corner of a room which it shares with two or three others, and a family which has one room per head is greater than the difference between the latter and a family which possesses a hundred or three hundred rooms. The difference between freezing and having adequate clothing is greater than the difference between having three and having three hundred suits. After a certain point possession of material goods ceases to contribute to enjoyment, and becomes purely a matter of rivalry for prestige; so that an increase in the total quantity of goods ceases to augment the sum of satisfactions, because some individuals will always have less than others, and suffer from invidious comparisons. There is no reason to believe that a Frenchman of modest income derives less pleasure from his 2 hp utility car than does his American counterpart from the fanciful vehicle which he has to change every year in order to maintain the respect of his neighbours. So if the Communist governments could ensure the level of relative affluence for their less privileged subjects which their counterparts enjoy now in Denmark or Britain, it would not matter much if the latter had moved by then to the American level, because the human and social significance of the relative differences in affluence would be negligible in comparison with the importance of the differences which exist today. An absolute rise would lessen the importance of discrepancies in virtue of the law of diminishing marginal utility. In this sense, therefore, there would be convergence.

Economic Structure

The top-heavy, over-centralized administrative machinery, plagued by red-tape, is now the chief obstacle to economic improvement

347

in the Soviet Empire, and all the remedies which have been suggested consist of proposals to introduce certain mechanisms of the market. In Yugoslavia an attempt is being made to build an economy reconciling the elements of free enterprise with the principle of collective ownership of the means of production: an individual can set up a business by organizing a co-operative and persuading a State bank to invest in it. The firms, whether state-owned or co-operative, have to compete, to show profit and pay interest on the loans obtained from the banks. Some prices are regulated while others are left to be determined by supply and demand. Thus the Yugoslav economy is regulated by a complicated interplay of central imperative planning with the mechanisms of the market. In view of more exiguous natural resources, its performance must be rated as higher than that of the Soviet economy, although to be fair we must discount the advantage accruing from American aid. In Poland the Soviet model of control over industry, with its detailed central planning, has remained in force with only slight modifications in the direction of capitalist calculation, but in agriculture Gomulka has carried out a full retreat from collectivism, allowed the peasants to break up the collective farms, to re-establish their individual farms and sell the produce on the markets, with the result that Poland is the only country in the Soviet Bloc where agricultural output has approached sufficiency. Artisans also are tolerated, with a considerable gain to the economy. In the Soviet Union itself no big retreats from collectivization have been carried out although certain features of a faint capitalist flavour have appeared: private bank accounts, interest on loans and a few others. The reforms aimed at improving the efficiency of the economy mainly affect the allocation of decision-making functions and the application of incentives.

It may be worth noting that in a way the Russians are repeating the achievement of Peter I who created large factories producing armaments and auxiliary materials, manned by serfs ascribed to them. At the end of the 18th century Russia had the biggest iron and armaments industry in the world while remaining backward in other fields. With the advent of steam and complex machinery the dependence of the arms industry on other branches of production increased, and for this reason Russian military power dwindled rapidly in the course of the 19th century in spite of the growth of population.

As the Soviet system has still not been able to provide decent economic conditions for its citizens, it seems strange that its leaders are unwilling to experiment with measures similar to those which have been tried with success in Yugoslavia and Poland. Three factors seem to be chiefly responsible for this conservatism: militarism, tradition and the expansionism of the bureaucracy.

Military power depends on the absolute quantity of arms, and only within wide limits on the productivity of labour employed in producing them, as low productivity can be compensated by greater numbers of workers and longer hours. Centralized totalitarian control may be less efficient as measured by productivity (ie product per man-hour) but more effective in raising the total quantity of production, by mobilizing and concentrating energies and resources. So far the Soviet government has been more concerned with squeezing out the effort than with employing it efficiently, but the decline in the growth of population combined with the increasing complexity of the industry should be conducive to a revaluation of this attitude and a more pragmatic approach to the problems of organizing the economy.

The impact of tradition is so clear that it requires little comment: the weight of centuries of serfdom and despotism makes authoritarian control seem the natural order of things, and colours correspondingly the interpretation of Marxist ideology.

Whereas the force of tradition may be gradually eroded, few forces can oppose the expansionist tendency of the bureaucratic machine. The most far-reaching example of the stripping of an absolutist bureaucracy of some of its prerogatives that we can find is the liberalization of the Prussian régime in the course of the 19th century. The political development of Japan between 1880 and 1930 proceeded along somewhat similar lines. However, even apart from the fact that neither Germany nor Japan have ever become strongholds of liberalism, we must remember that the chief incentive to liberalization from above which took place in these countries was the belief that industry, so indispensable to military strength, could be built only – or at least most effectively – by private enterprise operating under a liberal political régime. Having demonstrated that this belief is unfounded, the Communists can hardly be influenced by it. It seems therefore that – as suggested in the preceding chapter – a reversion from totalitarianism can occur only through a process of fission within the administrative machine because there are no forces which could push back the frontiers of its sway. But if such fission should occur, and the rulers' authority be checked by the power of semi-autonomous bodies, nobody will have absolute authority, and therefore the resistance against reforms involving dispersion of power should become less pronounced. Thus the way might be paved for an introduction of certain elements of the mechanism of the market.

The Polish reversion to private agriculture provides a political as well as an economic lesson. Collectivization of agriculture was only partly prompted by the misguided belief that this was the best way of squeezing out of the peasant the produce necessary for feeding the rapidly expanding urban population without giving him anything in return. No doubt, more has been wrung from the peasant in proportion to his output than could be achieved by any other method, but the output declined. So, it seems certain that larger quantities could have been obtained without depriving the peasants of their land, by judiciously planned taxation in kind. The chief motive behind forcible collectivization (as Lenin clearly said when laying plans for the future) was the determination to subdue the peasant by depriving him of his economic independence. Ever since Marx said in the 18th Brumaire of Louis Bonaparte that the French peasants, having become full proprietors of the soil, took the side of the *bourgeoisie* against the proletariat, the Communists regarded the peasants as their enemies, even when they wooed them. This doctrinal point had a character of a self-fulfilling prophecy, because by treating the peasants as sinners who must be forcibly converted into non-owning proletarians, the Communists did incur their wrath. By making peace with the peasants, the Polish Communists showed that peasant proprietors constitute no danger to a Communist state, thus perhaps paving the road for future reforms in the same direction in Russia.

One must not expect too much rationality in human behaviour as there are innumerable examples of how people have ruined themselves and their countries through blind passions or obstinate doctrinairism and ignorance or wilful disregard of their own long-term interests. Nevertheless, the rulers of Russia do not seem to be particularly irrational. Even the monstrous deeds of Stalin were perfectly rational from the point of view of a completely amoral man devoid of any feelings of sympathy for human beings, whose sole aim was to satisfy his lust for power and glorification. The scale of values of his successor does not seem to be so depraved, and given his aims and situation he does not behave irrationally. It must be remembered that, notwithstanding the primitive mentality of most of its adherents, the Communist doctrine (unlike the Fascist creeds and the notions of ultra-conservatives) puts quite a high value on the intellect. Moreover, with the spread of technical education more and more party functionaries gain some acquaintance with scientific modes of reasoning; and although such acquaintance cannot remove barriers to thought deeply rooted in sentiment, it should extend somewhat the area of rational choice. It seems therefore that Yugoslav and Polish demonstrations of how partial introductions of market mechanisms are profitable, should sooner or later induce the rulers of Russia to try some experiments along these lines. If such changes do take place, the Soviet economy will become less dissimilar from the economic systems of the Western countries than it is today. Up till now, however, if the dissimilarity between the systems has become less marked, it has been in virtue of the transformations of capitalism.

In many ways capitalism is stronger today than it was thirty years ago, when it was on the verge of collapsing under the weight of unemployment. Even more, it has recovered certain areas which it had partially lost, such as Western Germany, Spain and Italy. Neither Hitler nor Mussolini attacked the capitalists as a class, but they did limit their freedom of action and reduced their power. This is particularly true of Hitler, who also contributed more to the circulation of *élites* by creating a new ruling class superimposed upon the old out of his henchmen, who were of relatively humble origins. Economically the Nazi economic system was a half-way house between liberal capitalism and Communism; though its political system resembled Communism. The collapse of the Nazi and Fascist régimes produced greater freedom for the business-man, whilst the diplomatic realignment of Spain led eventually to a diminution of statist and corporatist controls over private enterprise. Owing to prosperity, there are no revolutionary movements in the chief capitalist countries, and the prospects of expropriations on a large scale are remote. Nevertheless, capitalism is continuously drifting towards a more or less collectivist model.

This general drift has four aspects: (1) concentration of control over private enterprise; (2) divorce between ownership and control; (3) extension of governmental regulation; (4) the expansion of the public sector of the economy.

Marx's law of industrial concentration constituted his greatest contribution to sociology and economics – far greater than his materialist interpretation of history, in which he had many (and more judicious) forerunners.[1] Marx coupled his diagnosis and prognosis of industrial concentration with the prophecy of the growing polarization of class structures and the increasing misery of the proletariat, which of course have been thoroughly disproved as far as the leading capitalist countries are concerned, although they can provide a plausible scheme for interpreting the social reality of countries like Colombia. There can be no doubt, however, that concentration is proceeding apace: larger and larger sectors of the economy are coming under the control of fewer and fewer firms. Among the newest technical factors which favour concentration we have the growing importance of large-scale research, economies of co-ordinated distribution, improvements in efficiency of direction due to better techniques of management and mechanical aids among which electronic computers take the first place. In the most important cases, however, concentration goes beyond the point at which the costs of production would be at a minimum, in order to secure greater profits by monopolizing the market. Even more important, though seldom acknowledged by economists, what propels concentration is the directors' sheer lust for power, similar to that which prompts soldiers and politicians to embark upon conquests. Such intra-economic imperialism often carries concentration even beyond the point of maximum profitability, because monopolistic profits can be obtained without formal fusion by cartels and price agreements. The fact that the trend towards concentration is much less pronounced in agriculture does not much affect the general trend because the agricultural population is declining.

Concentration of control over the economy can be interpreted as a movement towards collectivism only in so far as it is accompanied by a divorce between control and ownership, for so long as a firm is controlled by its owner it remains an individual enterprise regardless of size. As is well known, however, individual and

[1] Actually Proudhon has put it forth earlier but not so systematically.

family control is becoming rarer because concentration of owner-ship has not kept pace with concentration of control. When the shareholders are many, and no small group of them possesses the majority of votes, the directors become a practically autonomous governing body. Furthermore, the device of holding companies – as Berle and Means showed thirty years ago – permits crucially placed owners of as little as 2 per cent of the total capital to control whole chains of firms. Even family ownership does not always constitute a guarantee against control by salaried managers because the owners become less and less capable of running the business with the passage of the time, and come to resemble monarchs who reign but do not rule. In these ways directors are becoming autonomous and self-perpetuating bodies whose power is out of all proportion to their share in ownership. An economy dominated by giant concerns governed by semi-autonomous directorates recruited chiefly by co-option can no longer be described as a system based on free enterprise . . . but is it collec-tivism? Most certainly it is not economic individualism, and in a sense it is more collectivist than the Soviet economy because it is a system which has no boss, consisting of units none of which has an individual boss: the authority is diffused throughout the anonymous network of interlocking directorates. The fact that the top managers often come from the upper classes in no way disproves the thesis of collectivization of capitalism because the higher rungs of the army and the civil service – collective bodies *par excellence* – have often remained preserves of the privileged classes.

The expansion of the public sector of the economy offers the least debatable ground for maintaining that the Communist and capitalist systems are converging, if we take state ownership of the means of production as the chief criterion. Frequently the steps in that direction are motivated by considerations which are not ideological, and which may even be due to a fortuitous con-junction of circumstances. For instance, the French government expropriated Citroen, and so acquired the second largest motor factory in Europe, because M. Citroen collaborated with the Germans during the occupation. The Italian government came to own 80 per cent of the basic industries not because it adhered to the socialist doctrines but because private industry was sluggish, owing to lack of funds and the low initial profitability of many projects. Some of these state-owned industries are very well managed and show a great 'spirit of enterprise'. The most striking example is the oil company E.N.I. which under the directorship of Enrico Mattei achieved some outstanding victories in commercial competition against the old giants of international capitalism.

After the wave of nationalizations which swept Britain and France after the Second World War, there came a pause and even an ebb, although from a long-term point of view the trend has not been reversed. As the production of atomic energy will remain in Europe in the hands of governments, it seems certain that a very substantial expansion of the public sector will take place once this branch of technology reaches profitability. Nevertheless, at its present rate the expansion of the public sector is very far from being able to produce a fully collectivized economy. Barring wars and disasters, the internal dynamics of capitalist concentration will remain the chief agent of collectivization, extension of governmental control being the second.

Although during the First World War the governments instituted extensive controls over economies, they regarded them as temporary expedients. So, when the Bolsheviks proclaimed that they were going to plan economic development, they were regarded as madmen who could only bring about an economic collapse. This opinion was not unfounded. In their first attempt at economic planning the Bolsheviks came very near to this, but they learned quickly and proved to be very inventive, and so constructed a system which, though abhorrent by humane standards, was viable and even strong. The Communist example, however, had little influence on the economic policies of the Western countries until the Soviet industrial potential became the chief military menace. It was the terrible crisis of the thirties which caused the irrevocable abandonment of *laissez-faire*, by exposing the inability of private business to emerge from prostration without the help from the state.

Propounding his theory of aggravating crises of over-production, Marx was right once again in diagnosing the slow but mortal disease of *laissez-faire* capitalism. What he understandably could not foresee was that, shedding its aversion to governmental regulation, capitalism could survive with the aid of a therapy which he himself unwittingly helped to devise: for the ancestry of Keynes' theory of employment goes back to Quesnay, Malthus and Marx himself, whose concern with aggregate quantities stood in sharp contrast to the preoccupation of pre-Keynesian academic economists, and foreshadowed what is now called macroeconomics. (150 years before Keynes, Quesnay even arrived at a rudimentary form of the concept of the multiplier.) Keynes was acclaimed, although his forerunners like John A. Hobson and John Mackinnon Robertson were boycotted, because when he wrote no sane person could any longer believe in the automatic harmony of commercial economy.

The need to keep in check the forces which might produce unemployment is not the only root of the expansion of governmental control over industry and trade, because the sheer growth of complexity of economic structures requires more co-ordination, and the number of tasks which cannot be left to private initiative – such as prevention of soil erosion, traffic control, smoke abatement, and so on – grows incessantly. Moreover, governments are gradually accepting the responsibility not only for static welfare but for progress. In France there is a Planning Commission, and even in countries whose governments would feel too embarrassed about setting up such a body, its normal agencies engage in at least partial economic planning. Not even the West German economic miracle can be attributed to the automatic workings of free enterprise, because the government deliberately stimulated competition and steered business activity into the most productive channels by means of various laws and taxation policies. Italy has had a succession of plans for developing the South. Thus we can no longer contrast the planned economies of the Communists and the unplanned ones of the capitalists because the differences on the score of planning are of degree and of method.

Overwhelming difficulties would face anybody attempting to make a numerical estimate of the degrees of freedom which businessmen enjoy in different countries, but there is a general agreement that their freedom of action has been steadily diminishing during the last fifty years. Furthermore, there are ways of influencing people's behaviour other than by curtailing their freedom of choice. We must distinguish between imperative and inducive control. Reliance on definite commands constitutes the essence of the former, whereas the latter consists of influencing behaviour not by giving orders but by altering the environment in such a way that in pursuit of their interests people will behave

WAYNESBURG COLLEGE LIBRARY
WAYNESBURG, PA.

as we want them to behave. Thus, for instance, an increase in investment may be obtained by ordering businessmen to invest a higher share of their profits under the threat of imprisonment; but a more effective way is normally to grant tax exemptions on invested profits. The distinction between imperative and inducive control becomes blurred in many cases, and in strict logic we could regard the former as a special type of the latter, but for our present purpose the rough distinction will suffice, and we can leave aside the complications (which will be treated at length in a book on the general theory of organization which is in preparation). The relevance of this distinction to our present theme is that under statist and managerial capitalism inducive control is the most important notwithstanding a great deal of imperative control, whereas the opposite is the case in the Soviet economy. However, the place of inducive control in the Soviet economy is growing, although it has not reached the importance it has in Yugoslavia. This trend in the technique of planning and control has an interesting parallel in the recent changes in the internal structures of capitalist giants, many of which have been deliberately split into autonomous units with separate accounting, trading with each other notwithstanding common ownership, in order to stimulate competition and initiative, eliminate red-tape, and provide standards for measuring managerial achievement.

The conclusion which emerges from the foregoing brief survey is that during the last thirty years the capitalist and the Communist economic systems have moved in convergent directions although the differences remain very great. This convergence occurred more in virtue of the movement of the capitalist economies towards a form of collectivism, than because of the movement of the Communist economies towards a pluralistic system, which was almost negligible outside Poland and Yugoslavia. Moreover, it is possible that this convergence will remain partial because a movement towards collectivism need not reach monolithic totalitarianism. In the West it is a pluralistic diffuse collectivism which is replacing individualism.

Power

As the prospects of liberalization of the Soviet régime have been discussed in the preceding chapter, I shall consider here only the other side of the problem of convergence: namely, the question of whether the West is sliding towards totalitarianism.

Certain points are quite clear. A simple extrapolation of figures given in works on economic structures shows that at the present rate of industrial amalgamation, most national economies would come under control of a single company in less than a century. Such a situation would resemble the state of India under the East India Company, in so far as the nature of authority is concerned. However, the rule of an industrial owning company would be far more pervasive because it would own all the means of production, whereas the British as well as the Dutch East India Company held only the overall sovereignty and monopolized only the external trade. Moreover, we have no grounds for imagining that in such an eventuality the power of the owning company would be counter-balanced by that of a democratic government. What the opponents of socialism have been saying about the incompatibility of democracy with concentration of economic power in the hands of the state applies with equal force to private amalgamation. Whether the nominal title of ownership would be public or private is of minor importance in comparison with the brute fact of concentration of control over practically the entire wealth of the country in the hands of one small group.

Even a wide spread of share-owning would not help very much, because even if there were millions of owners, they could be reduced to impotence by the device of holding companies. The directors could easily whittle down the rights of the shareholders once the latter were deprived of opportunities of choice, and could not sell their shares in order to buy different ones. Under such circumstances the shareholders without access to the levers of power could not even defend their dividends, which the directors might easily reduce to nothingness in order to put everybody outside the *élite* into economic dependence. Why should the supreme directors wish to do such a thing? For the same reason that the members of the Politburo do not wish to relax their control over their poor 'comrades': out of sheer lust for power.

Up till now representative government has flourished only where there was in existence a large class of economically independent persons, not necessarily independent in the sense of enjoying unearned incomes but in the sense of having no boss. Whenever democratic constitutions were promulgated in countries where wealth was concentrated in the hands of the few, they existed only on paper. In districts dominated by one large estate, whose owner could deprive of their livelihood even the persons who were not in his employment, there could be no free elections. An industrialized country in which the means of production would be monopolized would provide a more complex and sophisticated equivalent of the large estate. There could be no freedom of expression if all the publishing and the Press were controlled by one cohesive clique. Nobody would dare to criticize the bosses for fear of being condemned to unemployment or to vegetation in an ill-paid job.

Karl Marx regarded the disappearance of the middle class to be the inevitable consequence of industrial concentration, and he has been frequently criticized on that score by writers who pointed out that in fact the middle class has been growing faster than any other class. Nevertheless, Marx was not entirely wrong: the middle class which he knew, consisting chiefly of independent merchants, artisans, farmers and the practitioners of the 'free professions', has declined radically in proportion to the population, and in some cases even dwindled in absolute numbers. Its decline, however, has been more than compensated by the multiplication of the better-paid employees of large organizations. The outlook and culture of this class has provided the subject of a number of sociological works, which included such famous books as *White Collar* by Wright Mills and *The Organization Man* by William C. Whyte. The political importance of this change in the character of the middle classes is enormous because it has greatly reduced the number of people who have the freedom to be politically active. Under a democratic régime an employee can vote any way he likes, but he might endanger his career if he engages in political activity on behalf of a party of which his employers disapprove. The manual workers who are not eligible for promotion, and who are protected by the unions, may not be affected very much, but for the members of the middle classes who are striving for promotion reticence seems to be the best policy. True, neither a small businessman nor a lawyer has absolute freedom either, as he must take care not to alienate his customers, but here the constraints are diffuse, contradictory and vacillating, whereas the control to which an employee is subject is organized and permanent. It must be noted that in many countries, the intermediate ranks of the private employees are under more astringent control than the employees of public authorities who are protected by rules defining security of tenure. This suggests a deduction that private amalgamation endangers political freedom even more than nationalization does.

The improvement in the standard of living of even the lowest paid employees, coupled with the swelling of the white collar category, has removed the possibility that capitalism could be toppled by a mass revolt. Indeed, the social order is becoming less vulnerable both because the means of control are becoming more powerful, and because the roots of mass discontent are withering.

It might be argued that a counterweight to concentrated economic power could be provided by the trade unions, which would prevent the encroachments upon the freedom of the employees. Unfortunately however, it seems that even this rampart would loose its effectiveness beyond a certain point of industrial concentration. Even the present sizes of the unions constitute the chief source of their internal weakness: red-tape and bureaucratic haughtiness creep in as the size grows. Moreover, the steeper the hierarchy, the stronger is the tendency of the highest union dignitaries to join the bosses whilst pretending to serve the workers. So long as the pluralist society exists and creates possibilities (even if remote) of organizing rival unions, there are certain limits on the abuse of power by the leaders; but extreme concentration of economic control would in all likelihood lead to the concrescence of the unions, and an emergence of an organization which under no circumstances could be challenged from below. Under such circumstances the leaders would be so remote from the rank and file, and so close to their opposite numbers on the side of management, that they would inevitably incline towards collusion, particularly as the alternative of struggle would be much less promising than it is today. An alliance with the managers could fortify the position of the union leaders in relation to their rank and file, and eliminate potential rivals, strangling at birth any new and more recalcitrant unions by refusing to negotiate with them.

The trade unions cannot survive as an independent power once control over the means of production had become completely concentrated, regardless of whether such concentration takes place through extensive nationalization or through amalgamation of giant joint-stock companies. The trade unionists oppose neither because neither harms immediately their personal interests. On the contrary: nationalizations create well-paid jobs for the union officials, whilst monopolization of a market enables a company to pay higher wages and to give greater security of employment.

The political influence of the lower employees has been insidiously undermined by a development which in itself furthers the cause of social justice: namely, the extension of educational opportunities for their children, necessitated by the growing demand for skills. For generations the labour movements fought for equality of educational opportunities, without realizing that its inevitable consequence must be a continuous creaming off from the working class of individuals who might become its leaders. As educational opportunities still remain unequal (though much less so than they were a generation ago) there are still many bright young men and women among the lower employees, but everything indicates that they are a great deal fewer than they were in the preceding generation. The impression one gets from living in different countries is that in more backward countries one meets more frequently unusually gifted men and women among the manual workers. Moreover, every advance in the effectiveness of educational selection enlarges the differences in the assorted categories, and the awareness of the correctness of the selection might have serious consequences on the self-esteem of the less successful, who might not be able to attribute their failures to unfairness. However, I shall not dwell upon the moral implications of this predicament which have been vividly depicted by Michael Young in his famous sociological satire, *The Rise of Meritocracy*. My sole concern at the moment is with the effects upon the political role of the lower employees. Unable to find competent leaders in their midst, the lower employees could choose as leaders either men who never shared their experience, or men who are inferior not only in knowledge but also in intelligence to those with whom they would have to negotiate. Without proper understanding of the situation, the inferior leaders would oscillate between docility and destructive truculence, neither of which would fortify their position. So long as managerial power remains fairly dispersed, the unions can retain theirs notwithstanding this handicap, but if faced with a monolithic and omni-comprehensive managerial hierarchy, they could do nothing except submit meekly or be squashed.

Totalitarianism implies a fusion of political and economic power, and therefore we must consider whether such a fusion would be necessitated by a concentration of power within each sphere. Conceivably, the supreme company and the government might live side by side, like the Church and the State in the Middle Ages, having delimited their respective spheres. A closer scrutiny, however, reveals that this is not likely. The feudal kingdoms were very loosely knit, whilst the Church, though better organized, remained incapable of ruling wide areas which came under its ideological sway. Notwithstanding the perpetual tug-of-war, the Church and the State could reach a *modus vivendi*, and agree on delimiting their respective spheres, because neither of them exercised control over more than a very small part of the activities of their subjects, and such control as they did exercise was chiefly in the nature of enforcing static customs, and rarely amounted to directing collective actions. Under the conditions of an industrial civilization, the necessity for continuous and detailed co-ordination, and for frequent re-adjustments of administrative structures, greatly favour unification of control, and would make a dualistic division extremely tenuous. Furthermore, we must take into account the fact that a system of balance of power requires for its maintenance a plurality of centres of power, so that a coalition can always be formed to contain the strongest. Once the number of the players is reduced to two, only technical and strategic impediments to a decisive victory, and not the sociological constellation, can prevent conquest or fusion under pressure. For these reasons, it seems that once the amalgamation of economic control proceeds beyond a certain point, the alternatives are that either the government takes over the business, or the supreme company takes over the government, or they fuse through interpenetration. True, the basic ambiguity of all social situations, due to the anti-social sociability of humanity, is such that the normal struggle for the good things of life produces an alternation between fusion and fission, of which the best exemplification we can find is the well-known phenomenon of discord breaking out among allies as soon as the victory is achieved. The process of internal decomposition of a totalitarian régime would belong to the same class of phenomena, regardless of whether the said totalitarianism came into existence violently through a revolution, or peacefully through amalgamation of free enterprise.

Managerial totalitarianism, which seems to be on the way towards supplanting capitalism and democracy, need not be savage and despotic like the régimes of Hitler and Stalin. Unburdened by the tradition of tyranny and obscurantism, unhampered by doctrinairism in its choice of techniques of control, without the handicap of the customs and attitudes generated by poverty and the bitter struggle for survival, managerial totalitarianism could be enlightened and suave; for modern technology has created the means of fully satisfying the material needs of the masses and of entertaining them, as well as the means of painless indoctrination. Moreover, the fairly intensive social mobility necessitated by the demands of a technological civilization greatly facilitates the enforcement of conformity, because threats stifle dissent less effectively than do prospects of promotion. No barbarous punishments are needed for foisting conformity upon a society where affluence, hedonism and discreet brain-washing are combined with the generalized rat-race.

Notwithstanding the size of the giant companies and their enormous power, in the West we are still living in pluralist societies. The process of concrescence of centres of power has gone quite far but it has not yet produced a unified *élite* compressed into a single hierarchy. On the other side, Soviet totalitarianism has become somewhat attenuated and has undergone a process of limited liberalization. We must conclude, therefore, that the evolution of the two systems has been somewhat convergent. But we must not exaggerate: they are still very far from having converged, and their differences remain radical and basic. Nor must we conclude that this convergence undermines the importance of resisting Communism, because the worst features of Communist ideology will be upheld so long as they appear to provide a weapon for effortless subjugation of foreign lands through subversion. A decline in the prospects of expanding its frontiers by this method would greatly stimulate a further liberalization of the Soviet Empire.

In comparison with 1938 the process of concentration of power in the leading capitalist countries is more noticeable than the process of dispersion of power in Russia. In contrast, the attenuation of terror in Russia and its satellites constitutes an event of far greater portent than the spread of submissiveness in the West, which is only barely noticeable. The explanation of this discrepancy between the structural changes and the trends of the political climate is that the influence of the former finds a counterweight in the traditions of liberalism on the one side, and of tyranny on the other.

It seems that the heritage of liberalism and democracy can be conserved only if these ideals, together with improved sociological knowledge, can inspire effective action deliberately aimed at preserving a balance of power within society, which the spontaneous dynamics of capitalism, operating within the environment of contemporary technology, cannot fail to undermine. Just as the framers of the constitution of the USA, guided by the ideas of Montesquieu, established a division of political authority which sufficed to guarantee freedom when there were no concentrations of power of a different nature, so must the liberals of today devise institutional arrangements which would ensure the polycentricity of the structure of power. In discussions of the problem of the concentration of economic control the accent is usually laid upon the deleterious effects of monopolies on production and welfare; but from a wider point of view restricting production is relatively unimportant in comparison with the significance of the mere concentration of power.

Karl Marx was right about the tendency of unfettered capitalism to work itself into a state of collapse through crises of overproduction, but he could not foresee that capitalism could be saved from this apparently lethal disease by having its freedom curtailed by the State's therapeutic action. He also seems to have been right in regarding industrial concentration as another mortal disease of capitalism, although he imagined that out of this unpleasant process a beautiful, free and humane socialist society would emerge, whereas we know that this road leads to bureaucratic totalitarianism, and that the remedies proposed by orthodox socialists tend to accelerate the progression towards that state of affairs. Whether the concentration of economic power will kill democracy depends on whether Marx was right on another point: namely, his interpretation of history. According to this interpretation (and I am referring to how Marx interpreted past events, not to how he envisaged the future establishment of socialism) men act solely in pursuit of their own material advantage, and collective actions consist of cumulative vectors of thus motivated individual actions. In this scheme no influence is attributed to the regard for the common interest. If this is correct, and neither the appreciation of long-term general interest nor the desire to conserve and further cultural values can prompt effective collective action, then there can be little doubt that the cumulative effect of the unbridled pursuit of personal advantage by each and all will be to push the pluralist polities towards a managerial totalitarianism – the direction of least resistance under the circumstances created by contemporary technology.

NOTES

A popularised version of Chapter Seven was published by Aldus Books in their Encyclopædia of Knowledge.

1. Chapter Eight appeared in the *European Journal of Sociology* in 1961. Parts of Chapter Twelve were published in the *American Sociological Review*, December, 1949, and most of Chapter Sixteen in *Social Forces*, October, 1950. Earlier versions of Chapters One, Two, Three, Five, Ten, Fourteen and Twenty-one have been circulating in mimeographed form since 1961. Chapter Twenty-one has appeared in the *Jewish Journal of Sociology*, December, 1963. The material from Chapters Five and Thirteen has appeared in the article 'Method and Substantive Theory in Max Weber', in the *British Journal of Sociology*, March, 1964.

APPENDIX

On the Concept of Industrial Society

IN CONSIDERING how to define a concept we must not forget that a definition is a very special and limited kind of description; and that only those traits need be included in the definition which are indispensable for identifying the phenomena which the given concept denotes. In the case in hand, we need to specify only the minimal cluster of the features which distinguish an industrial society from other societies. This statement does not, of course, dispose of the question of what we mean by 'industrial' but our freedom to choose the core of the meaning of this word is limited by the general acceptance among sociologists and laymen alike that 'industrial' must have something to do with factories and machines.

The quest for cognitive economy constitutes the first of the reasons why we ought to leave out of the definition the traits which are not necessary for identifying the object of our discourse. The pursuit of the ideal of economy does not depend on the belief that it reflects some characteristic of the structure of the universe, because the limited nature of our mental powers constitutes a sufficient justification for striving to make our formulations as simple as possible in order not to get lost in the maze. With respect to definitions there is also a special reason for making them as brief as possible: namely the danger of pre-judging by definition questions which in fact have not yet been solved, and of rendering unusable the terms needed for discussing them, as has happened on various occasions in connection with the idea of industrial society.

In Herbert Spencer's works, for instance, 'industrial' appears as the opposite of 'militant' or, as we would say today, militaristic. This may have sounded plausible in the second half of the 19th century but appears utterly untenable now, unless we divest the term 'industrial' of any associations with factories and machines, and choose to make it equivalent to 'pacific'. To take another example: some sociologists take the waning of ideological fervour (together with a diminution of inequality of classes) to be an essential feature of the industrial society. Personally, I doubt whether there is a necessary connection between a high degree of industrialization and ideological tepidity. After all, Germany in 1938 was in many ways more industrialized than is France or Denmark today. The cooling off of class struggles and ideological controversies which took place in Western Europe since the Second World War was due chiefly to the fairly steady economic improvement; and there is no evidence that even the most highly industrialized of contemporary societies would have an immunity against ideological mass frenzies if it were hit by a calamity like the great depression of the thirties. Moreover, there is no proof that a highly industrialized society must be prosperous. Indeed, unless the rate of population growth falls rapidly, the present affluence of the more fortunate polities may soon vanish and we might enter into an era of brutal struggle for space and resources, which might completely reverse the trend towards lesser inequality and produce a crop of barbarously iniquitous régimes. Such calamities may, let us hope, be averted, but only if something is done about it. Therefore, a concept of industrial society, which implies a necessary connection between a high degree of industrialization and the absence of the said evils, is not only scientifically defective but also politically undesirable, as it may lull us into groundless complacency.

Unless we insist on creating needless difficulties by including the characteristics which may be only fortuitously and temporarily connected with the central and generally acknowledged meaning of the word industrial, the problem of the concept of industrial society resolves itself: we can simply define it as a society which subsists on products of big and complicated machines. Naturally, we are faced with the ubiquitous problem of how to classify the intermediate grades, but it is no more difficult in this case than with any other definition in sociology. In any case, the shading off applies both to the features which are regarded as constituting the concept and to those which may be empirically associated with them. If, for instance, we believe that a high degree of industrialization necessitates a high degree of social mobility, then we would surmise that a society which is 10 per cent industrial should have less mobility than one which is 80 per cent industrial; although on this particular point the question is complicated by the fact that becoming industrialized may necessitate more mobility than being industrialized.

Taking the dependence on machines as the sole essential feature of industrial society, we avoid pre-judging empirical issues by definition, and leave open to study and debate the question of which of the features exhibited by the most highly industrialized societies of today are intrinsically concatenated with the high degree of industrialization, and which are more or less fortuitous.

WAYNESBURG COLLEGE LIBRARY
WAYNESBURG, PA.